Authors In Depth

· · · ·

SILVER LEVEL

PRENTICE HALL
Upper Saddle River, New Jersey
Glenview, Illinois
Needham, Massachusetts

ISBN 0-13-052385-2
6 7 8 9 10   08 07 05 04

PRENTICE HALL

Acknowledgments

Grateful acknowledgment is made to the following for copyrighted material:

The Estate of Toni Cade Bambara
"The War of the Wall" by Toni Cade Bambara from *THE WAR OF THE WALL*. Copyright © 1981 by Toni Cade Bambara.

Bancroft Library for the Estate of Uchida
"Of Dry Goods and Black Bow Ties" by Yoshiko Uchida from *OF DRY GOODS AND BLACK BOW TIES*. Copyright © 1979, Yoshiko Uchida. From *THE HAPPIEST ENDING* by Yoshiko Uchida. Copyright © 1985 by Yoshiko Uchida. "Letter From a Concentration Camp" by Yoshiko Uchida from *THE BIG BOOK FOR PEACE*. Text copyright © 1990 by Yoshiko Uchida. "Prologue and Strangers at the Door" by Yoshiko Uchida from *JOURNEY TO TOPAZ*. Text copyright © 1971 by Yoshiko Uchida. All rights reserved.

Susan Bergholz Literary Services
From *BLESS ME, ULTIMA* by Rudolfo Anaya. Copyright © 1972 by Rudolfo Anaya. Published by Warner Books in 1994 and originally published by TQS Publications. "Take Tortillas Out of Poetry" by Rudolfo Anaya from *THE ANAYA READER*. Copyright © 1995 by Rudolfo Anaya. All rights reserved.

Jonathan Clowes Ltd.
From "A Study in Scarlet" by Sir Arthur Conan Doyle from *THE COMPLETE SHERLOCK HOLMES*. Copyright © 1905, 1917, 1927, 1930, by Doubleday & Company, Inc. "The Recollections of Captain Wilkie," Chambers' Journal, January 19, 1895, London.

Don Congdon Associates, Inc.
From *FAHRENHEIT 451* by Ray Bradbury. Copyright © 1953 by Ray Bradbury. "Hail and Farewell" by Ray Bradbury from *TWICE TWENTY-TWO*. Copyright © 1959 by Ray Bradbury. From "Just This Side of Byzantium" by Ray Bradbury from *DANDELION WINE*. Introduction Copyright © 1975 by Ray Bradbury. All Rights Reserved.

Acknowledgments continue on page 212.

Contributing Writer: Carroll Moulton, former English teacher, Stoughton High School, Stoughton, Massachusetts.

ontents

William Shakespeare

E. E. Cummings

Rudolfo Anaya

Authors
In
Depth

. . . .

SILVER LEVEL

*R*ay Bradbury In Depth

"This book, like most of my books and stories, was a surprise."
— Ray Bradbury, Introduction to Dandelion Wine

RAY **B**RADBURY is acknowledged today as one of the pioneers of science fiction. Unusually versatile and the author of over 500 works, Bradbury has written short stories, novels, poetry, plays, and screenplays. Bradbury's ingenious, thoughtful use of fantasy always engages the reader, and his gracefully poetic style has won him the admiration of many literary critics.

Childhood and Youth Born in Waukegan, Illinois, in 1920, Ray Bradbury recalls a childhood fear of the dark and an intense fascination with monsters, magicians, and adventure films. He began to write stories at the age of twelve. Two years later, in 1934, the Bradbury family moved to Los Angeles, California, where young Ray attended high school and haunted the Uptown Theatre to see films. He saved his lunch money to buy a typewriter and began to submit his stories to national magazines. From the beginning, Bradbury was attracted to science fiction, although this type of writing enjoyed little popularity at the time. In search of professional mentors, Bradbury joined the Los Angeles Science Fiction League, where he met a number of published authors who encouraged him.

First Steps to a Career Bradbury graduated from high school in 1938. Despite his energy and talent, he had little success with his writing for nearly three years. Bradbury sold newspapers on a street corner to support himself, but he never stopped writing stories, producing one new tale every week. Finally, in late 1940, he sold his first story, which was published the following year.

Two years later, he was making enough money from story sales so that he could abandon his newspaper job and begin writing full time. In 1947, Bradbury published his first collection of tales, *Dark Carnival*. The same year, he married Margaret McClure, and the two settled in an apartment just outside Los Angeles.

As a child, Bradbury had wanted to write stories about Mars and Martians. In 1950, he fulfilled that goal with the publication of *The Martian Chronicles,* his first novel. The book describes humankind's first attempt to colonize the planet Mars.

In *The Martian Chronicles,* Bradbury combines science fiction with social commentary—an approach that characterizes much of his later work. The book's focus on the human colonization of an already-inhabited planet allowed Bradbury to explore social concerns such as the threat of nuclear war, cencorship, racism, and the dangers of technology. Significantly, these issues of the 1950's continue to be major concerns today.

Recognition and Success The year 1953 was a turning point in Bradbury's career. The respected film director John Huston invited the young writer to co-author the screenplay for an adaptation of the classic novel by Herman Melville, *Moby-Dick*. Also in 1953, Bradbury published *Fahrenheit 451,* which took its title from the temperature at which book paper catches fire. In the novel's future society, all books are forbidden, and squads of "firemen" stand ready to search citizens' houses for any literary contraband and destroy it. In this novel, Bradbury launched a powerful attack on censorship and on how mass culture pressures the individual to conform.

In 1957, Bradbury published *Dandelion Wine,* a semi-autobiographical novel about his own childhood. Its gentle nostalgia and imaginative recreation of a vanished past proved Bradbury to be a writer of great range, and helped confirm his success.

◆ Technology

Technology is the development of machines and other tools that help humans control, study, or make use of parts of our environment. Some modern examples are space technologies and the many new advances in Internet technology. Technological innovation has inspired many writers of science fiction such as Ray Bradbury.

In the last few centuries, technological advances have been occurring at a faster and faster rate. Although the benefits of these inventions often seem obvious, technology can have unpredictable consequences for society. It can change cultural traditions, economic systems, and individual life styles. The pervasiveness of technological change can prompt nostalgia, such as the yearning for the past that fills *Dandelion Wine.*

By the 1950's, it seemed as if technology had triumphed. Nevertheless, some began to feel that its ascendency had brought many problems. Air and water were increasingly polluted. Possession of the latest technological devices often divided people economically. Only the rich could afford them.

In response to the disadvantages of technology, some steps have been taken. Government agencies and public spokespeople monitor the effects of each technological advance upon society or the environment. Meanwhile, the rate of technological advance continues to increase by leaps and bounds.

◆ Literary Works

Short Story Collections
- *Dark Carnival* (1947)
- *The Illustrated Man* (1951)
- *The Machineries of Joy* (1964)
- *I Sing the Body Electric!* (1969)
- *Selected Stories* (1975)
- *Driving Blind* (1997)

Novels
- *The Martian Chronicles* (1950)
- *Fahrenheit 451* (1953)
- *Dandelion Wine* (1957)
- *Something Wicked This Way Comes* (1962)
- *Quicker Than the Eye* (1996)

Ray Bradbury

from Fahrenheit 451

*Books have been banned; each community's fire department
searches out and burns the homes and libraries of criminal readers. In the following selection, renegade fireman Guy Montag
receives a visit from his suspicious boss, Captain Beatty.
Pretending to be ill, Montag plays for time while he conceals a contraband book from his video-addicted, near-illiterate wife Mildred.*

Beatty took a full minute to settle himself in and think back
for what he wanted to say.

"When did it all start, you ask, this job of ours, how did it come
about, where, when? Well, I'd say it really got started around about
a thing called the Civil War. Even though our rule book claims it
was founded earlier. The fact is we didn't get along well until photography came into its own. Then—motion pictures in the early
twentieth century. Radio. Television. Things began to have *mass*.[1]"

Montag sat in bed, not moving.

"And because they had mass, they became simpler," said
Beatty. "Once, books appealed to a few people, here, there, everywhere. They could afford to be different. The world was roomy.
But then the world got full of eyes and elbows and mouths.
Double, triple, quadruple population. Films and radios, magazines, books leveled down to a sort of pastepudding[2] norm, do
you follow me?"

"I think so."

Beatty peered at the smoke pattern he had put out on the air.
"Picture it. Nineteenth-century man with his horses, dogs, carts,
slow motion. Then, in the twentieth century, speed up your cam-
era. Books cut shorter. Condensations. Digests.[3] Tabloids.[4]
Everything boils down to the gag, the snap ending."

"Snap ending," Mildred nodded.

"Classics cut to fit fifteen-minute radio shows, then cut again
to fill a two-minute book column, winding up at last as a ten- or
twelve-line dictionary résumé.[5] I exaggerate, of course. The dictio-
naries were for reference. But many were those whose sole
knowledge of *Hamlet* (you know the title certainly, Montag; it is
probably only a faint rumor of a title to you, Mrs. Montag) whose
sole knowledge, as I say, of *Hamlet* was a one-page digest in a

---

1. **mass:** Weight; bulk; magnitude.
2. **pastepudding:** Homogenized; bland; tasteless.
3. **condensations; digests:** Books reduced in size and content.
4. **tabloids:** Half-size newspapers.
5. **resume:** Summary; synopsis.

book that claimed: *now at last you can read all the classics; keep up with your neighbors.* Do you see? Out of the nursery into the college and back to the nursery; there's your intellectual pattern for the past five centuries or more."

Mildred rose and began to move around the room, picking things up and putting them down. Beatty ignored her and continued:

"Speed up the film, Montag, quick. *Click, Pic, Look, Eye, Now, Flick, Here, There, Swift, Pace, Up, Down, In, Out, Why, How, Who, What, Where, Eh? Uh! Bang! Smack! Wallop, Bing, Bong, Boom!* Digest-digests, digest-digest-digests. Politics? One column, two sentences, a headline! Then, in midair, all vanishes! Whirl man's mind around about so fast under the pumping hands of publishers, exploiters, broadcasters that the centrifuge flings off all unnecessary, time-wasting thought!"

Mildred smoothed the bedclothes. Montag felt his heart jump and jump again as she patted his pillow. Right now she was pulling at his shoulder to try to get him to move so she could take the pillow out and fix it nicely and put it back. And perhaps cry out and stare or simply reach down her hand and say, "What's this?" and hold up the hidden book with touching innocence.

"School is shortened, discipline relaxed, philosophies, histories, languages dropped, English and spelling gradually gradually neglected, finally almost completely ignored. Life is immediate, the job counts, pleasure lies all about after work. Why learn anything save pressing buttons, pulling switches, fitting nuts and bolts?"

"Let me fix your pillow," said Mildred.

"No!" whispered Montag.

"The zipper displaces the button and a man lacks just that much time to think while dressing at dawn, a philosophical hour, and thus a melancholy hour."

Mildred said. "Here."

"Get away," said Montag.

"Life becomes one big pratfall, Montag; everything bang, boff, and wow!"

"Wow," said Mildred, yanking at the pillow.

"For God's sake, let me be!" cried Montag passionately.

Beatty opened his eyes wide.

Mildred's hand had frozen behind the pillow. Her fingers were tracing the book's outline and as the shape became familiar her face looked surprised and then stunned. Her mouth opened to ask a question . . .

"Empty the theaters save for clowns and furnish the rooms with glass walls and pretty colors running up and down the walls like confetti or blood or sherry or sauterne.[6] You like baseball, don't you, Montag?"

---

6. **sherry or sauterne:** Heavy wines that make patterns on the side of a glass.

"Baseball's a fine game."

Now Beatty was almost invisible, a voice somewhere behind a screen of smoke.

"What's this?" asked Mildred, almost with delight. Montag heaved back against her arms. "What's this here?"

☑ Check Your Comprehension

1. According to Beatty, when did "this job of ours" get started?
2. What does Beatty claim is the "intellectual pattern for the past five centuries or more"?
3. Why does Mildred pull at Montag's shoulder?
4. Toward the end of the passage, what does Mildred discover?

◆ Critical Thinking

1. How do Beatty's comments about *Hamlet* hint at the era in which this episode is set? **[Infer]**
2. According to Beatty, what have been the effects of ever-expanding media such as photography, film, radio, and television? **[Interpret]**
3. How do you explain Montag's abrupt treatment of Mildred? **[Interpret]**
4. Do you agree with Beatty's claims about the effects of technology? Briefly explain why or why not. **[Apply]**

ay Bradbury

HAIL AND FAREWELL

But of course he was going away, there was nothing else to do, the time was up, the clock had run out, and he was going very far away indeed. His suitcase was packed, his shoes were shined, his hair was brushed, he had expressly washed behind his ears, and it remained only for him to go down the stairs, out the front door, and up the street to the small-town station where the train would make a stop for him alone. Then Fox Hill, Illinois, would be left far off in his past. And he would go on, perhaps to Iowa, perhaps to Kansas, perhaps even to California; a small boy, twelve years old, with a birth certificate in his valise to show he had been born forty-three years ago.

"Willie!" called a voice belowstairs.

"Yes!" He hoisted his suitcase. In his bureau mirror he saw a face made of June dandelions and July apples and warm summer-morning milk. There, as always, was his look of the angel and the innocent, which might never, in the years of his life, change.

"Almost time," called the woman's voice.

"All right!" And he went down the stairs, grunting and smiling. In the living room sat Anna and Steve, their clothes painfully neat.

"Here I am!" cried Willie in the parlor door.

Anna looked like she was going to cry. "Oh, good Lord, you can't really be leaving us, can you, Willie?"

"People are beginning to talk," said Willie quietly. "I've been here three years now. But when people begin to talk, I know it's time to put on my shoes and buy a railway ticket."

It's all so strange. I don't understand. It's so sudden," Anna said. "Willie, we'll miss you."

"I'll write you every Christmas, so help me. Don't you write me."

"It's been a great pleasure and satisfaction," said Steve, sitting there, his words the wrong size in his mouth. "It's a shame it had to stop. It's a shame you had to tell us about yourself. It's an awful shame you can't stay on."

"You're the nicest folks I ever had," said Willie, four feet high, in no need of a shave, the sunlight on his face.

And then Anna *did* cry. "Willie, Willie." And she sat down and looked as if she wanted to hold him but was afraid to hold him now; she looked at him with shock and amazement and her hands empty, not knowing what to do with him now.

"It's not easy to go," said Willie. "You get used to things. You want to stay. But it doesn't work. I tried to stay on once after people began to suspect. 'How horrible!' people said. 'All these years, playing with our innocent children,' they said, 'and us not guessing! Awful!' they said. And finally I had to just leave town one night. It's not easy. You know darned well how much I love both of you. Thanks for three swell years."

They all went to the front door. "Willie, where're you going?"

"I don't know. I just start traveling. When I see a town that looks green and nice, I settle in."

"Will you ever come back?"

"Yes," he said earnestly with his high voice. "In about twenty years it should begin to show in my face. When it does, I'm going to make a grand tour of all the mothers and fathers I've ever had."

They stood on the cool summer porch, reluctant to say the last words. Steve was looking steadily at an elm tree. "How many other folks've you stayed with, Willie? How many adoptions?"

Willie figured it, pleasantly enough. "I guess it's about five towns and five couples and over twenty years gone by since I started my tour."

"Well, we can't holler," said Steve. "Better to've had a son thirty-six months than none whatever."

"Well," said Willie, and kissed Anna quickly, seized at his luggage, and was gone up the street in the green noon light, under the trees, a very young boy indeed, not looking back, running steadily.

The boys were playing on the green park diamond when he came by. He stood a little while among the oak-tree shadows, watching them hurl the white, snowy baseball into the warm summer air, saw the baseball shadow fly like a dark bird over the grass, saw their hands open in mouths to catch this swift piece of summer that now seemed most especially important to hold onto. The boys' voices yelled. The ball lit on the grass near Willie.

Carrying the ball forward from under the shade trees, he thought of the last three years now spent to the penny, and the five years before that, and so on down the line to the year when he was really eleven and twelve and fourteen and the voices saying: "What's wrong with Willie, missus?" "Mrs. B., is Willie late a-growin'?" "Willie, you smokin' *cigars* lately?" The echoes died in summer light and color. His mother's voice: "Willie's twenty-one today!" And a thousand voices saying: "Come back, son, when you're fifteen; *then* maybe we'll give you a job."

He stared at the baseball in his trembling hand, as if it were his life, an interminable[1] ball of years strung around and around and around, but always leading back to his twelfth birthday. He heard the kids walking toward him; he felt them blot out the sun, and they were older, standing around him.

"Willie! Where you goin'?" They kicked his suitcase.

How tall they stood to the sun. In the last few months it seemed the sun had passed a hand above their heads, beckoned, and they were warm metal drawn melting upward; they were golden taffy pulled by an immense gravity to the sky, thirteen, fourteen years old, looking down upon Willie, smiling, but already beginning to neglect him. It had started four months ago:

"Choose up sides! Who wants Willie?"

"Aw, Willie's too little; we don't play with 'kids.'"

And they raced ahead of him, drawn by the moon and the sun and the turning seasons of leaf and wind, and he was twelve years old and not of them any more. And the other voices beginning again on the old, the dreadfully familiar, the cool refrain: "Better feed that boy vitamins, Steve." "Anna, does shortness *run* in your family?" And the cold fist kneading at your heart again and knowing that the roots would have to be pulled up again after so many good years with the "folks."

"Willie, where you goin'?"

He jerked his head. He was back among the towering, shadowing boys who milled around him like giants at a drinking fountain bending down.

"Goin' a few days visitin' a cousin of mine."

"Oh," There was a day, a year ago, when they would have cared very much indeed. But now there was only curiosity for his luggage, their enchantment with trains and trips and far places.

"How about a coupla fast ones?" said Willie.

They looked doubtful, but, considering the circumstances, nodded. He dropped his bag and ran out; the white baseball was up in the sun, away to their burning white figures in the far meadow, up in the sun again, rushing, life coming and going in a pattern. Here, *there*! Mr. And Mrs. Robert Hanlon, Creek Bend, Wisconsin, 1932, the first couple, the first year! Here, there! Henry and Alice Boltz, Limeville, Iowa, 1935! The baseball flying. The Smiths, the Eatons, the Robinsons! 1939! 1945! Husband and wife, husband and wife, husband and wife, no children, no children, no children! A knock on this door, a knock on that.

"Pardon me. My name is William. I wonder if—"

"A sandwich? Come in, sit down. Where you *from*, son?"

The sandwich, a tall glass of cold milk, the smiling, the nodding, the comfortable, leisurely talking.

---

1. **interminable:** Endless.

"Son, you look like you been traveling. You run *off* from somewhere?"

"No."

"Boy, are you an orphan?"

Another glass of milk.

"We always wanted kids. It never worked out. Never knew why. One of those things. Well, well. It's getting late, son. Don't you think you better hit for home?"

"Got no home."

"A boy like you? Not dry behind the ears? Your mother'll be worried."

"Got no home and no folks anywhere in the world. I wonder if—I wonder—could I sleep here tonight?"

"Well, now, son, I don't just *know*. We never considered taking in—" said the husband.

"We got chicken for supper tonight," said the wife, "enough for extras, enough for company. . . ."

And the years turning and flying away, the voices, and the faces, and the people, and always the same first conversations. The voice of Emily Robinson, in her rocking chair, in summernight darkness, the last night he stayed with her, the night she discovered his secret, her voice saying:

"I look at all the little children's faces going by. And I sometimes think, What a shame, what a shame, that all these flowers have to be cut, all these bright fires have to be put out. What a shame these, all of these you see in schools or running by, have to get tall and unsightly and wrinkle and turn gray or get bald, and finally, all bone and wheeze, be dead and buried off away. When I hear them laugh I can't believe they'll ever go the road I'm going. Yet here they *come*! I still remember Wordsworth's poem: 'When all at once I saw a crowd, A host of golden daffodils; Beside the lake, beneath the trees, Fluttering and dancing in the breeze.' That's how I think of children, cruel as they sometimes are, mean as I know they can be, but not yet showing the meanness around their eyes or *in* their eyes, not yet full of tiredness. They're so eager for everything! I guess that's what I miss most in older folks, the eagerness gone nine times out of ten, the freshness gone, so much of the drive and life down the drain. I like to watch school let out each day. It's like someone threw a bunch of flowers out the school front doors. How does it feel, Willie? How does it feel to be young forever? To look like a silver dime new from the mint? Are you happy? Are you as fine as you *seem*?"

The baseball whizzed from the blue sky, stung his hand like a great pale insect. Nursing it, he hears his memory say:

"I worked with what I had. After my folks died, after I found I couldn't get man's work anywhere, I tried carnivals, but they only laughed. 'Son,' they said, 'you're not a midget, and even if you are, you look like a *boy!* We want midgets with midgets' *faces!* Sorry, son, sorry.' So I left home, started out, thinking: What *was* I? A boy. I looked like a boy, sounded like a boy, so I might as well go on being a boy. No use fighting it. No use screaming. So what could I do? What job was handy? And then one day I saw this man in a restaurant looking at another man's pictures of his children. 'Sure wish I had kids,' he said. 'Sure wish I had kids.' He kept shaking his head. And me sitting a few seats away from him, a hamburger in my hands. I sat there, *frozen!* At that very instant I knew what my job would be for all of the rest of my life. There *was* work for me, after all. Making lonely people happy. Keeping myself busy. Playing forever. I knew I had to play forever. Deliver a few papers, run a few errands, mow a few lawns, maybe. But *hard* work? No. All I had to do was be a mother's son and a father's pride. I turned to the man down the counter from me. 'I beg your pardon,' I said. I *smiled* at him. . . ."

"But, Willie," said Mrs. Emily long ago, "didn't you ever get lonely? Didn't you ever want—*things*—that grownups wanted?"

"I fought that out alone," said Willie. "I'm a boy, I told myself, I'll have to live in a boy's world, read boys' books, play boys' games, cut myself off from everything else. I can't be both. I got to be only one thing—young. And so I played that way. Oh, it wasn't easy. There were times—" He lapsed into silence.

"And the family you lived with, they never knew?"

"No. Telling them would have spoiled everything. I told them I was a runaway; I let them check through official channels, police. Then, when there was no record, let them put in to adopt me. That was best of all; as long as they never guessed. But then, after three years, or five years, they guessed, or a traveling man came through, or a carnival man saw me, and it was over. It always had to end."

"And you're *very* happy and it's *nice* being a child for over forty years?"

"It's a living, as they say. And when you make other people happy, then you're almost happy too. I got my job to do and I do it. And anyway, in a few years now I'll be in my second child-hood. All the fevers will be out of me and all the unfulfilled things and most of the dreams. Then I can relax, maybe, and play the role all the way."

He threw the baseball one last time and broke the reverie.[2] Then he was running to seize his luggage. Tom, Bill, Jamie, Bob, Sam—their names moved on his lips. They were embarrassed at his shaking hands.

---

2. **reverie:** Musing; daydream.

"After all, Willie, it ain't as if you're going to China or Timbuktu."

"That's right, isn't it?" Willie did not move.

"So long, Willie. See you next week!"

"So long, so long!"

And he was walking off with his suitcase again, looking at the trees, going away from the boys and the street where he had lived, and as he turned the corner a train whistle screamed, and he began to run.

The last thing he saw and heard was a white ball tossed at a high roof, back and forth, back and forth, and two voices crying out as the ball pitched now up, down, and back through the sky, "Annie, Annie, over! Annie, Annie, over!" like the crying of birds flying off to the far south.

In the early morning, with the smell of the mist and the cold metal, with the iron smell of the train around him and a full night of traveling shaking his bones and his body, and a smell of the sun beyond the horizon, he awoke and looked out upon a small town just arising from sleep. Lights were coming on, soft voices muttered, a red signal bobbed back and forth, back and forth in the cold air. There was that sleeping hush in which echoes are dignified by clarity, in which echoes stand nakedly alone and sharp. A porter moved by, a shadow in shadows.

"Sir," said Willie.

The porter stopped.

"What town's this?" whispered the boy in the dark.

"Valleyville."

"How many people?"

"Ten thousand. Why? This your stop?"

"It looks green." Willie gazed out at the cold morning town for a long time. "It looks nice and quiet," said Willie.

"Son," said the porter, "you know where you *going*?"

"Here," said Willie, and got up quietly in the still, cool, iron-smelling morning, in the train dark, with a rustling and stir.

"I hope you know what you're doing, boy," said the porter.

"Yes, sir," said Willie. "I know what I'm doing." And he was down the dark aisle, luggage lifted after him by the porter, and out in the smoking, steaming-cold, beginning-to-lighten morning. He stood looking up at the porter and the black metal train against the few remaining stars. The train gave a great wailing blast of whistle, the porters cried out all along the line, the cars jolted, and his special porter waved and smiled down at the boy there, the small boy there with the big luggage who shouted up to him, even as the whistle screamed again.

"What?" shouted the porter, hand cupped to ear.

"Wish me luck!" cried Willie.

"Best of luck, son," called the porter, waving, smiling. "Best of luck, boy!"

"Thanks!" said Willie, in the great sound of the train, in the steam and roar.

He watched the black train until it was completely gone away and out of sight. He did not move all the time it was going. He stood quietly, a small boy twelve years old, on the worn wooden platform, and only after three entire minutes did he turn at last to face the empty streets below.

Then, as the sun was rising, he began to walk very fast, so as to keep warm, down into the new town.

☑ **Check Your Comprehension**

1. As the story opens, what is Willie preparing to do, and why?
2. What does Emily Robinson tell Willie that she misses most in grownups?
3. In the restaurant, what job does Willie discover he wants to do for the rest of his life?
4. At the end of the story, what new beginning does Willie make?

◆ **Critical Thinking**

1. How might Willie's life be described as both a blessing and a curse? **[Interpret]**

2. Fantasy is imaginative writing that contains elements not found in real life. Suspense is a reader's feeling of anxious uncertainty. Explain how Bradbury combines fantasy with suspense in the opening section of the story. **[Analyze]**
3. The theme of a literary work is its central idea or overall message. What is Bradbury's theme in this story, in your opinion? **[Interpret]**
4. Bradbury has said, "The important thing [in life] is to have a ball, to be joyful, to be loving." How is this idea represented in "Hail and Farewell"? **[Apply]**

ay Bradbury

from Just This Side of Byzantium: An Introduction *from* Dandelion Wine

This book, like most of my books and stories, was a surprise. I began to learn the nature of such surprises, thank God, when I was fairly young as a writer. Before that, like every beginner, I thought you could beat, pummel, and thrash an idea into existence. Under such treatment, of course, any decent idea folds up its paws, turns on its back, fixes its eyes on eternity, and dies.

It was with great relief, then, that in my early twenties I floundered into a word-association process in which I simply got out of bed each morning, walked to my desk, and put down any word or series of words that happened along in my head.

I would then take arms against the word, or for it, and bring on an assortment of characters to weigh the word and show me its meaning in my own life. An hour or two hours later, to my amazement, a new story would be finished and done. The surprise was total and lovely. I soon found that I would have to work this way for the rest of my life.

First I rummaged my mind for words that could describe my personal nightmares, fears of night and time from my childhood, and shaped stories from these.

Then I took a long look at the green apple trees and the old house I was born in and the house next door where lived my grandparents, and all the lawns of the summers I grew up in, and I began to try words for all that.

What you have here in this book then is a gathering of dandelions from all those years. The wine metaphor which appears again and again in these pages is wonderfully apt. I was gathering images all of my life, storing them away, and forgetting them. Somehow I had to send myself back, with words as catalysts,[1] to open the memories out and see what they had to offer.

So from the age of twenty-four to thirty-six hardly a day passed when I didn't stroll myself across a recollection of my grandparents' northern Illinois grass, hoping to come across some old half-burnt firecracker, a rusted toy, or a fragment of letter written to myself in some young year hoping to contact the older person I became to remind him of his past, his life, his people, his joys, and his drenching sorrows.

It became a game that I took to with immense gusto: to see how much I could remember about dandelions themselves, or

---

1. catalysts: Things that precipitate change.

picking wild grapes with my father and brother, rediscovering the mosquito-breeding ground rain barrel by the side bay window, or searching out the smell of the gold-fuzzed bees that hung around our back porch grape arbor. Bees do have a smell, you know, and if they don't they should, for their feet are dusted with spices from a million flowers.

And then I wanted to call back what the ravine was like, especially on those nights when walking home late across town, after seeing Lon Chaney's delicious fright *The Phantom of the Opera*, my brother Skip would run ahead and hide under the ravine-creek bridge like the Lonely One and leap out and grab me, shrieking, so I ran, fell, and ran again, gibbering all the way home. That was great stuff.

Along the way I came upon and collided, through word-association, with old and true friendships. I borrowed my friend John Huff from my childhood in Arizona and shipped him East to Green Town so that I could say goodbye to him properly.

Along the way, I sat me down to breakfasts, lunches, and dinners with the long dead and much loved. For I was a boy who did indeed love his parents and grandparents and his brother, even when that brother "ditched" him.

Along the way, I found myself in the basement working the wine-press for my father, or on the front porch Independence night helping my Uncle Bion load and fire his homemade brass cannon.

Thus I fell into surprise. No one told me to surprise myself, I might add. I came on the old and best ways of writing through ignorance and experiment and was startled when truths leaped out of bushes like quail before gunshot. I blundered into creativity as blindly as any child learning to walk and see. I learned to let my senses and my Past tell me all that was somehow true.

So, I turned myself into a boy running to bring a dipper of clear rainwater out of that barrel by the side of the house. And, of course, the more water you dip out the more flows in. The flow has never ceased. Once I learned to keep going back and back again to those times, I had plenty of memories and sense impressions to play with, not work with, no, play with. *Dandelion Wine* is nothing if it is not the boy-hid-in-the-man playing in the fields of the Lord on the green grass of other Augusts in the midst of starting to grow up, grow old, and sense darkness waiting under the trees to seed the blood.

I was amused and somewhat astonished at a critic a few years back who wrote an article analyzing *Dandelion Wine* plus the more realistic works of Sinclair Lewis, wondering how I could have been born and raised in Waukegan, which I renamed Green Town for my novel, and not noticed how ugly the harbor was and how depressing the coal docks and railyards down below the town.

But, of course, I had noticed them and, genetic enchanter that I was, was fascinated by their beauty. Trains and boxcars and the smell of coal and fire are not ugly to children. Ugliness is a concept that we happen on later and become self-conscious about. Counting boxcars is a prime activity of boys. Their elders fret and fume and jeer at the train that holds them up, but boys happily count and cry the names of the cars as they pass from far places.

And again, that supposedly ugly railyard was where carnivals and circuses arrived with elephants who washed the brick pavements with mighty steaming acid waters at five in the dark morning.

As for the coal from the docks, I went down in my basement every autumn to await the arrival of the truck and its metal chute, which clanged down and released a ton of beauteous meteors that fell out of far space into my cellar and threatened to bury me beneath dark treasures.

In other words, if your boy is a poet, horse manure can only mean flowers to him; which is, of course, what horse manure has always been about.

☑ Check Your Comprehension

1. According to the writer, what surprising result emerged in an hour or two from his "word-association process"?

2. Identify two specific objects that the writer recalls in his memories of his grandparents' house in Illinois.

3. What game did the young Bradbury play with his brother Skip?

4. What does Bradbury claim about people's ideas of ugliness?

◆ Critical Thinking

1. From the evidence of this excerpt, what role do memories of the past play in Bradbury's writing? **[Interpret]**

2. What three adjectives would you choose to describe the young Bradbury's personality? Briefly explain your choices. **[Analyze]**

3. Bradbury says he changed the name of his childhood home, Waukegan, Illinois, to Green Town in *Dandelion Wine*. Why do you think Bradbury made this change? **[Speculate]**

4. Do you agree with Bradbury's assessment of people's perception of what is ugly? Do you think his comments can be applied to everyday life? **[Evaluate/Apply]**

Ray Bradbury
Comparing and Connecting the Author's Works

◆ Literary Focus: Science Fiction

Science fiction combines elements of fiction and fantasy with scientific fact. This type of writing is most effective when the writer creates a believable setting and characters and balances new ideas with familiar details. Science fiction became especially popular toward the end of the nineteenth century, with such stories as Jules Verne's *Twenty Thousand Leagues Under the Sea* and H. G. Wells's *The Time Machine* and *The War of the Worlds*. Leading writers of science fiction in the twentieth century have included Isaac Asimov, Robert Heinlein, Ursula K. LeGuin, and, of course, Ray Bradbury.

Time travel and the ingenious manipulation of time are leading techniques in science fiction.

1. Ray Bradbury has said, "A man cannot possibly speak futures (write or talk about the future) unless he has a strong sense of the past." How might you apply this idea to the passage from *Fahrenheit 451*?

2. What fantasy about time is central to the plot in "Hail and Farewell"?

3. In his introduction to *Dandelion Wine*, what link does Bradbury stress between the creative process and a writer's memories of the past?

◆ Drawing Conclusions About Bradbury's Work

In a magazine interview, Bradbury remarked that poetry plays an important role in his writing. Many critics have singled out Bradbury's prose style as notably poetic. One prominent feature of this style is Bradbury's use of figurative language, especially similes and metaphors. A **simile** uses *like* or *as* to make a direct comparison between two unlike things; the phrase *fresh as a daisy* is a simile. In a **metaphor** something is described as though it were something else; the saying *life is just a bowl of cherries* is a metaphor.

Together with a partner, create two Sunburst Organizers like the one shown below, one for simile and one for metaphor. In the boxes at the right, use the lines to record examples of similes and metaphors from each of the three selections you have read.

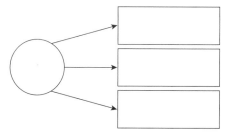

◆ Idea Bank

Writing

1. **Letter** Evaluate the three selections you have read, using criteria such as suspense, style, and theme. Then write a letter to Ray Bradbury in which you identify your favorite selection and tell the author why you enjoyed it.

2. ***What If?* Scenario** Science fiction relies on a *What if . . .?* question. For example, "Hail and Farewell" is built around the concept of a boy trapped in time at his twelfth birthday. Think of a different *What If?* scenario that might serve as the basis for a science fiction story. In a paragraph or two, sketch the plot of your story.

3. **Op-Ed Column** One of Bradbury's major themes is his concern over the advantages and disadvantages of technology. Choose a technological advance in the news today, such as the Internet or bioengineering. Research some of the advantages and disadvantages of this technology. Then write an Op-Ed column in which you present your results and express your own opinion.

Speaking and Listening

4. **Dramatic Reading** Choose a speech or a sequence of paragraphs from one of the selections: for example, one of Beatty's speeches to Montag in *Fahrenheit 451* or Emily Robinson's long speech to Willie in "Hail and Farewell." Practice a dramatic reading of the passage, using pace, emphasis, tone, and volume to bring it to life. Then perform your reading for an audience of classmates or friends. **[Performing Arts Link]**

5. **Sound Track** Together with a small group, produce a sound track of suitable recorded music and other sound effects for a filmed version of "Hail and Farewell." Then give a demonstration of your sound track to the class as a whole. Be prepared to explain and defend your choices. **[Music Link] [Group Activity]**

Researching and Representing

6. **Collage** Using Internet and library resources, prepare a collage that illustrates the lives and major works of three or four leading science fiction writers during the past one hundred years. Use photographs, original art work, capsule biographies, cartoons, charts, and other graphic devices. When you have finished work, display your collage to the class as a whole. **[Art Link]**

◆ Further Reading, Listening, and Viewing

- Bradbury, Ray: *Dandelion Wine* (1957). This boyhood reminiscence vividly recalls life in the Midwest in an earlier era.

- Bradbury, Ray: *Classic Stories 1: The Golden Apples of the Sun/R is for Rocket* (1990). This volume contains some of Bradbury's most popular stories.

- Bradbury, Ray: *Dark They Were and Golden-Eyed* (1994). This audiocassette dramatizes a compelling story about a family who comes to colonize Mars.

- *Ray Bradbury: An American Icon* (1997). This videocassette chronicles Bradbury's life and career.

On the Web:

http://www.phschool.com/atschool/literature
Go to the student edition *Silver*. Proceed to Unit 1. Then, click Hot Links to find Web sites featuring Ray Bradbury.

Jack London In Depth

"[Buck] walked to the center of the open space and listened. It was the call, the many-noted call, sounding more luringly and compelling than ever before. And as never before, he was ready to obey. John Thornton was dead. The last tie was broken. Man and the claims of man no longer bound him."

—*Jack London,* **The Call of the Wild**

JACK LONDON's wildly popular fiction made him the highest-paid writer of his time, just after the dawn of the twentieth century. His books continue to be read by legions of devoted fans. What explains the enduring appeal of London's works to generations of readers? Perhaps one critic of the day grasped the secret of London's success: in his novels and short stories, wrote Granville Hicks, London had discovered "a dreamland of heroic opportunity."

Youthful Adventure One of the author's biographers, Alex Kershaw, has written that "more than any other American writer, Jack London had an insatiable appetite for life." London was born in San Francisco, California, in 1876. After completing grammar school at age fourteen, he worked in a cannery and on the docks as a longshoreman. Together with some friends, he bought a boat and risked arrest by raiding oyster beds in San Francisco Bay. Signing up as a sailor at the age of seventeen, he joined a seal-hunting cruise to Japan; he recalls some of his experiences on this journey in the memoir entitled "That Dead Men Rise Up Never." Returning home, he took a tramping trip through the United States and Canada, completed his high school courses in one year, and studied for one semester at the University of California. Finally, at the age of twenty-one, London embarked on an adventure that would change his life: he joined the gold rush to the Klondike.

The Far North The Klondike region lies in the Yukon Territory of northwest Canada near the Alaskan border. Rich gold deposits were discovered there in 1896, triggering a rush of thousands of prospectors to the almost uninhabited region. Like most of these fortune hunters, Jack London found no gold. However, in the far North he discovered something even more valuable: the inspiration for some of his best fiction. For London, the forbidding landscape and unforgiving climate of the Klondike posed a stark challenge to human strength and survival. The conflicts of man vs. nature and civilization vs. barbarity were to become some of the writer's main themes.

Early Career Soon after his return from the Klondike, London began to write about his experiences. His stories appeared in two popular magazines, the *Overland Monthly* and the *Atlantic Monthly*. London's reputation gathered steam rapidly. Within three years, he had published two collections of stories, a lengthy report on slum conditions in England, and the novel that gained him international fame, *The Call of the Wild*. The story of the kidnapped pet dog Buck—half St. Bernard, half shepherd— and his transformation into a wild dog in the Yukon was written in a little over three months. Upon publication, it was instantly hailed as a classic. In the course of nearly a century, it has become one of the most widely-read American novels.

Riches and Fame A prolific writer, London soon capitalized on his success with a series of novels and stories: *The Sea-Wolf* (1904), *White Fang* (1906), and *Love of Life and Other Stories* (1907). He took a journalism assignment to report on the Russo-Japanese War in 1904. He made lecture tours, sailed in the Pacific, and bought an estate in California. London's interest in philosophy and sociology, dating back to his university days, inspired him to write a number of essays on class struggle and primitive violence. In 1909, he published a semi-autobiographical novel, *Martin Eden,* about the struggles of a young writer.

With rare exceptions such as the story "To Build a Fire," however, London's work toward the end of his career failed to recapture the brilliance of his early stories and novels. In the final years of his brief life, poor management caused him financial problems and the excesses of hard living broke his health. London died at his ranch in California, aged only forty.

◆ Naturalism

Jack London's fiction reveals many of the features of naturalism, a literary movement among novelists at the end of the nineteenth century. Naturalism had its origins in the theory and practice of the French novelist Émile Zola (1840–1902), who believed that fiction should depict human society with scientific precision and unflinching accuracy. Naturalist writers tended to view human beings as the helpless victims of either heredity or environment. In the face of such supremely strong forces, human

beings had to develop brute strength in order to survive. Other early exponents of naturalism in American literature included Stephen Crane, author of the classic Civil War novel, *The Red Badge of Courage;* Frank Norris, whose characters struggled with economic oppression; and Theodore Dreiser, who portrayed characters trapped or crushed by social forces beyond their control. Although it is difficult to generalize about such a complex movement, the following short poem by Jack London's contemporary Stephen Crane suggests some of the bleakness of naturalism's vision of the power of the individual:

A man said to the universe:
"Sir, I exist!"
"However," replied the universe,
"The fact has not created in me
A sense of obligation."

◆ Literary Works

Short Story Collections
- *The Son of the Wolf* (1900)
- *The God of His Fathers and Other Stories* (1901)
- *Love of Life and Other Stories* (1907)
- *South Sea Tales* (1911)
- *The Strength of the Strong* (1914)

Novels
- *The Call of the Wild* (1903)
- *The Sea-Wolf* (1904)
- *White Fang* (1906)
- *The Iron Heel* (1908)
- *Martin Eden* (1909)
- *The Valley of the Moon* (1913)

Jack London

from The Call of the Wild

In the following excerpt from The Call of the Wild, *the dog Buck, kidnapped to the Yukon to serve as a sled dog, demonstrates his love for and loyalty to the man who rescued him from abusive owners.*

That winter, at Dawson, Buck performed another exploit, not so heroic, perhaps, but one that put his name many notches higher on the totem-pole of Alaskan fame. This exploit was particularly gratifying to the three men; for they stood in need of the outfit which it furnished, and were enabled to make a long-desired trip into the virgin East, where miners had not yet appeared. It was brought about by a conversation in the Eldorado Saloon, in which men waxed boastful of their favorite dogs. Buck, because of his record, was the target for these men, and Thornton was driven stoutly to defend him. At the end of half an hour one man stated that his dog could start a sled with five hundred pounds and walk off with it; a second bragged six hundred for his dog; and a third, seven hundred.

"Pooh! pooh!" said John Thornton; "Buck can start a thousand pounds."

"And break it out? and walk off with it for a hundred yards?" demanded Matthewson, a Bonanza King, he of the seven hundred vaunt.

"And break it out, and walk off with it for a hundred yards," John Thornton said coolly.

"Well," Matthewson said, slowly and deliberately, so that all could hear, "I've got a thousand dollars that says he can't. And there it is." So saying, he slammed a sack of gold dust the size of a bologna sausage down upon the bar.

Nobody spoke. Thornton's bluff, if bluff it was, had been called. He could feel a flush of warm blood creeping up his face. His tongue had tricked him. He did not know whether Buck could start a thousand pounds. Half a ton! The enormousness of it appalled him. He had great faith in Buck's strength and had often thought him capable of starting such a load; but never, as now, had he faced the possibility of it, the eyes of a dozen men fixed upon him, silent and waiting. Further, he had no thousand dollars; nor had Hans or Pete.

"I've got a sled standing outside now, with twenty fifty-pound sacks of flour on it," Matthewson went on with brutal directness; "so don't let that hinder you."

Thornton did not reply. He did not know what to say. He glanced from face to face in the absent way of a man who has lost the power of thought and is seeking somewhere to find the thing that will start it going again. The face of Jim O'Brien, a Mastodon King and old-time comrade, caught his eyes. It was a cue to him, seeming to rouse him to do what he would never have dreamed of doing.

"Can you lend me a thousand?" he asked, almost in a whisper.

"Sure," answered O'Brien, thumping down a plethoric sack by the side of Matthewson's. "Though it's little faith I'm having, John, that the beast can do the trick."

The Eldorado emptied its occupants into the street to see the test. The tables were deserted, and the dealers and gamekeepers came forth to see the outcome of the wager and to lay odds. Several hundred men, furred and mittened, banked around the sled within easy distance. Matthewson's sled, loaded with a thousand pounds of flour, had been standing for a couple of hours, and in the intense cold (it was sixty below zero) the runners had frozen fast to the hard-packed snow. Men offered odds of two to one that Buck could not budge the sled. A quibble arose concerning the phrase "break out." O'Brien contended it was Thornton's privilege to knock the runners loose, leaving Buck to "break it out" from a dead standstill. Matthewson insisted that the phrase included breaking the runners from the frozen grip of the snow. A majority of the men who had witnessed the making of the bet decided in his favor, whereat the odds went up to three to one against Buck.

There were no takers. Not a man believed him capable of the feat. Thornton had been hurried into the wager, heavy with doubt; and now that he looked at the sled itself, the concrete fact, with the regular team of ten dogs curled up in the snow before it, the more impossible the task appeared. Matthewson waxed jubilant.

"Three to one!" he proclaimed. "I'll lay you another thousand at that figure, Thornton. What d'ye say?"

Thornton's doubt was strong in his face, but his fighting spirit was aroused—the fighting spirit that soars above odds, fails to recognize the impossible, and is deaf to all save the clamor for battle. He called Hans and Pete to him. Their sacks were slim, and with his own the three partners could rake together only two hundred dollars. In the ebb of their fortunes, this sum was their total capital; yet they laid it unhesitatingly against Matthewson's six hundred.

The team of ten dogs was unhitched, and Buck, with his own harness, was put into the sled. He had caught the contagion of the excitement, and he felt that in some way he must do a great thing for John Thornton. Murmurs of admiration at his splendid appearance went up. He was in perfect condition, without an ounce of superfluous flesh, and the one hundred and fifty pounds that he weighed were so many pounds of grit and virility. His furry coat shone with the sheen of silk. Down the neck and across the shoulders, his mane, in repose as it was, half bristled and seemed to lift with every movement, as though excess of vigor made each particular hair alive and active. The great breast and heavy fore legs were no more than in proportion with the rest of the body, where the muscles showed in tight rolls underneath the skin. Men felt these muscles and proclaimed them hard as iron, and the odds went down to two to one.

"Gad, sir! Gad, sir!" stuttered a member of the latest dynasty, a king of the Skookum Benches. "I offer you eight hundred for him, sir, before the test, sir; eight hundred just as he stands."

Thornton shook his head and stepped to Buck's side.

"You must stand off from him," Matthewson protested. "Free play and plenty of room."

The crowd fell silent; only could be heard the voices of the gamblers vainly offering two to one. Everybody acknowledged Buck a magnificent animal, but twenty fifty-pound sacks of flour bulked too large in their eyes for them to loosen their pouch-strings.

Thornton knelt down by Buck's side. He took his head in his two hands and rested cheek on cheek. He did not playfully shake him, as was his wont, or murmur soft love curses; but he whispered in his ear. "As you love me, Buck. As you love me," was what he whispered. Buck whined with suppressed eagerness.

The crowd was watching curiously. The affair was growing mysterious. It seemed like a conjuration. As Thornton got to his feet, Buck seized his mittened hand between his jaws, pressing in with his teeth and releasing slowly, half-reluctantly. It was the answer, in terms, not of speech, but of love. Thornton stepped well back.

"Now, Buck," he said.

Buck tightened the traces, then slacked them for a matter of several inches. It was the way he had learned.

"Gee!" Thornton's voice rang out, sharp in the tense silence.

Buck swung to the right, ending the movement in a plunge that took up the slack and with a sudden jerk arrested his one hundred and fifty pounds. The load quivered, and from under the runners arose a crisp crackling.

"Haw!" Thornton commanded.

Buck duplicated the manoeuvre, this time to the left. The crackling turned into a snapping, the sled pivoting and the runners slipping and grating several inches to the side. The sled was broken out. Men were holding their breaths, intensely unconscious of the fact.

"Now, MUSH!"

Thornton's command cracked out like a pistol-shot. Buck threw himself forward, tightening the traces with a jarring lunge. His whole body was gathered compactly together in the tremendous effort, the muscles writhing and knotting like live things under the silky fur. His great chest was low to the ground, his head forward and down, while his feet were flying like mad, the claws scarring the hard-packed snow in parallel grooves. The sled swayed and trembled, half-started forward. One of his feet slipped, and one man groaned aloud. Then the sled lurched ahead in what appeared a rapid succession of jerks, though it never really came to a dead stop again . . . half an inch . . . an inch . . . two inches. . . . The jerks perceptibly diminished; as the sled gained momentum, he caught them up, till it was moving steadily along.

Men gasped and began to breathe again, unaware that for a moment they had ceased to breathe. Thornton was running behind, encouraging Buck with short, cheery words. The distance had been measured off, and as he neared the pile of firewood which marked the end of the hundred yards, a cheer began to grow and grow, which burst into a roar as he passed the firewood and halted at command. Every man was tearing himself loose, even Matthewson. Hats and mittens were flying in the air. Men were shaking hands, it did not matter with whom, and bubbling over in a general incoherent babel.

But Thornton fell on his knees beside Buck. Head was against head, and he was shaking him back and forth. Those who hurried up heard him cursing Buck, and he cursed him long and fervently, and softly and lovingly.

"Gad, sir! Gad, sir!" spluttered the Skookum Bench king. "I'll give you a thousand for him, sir, a thousand, sir—twelve hundred, sir."

Thornton rose to his feet. His eyes were wet. The tears were streaming frankly down his cheeks. "Sir," he said to the Skookum Bench king, "no, sir. You can go to hell, sir. It's the best I can do for you, sir."

Buck seized Thornton's hand in his teeth. Thornton shook him back and forth. As though animated by a common impulse, the onlookers drew back a respectful distance; nor were they again indiscreet enough to interrupt.

☑ Check Your Comprehension

1. (a) In the Eldorado Saloon, what claim does Thornton make about Buck? (b) What does Thornton do to back up this claim?
2. How does Jim O'Brien help Thornton?
3. What disagreement arises among the men concerning the phrase "break out"?
4. (a) What three commands does Thornton give Buck? (b) What is the result?

◆ Critical Thinking

1. Soon after this episode begins, why does Thornton feel that his tongue has tricked him? **[Interpret]**

2. Suspense is a feeling of anxious uncertainty about the outcome of events. Identify two ways in which London creates and maintains suspense in this passage. **[Analyze]**
3. Cite three details from the passage that portray the unique bond between Thornton and Buck. **[Support]**
4. (a) Why do you think the men react as they do to Buck's "exploit"? (b) How might this reaction be related to London's overall theme in the passage? **[Infer]**

Jack London

from That Dead Men Rise Up Never

The month in which my seventeenth birthday arrived I signed on before the mast on the *Sophie Sutherland,* a three-topmast schooner bound on a seven-months' seal-hunting cruise to the coast of Japan. We sailed from San Francisco, and immediately I found confronting me a problem of no inconsiderable proportions. There were twelve men of us in the forecastle, ten of whom were hardened, tarry-thumbed sailors. Not alone was I a youth and on my first voyage, but I had for shipmates men who had come through the hard school of the merchant service of Europe. As boys, they had had to perform their ship's duty, and, in addition, by immemorial sea custom, they had had to be the slaves of the ordinary and able-bodied seamen. When they became ordinary seamen they were still the slaves of the able-bodied. Thus, in the forecastle, with the watch below, an able seaman, lying in his bunk, will order an ordinary seaman to fetch him his shoes or bring him a drink of water. Now the ordinary seaman may be lying in *his* bunk. He is just as tired as the able seaman. Yet he must get out of his bunk and fetch and carry. If he refuses, he will be beaten. If, perchance, he is so strong that he can whip the able seaman, then all the able seamen, or as many as may be necessary, pitch upon the luckless devil and administer the beating.

My problem now becomes apparent. These hard-bit Scandinavian sailors had come through a hard school. As boys they had served their mates, and as able seamen they looked to be served by other boys. I was a boy—withal with a man's body. I had never been to sea before—withal I was a good sailor and knew my business. It was either a case of holding my own with them or of going under. I had signed on as an equal, and an equal I must maintain myself, or else endure seven months of hell at their hands. And it was this very equality they resented. By what right was I an equal? I had not earned that high privilege. I had not endured the miseries they had endured as maltreated boys or bullied ordinaries. Worse than that, I was a landlubber making his first voyage. And yet, by the injustice of fate, on the ship's articles I was their equal.

My method was deliberate, and simple, and drastic. In the first place, I resolved to do my work, no matter how hard or dangerous it might be, so well that no man would be called upon to do it for me. Further, I put ginger in my muscles. I never malingered when pulling on a rope, for I knew the eagle eyes of my forecastle mates were squinting for just such evidences of my inferiority. I made it a point to be among the first of the watch going on deck, among the last going below, never leaving a sheet or tackle for some one else to coil over a pin. I was always eager for the run aloft for the shifting of topsail sheets and tacks, or for the setting or taking in of topsails; and in these matters I did more than my share.

Furthermore, I was on a hair-trigger of resentment myself. I knew better than to accept any abuse or the slightest patronizing. At the first hint of such, I went off—I exploded. I might be beaten in the subsequent fight, but I left the impression that I was a wild-cat and that I would just as willingly fight again. My intention was to demonstrate that I would tolerate no imposition. I proved that the man who imposed on me must have a fight on his hands. And, doing my work well, the innate justice of the men, assisted by their wholesome dislike for a clawing and rending wild-cat ruction, soon led them to give over their hectoring. After a bit of strife, my atti-tude was accepted, and it was my pride that I was taken in as an equal in spirit as well as in fact. From then on, everything was beautiful, and the voyage promised to be a happy one.

But there was one other man in the forecastle. Counting the Scandinavians as ten, and myself as the eleventh, this man was the twelfth and last. We never knew his name, contenting our-selves with calling him the "Bricklayer." He was from Missouri—at least he so informed us in the one meagre confidence he was guilty of in the early days of the voyage. Also, at that time, we learned several other things. He was a bricklayer by trade. He had never even seen salt water until the week before he joined us, at which time he had arrived in San Francisco and looked upon San Francisco Bay. Why he, of all men, at forty years of age, should have felt the prod to go to sea, was beyond all of us; for it was our unanimous conviction that no man less fitted for the sea had ever embarked on it. But to sea he had come. After a week's stay in a sailors' boardinghouse, he had been shoved aboard of us as an able seaman.

All hands had to do his work for him. Not only did he know nothing, but he proved himself unable to learn anything. Try as they would, they could never teach him to steer. To him the com-pass must have been a profound and awful whirligig. He never mastered its cardinal points, much less the checking and steady-ing of the ship on her course. He never did come to know whether ropes should be coiled from left to right or from right to left. It was mentally impossible for him to learn the easy muscu-lar trick of throwing his weight on a rope in pulling and hauling. The simplest knots and turns were beyond his comprehension, while he was mortally afraid of going aloft. Bullied by captain and mate, he was one day forced aloft. He managed to get under-neath the crosstrees, and there he froze to the ratlines. Two sailors had to go after him to help him down.

All of which was bad enough had there been no worse. But he was vicious, malignant, dirty, and without common decency. He was a tall, powerful man, and he fought with everybody. And there was no fairness in his fighting. His first fight on board, the first day out, was with me, when he, desiring to cut a plug of chewing tobacco, took my personal table-knife for the purpose, and whereupon, I, on a hair-trigger, promptly exploded. After that he fought with nearly every member of the crew. When his clothing became too filthy to be bearable by the rest of us, we put it to soak and stood over him while he washed it. In short, Bricklayer was one of those horrible monstrous things one must see in order to be convinced that they exist.

I will only say that he was a beast, and that we treated him like a beast. It is only by looking back through the years that I realise how heartless we were to him. He was without sin. He could not, by the very nature of things, have been anything else than he was. He had not made himself, and for his making he was not responsible. Yet we treated him as a free agent and held him personally responsible for all that he was and that he should not have been. As a result, our treatment of him was as terrible as he was himself terrible. Finally we gave him the silent treatment, and for weeks before he died we neither spoke to him nor did he speak to us. And for weeks he moved among us, or lay in his bunk in our crowded house, grinning at us his hatred and malignancy. He was a dying man, and he knew it, and we knew it. And furthermore, he knew that we wanted him to die. He cumbered our life with his presence, and ours was a rough life that made rough men of us. And so he died, in a small space crowded by twelve men and as much alone as if he had died on some desolate mountain peak. No kindly word, no last word, was passed between. He died as he had lived, a beast, and he died hating us and hated by us.

✓ **Check Your Comprehension**

1. (a) How old was London when he signed up for the seal-hunting cruise? (b) What ancient seafaring custom is he forced to observe?
2. Identify two elements of the "method" the writer adopts to get along with the other sailors.
3. (a) Who is the "Bricklayer"? (b) How do the other sailors treat him? (c) What finally happens to him?

◆ **Critical Thinking**

1. What do you think London's method of coping on board ship reveals about his personality? **[Interpret]**
2. How does London's attitude toward his duties and his shipmates contrast with the Bricklayer's outlook? **[Compare and Contrast]**
3. Do you find London's judgments about the Bricklayer brutal or shocking? How else might the situation have been resolved? Explain your answer. **[Evaluate]**

Jack London

Love of Life

They limped painfully down the bank, and once the foremost of the two men staggered among the rough-strewn rocks. They were tired and weak, and their faces had the drawn expression of patience which comes of hardship long endured. They were heavily burdened with blanket packs which were strapped to their shoulders. Headstraps, passing across the forehead, helped support these packs. Each man carried a rifle. They walked in a stooped posture, the shoulders well forward, the head still farther forward, the eyes bent upon the ground.

"I wish we had just about two of them cartridges that's layin' in that cache[1] of ourn," said the second man.

His voice was utterly and drearily expressionless. He spoke without enthusiasm; but the first man, limping into the milky stream that foamed over the rocks, vouchsafed no reply.

The other man followed at his heels. They did not remove their foot-gear, though the water was icy cold—so cold that their ankles ached and their feet went numb. In places the water dashed against their knees, and both men staggered for footing.

The man who followed slipped on a smooth boulder, nearly fell, but recovered himself with a violent effort, at the same time uttering a sharp exclamation of pain. He seemed faint and dizzy, and put out his free hand while he reeled, as though seeking support against the air. When he had steadied himself he stepped forward, but reeled again and nearly fell. Then he stood still and looked at the other man, who had never turned his head.

The man stood still for fully a minute, as though debating with himself. Then he called out:

"I say, Bill, I've sprained my ankle."

Bill staggered on through the milky water. He did not look around. The man watched him go, and though his face was expressionless as ever, his eyes were like the eyes of a wounded deer.

The other man limped up the farther bank and continued straight on without looking back. The man in the stream watched him. His lips trembled a little, so that the rough thatch of brown hair which covered them was visibly agitated. His tongue even strayed out to moisten them.

"Bill!" he cried out.

It was the pleading cry of a strong man in distress, but Bill's head did not turn. The man watched him go, limping grotesquely

---

1. **cache** (cash): A place in which stores of food or supplies are hidden.

and lurching forward with stammering gait up the slow slope toward the soft sky-line of the low-lying hill. He watched him go till he passed over the crest and disappeared. Then he turned his gaze and slowly took in the circle of the world that remained to him now that Bill was gone.

Near the horizon the sun was smoldering dimly, almost obscured by formless mists and vapors, which gave an impression of mass and density without outline or tangibility. The man pulled out his watch, the while resting his weight on one leg. It was four o'clock, and as the season was near the last of July or first of August—he did not know the precise date within a week or two—he knew that the sun roughly marked the northwest. He looked to the south and knew that somewhere beyond those bleak hills lay the Great Bear Lake; also, he knew that in that direction the Arctic Circle cut its forbidding way across the Canadian Barrens. This stream in which he stood was a feeder to the Coppermine River, which in turn flowed north and emptied into Coronation Gulf and the Arctic Ocean. He had never been there, but he had seen it, once, on a Hudson Bay Company chart.

Again his gaze completed the circle of the world about him. It was not a heartening spectacle. Everywhere was soft sky-line. The hills were all low-lying. There were no trees, no shrubs, no grasses—naught but a tremendous and terrible desolation that sent fear swiftly dawning into his eyes.

"Bill!" he whispered, once and twice; "Bill!"

He cowered in the mist of the milky water, as though the vastness were pressing in upon him with overwhelming force, brutally crushing him with its complacent awfulness. He began to shake as with an ague-fit, till the gun fell from his hand with a splash. This served to rouse him. He fought with his fear and pulled himself together, groping in the water and recovering the weapon. He hitched his pack farther over his left shoulder, so as to take a portion of its weight from off the injured ankle. Then he proceeded, slowly and carefully, wincing with pain, to the bank.

He did not stop. With a desperation that was madness, unmindful of the pain, he hurried up the slope to the crest of the hill over which his comrade had disappeared—more grotesque and comical by far than that limping, jerking comrade. But at the crest he saw a shallow valley, empty of life. He fought with his fear again, overcame it, hitched the pack still farther over on his left shoulder, and lurched on down the slope.

The bottom of the valley was soggy with water, which the thick moss held, spongelike, close to the surface. This water squirted out from under his feet at every step, and each time he lifted a foot the action culminated in a sucking sound as the wet moss reluctantly released its grip. He picked his way from muskeg to muskeg, and followed the other man's footsteps along and across the rocky ledges which thrust like islets through the sea of moss.

Though alone he was not lost. Farther on he knew he would come to where dead spruce and fir, very small and weazened, bordered the shore of a little lake, the *tit-chinnichile*—in the tongue of the country, the "land of little sticks." And into that lake flowed a small stream, the water of which was not milky. There was rushgrass on that stream—this he remembered well— but no timber, and he would follow it till its first trickle ceased at a divide. He would cross this divide to the first trickle of another stream, flowing to the west, which he would follow until it emp- tied into the River Dease, and here he would find a cache under an upturned canoe and piled over with many rocks. And in this cache would be ammunition for his empty gun, fish-hooks and lines, a small net—all the utilities for the killing and snaring of food. Also, he would find flour—not much—a piece of bacon and some beans.

Bill would be waiting for him there, and they would paddle away south down the Dease to the Great Bear Lake. And south across the lake they would go, ever south, till they gained the Mackenzie. And south, still south, they would go, while the win- ter raced vainly after them, and the ice formed in the eddies, and the days grew chill and crisp, south to some warm Hudson Bay Company post, where timber grew tall and generous and there was grub without end.

These were the thoughts of the man as he strove onward. But hard as he strove with his body, he strove equally hard with his mind, trying to think that Bill had not deserted him, that Bill would surely wait for him at the cache. He was compelled to think this thought, or else there would not be any use to strive, and he would have lain down and died. And as the dim ball of the sun sank slowly into the northwest he covered every inch, and many times, of his and Bill's flight south before the down- coming winter. And he conned the grub of the cache and the grub of the Hudson Bay Company post over and over again. He had not eaten for two days; for a far longer time he had not had all he wanted to eat. Often he stooped and picked pale muskeg berries, put them into his mouth and chewed and swallowed them. A muskeg berry is a bit of seed enclosed in a bit of water. In the mouth the water melts away and the seed chews sharp and bitter. The man knew there was no nourishment in the berries, but he chewed them patiently with a hope greater than knowledge and defying experience.

At nine o'clock he stubbed his toe on a rocky ledge, and from sheer weariness and weakness staggered and fell. He lay for some time, without movement, on his side. Then he slipped out of the pack straps and clumsily dragged himself into a sitting posture. It was not yet dark, and in the lingering twilight he groped about among the rocks for shreds of dry moss. When he had gathered a heap he built a fire—a smoldering, smudgy fire— and put a tin pot of water on to boil.

He unwrapped his pack and the first thing he did was to count his matches. There were sixty-seven. He counted them three times to make sure. He divided them into several portions, wrapping them in oil paper, disposing of one bunch in his empty tobacco pouch, of another bunch in the inside band of his battered hat, of a third bunch under his shirt on the chest. This accomplished, a panic came upon him and he unwrapped them all and counted them again. There were still sixty-seven.

He dried his wet foot-gear by the fire. The moccasins were in soggy shreds. The blanket socks were worn through in places and his feet were raw and bleeding. His ankle was throbbing and he gave it an examination. It had swollen to the size of his knee. He tore a long strip from one of his two blankets and bound the ankle tightly. He tore other strips and bound them about his feet to serve for both moccasins and socks. Then he drank the pot of water, steaming hot, wound his watch, and crawled between his blankets.

He slept like a dead man. The brief darkness around midnight came and went. The sun arose in the northeast—at least the day dawned in that quarter, for the sun was hidden by gray clouds.

At six o'clock he awoke, quietly lying on his back. He gazed straight up into the gray sky and knew that he was hungry. As he rolled over on his elbow he was startled by a loud snort, and saw a bull caribou regarding him with alert curiosity. The animal was not more than fifty feet away, and instantly into the man's mind leaped the vision and the savor of a caribou steak sizzling and frying over a fire. Mechanically he reached for the empty gun, drew a bead, and pulled the trigger. The bull snorted and leaped away, his hoofs rattling and clattering as he fled across the ledges.

The man cursed and flung the empty gun from him. He groaned aloud as he started to drag himself to his feet. It was a slow and arduous task. His joints were like rusty hinges. They worked harshly in their sockets, with much friction, and each bending or unbending was accomplished only through a sheer exertion of will. When he finally gained his feet another minute or so was consumed in straightening up, so that he could stand erect as a man should stand.

He crawled up a small knoll and surveyed the prospect. There were no trees, no bushes, nothing but a gray sea of moss scarcely diversified by gray rocks, gray-colored lakelets, and gray streamlets. The sky was gray. There was no sun or hint of sun. He had no idea of north, and he had forgotten the way he had come to this spot the night before. But he was not lost. He knew that. Soon he would come to the land of the little sticks. He felt that it lay off to the left somewhere, not far—possibly just over the next low hill.

He went back to put his pack into shape for travelling. He assured himself of the existence of his three separate parcels of matches, though he did not stop to count them. But he did linger, debating over a squat moose-hide sack. It was not large. He could hide it under his two hands. He knew that it weighed fifteen pounds—as much as all the rest of the pack—and it worried him. He finally set it to one side and proceeded to roll the pack. He paused to gaze at the squat moose-hide sack. He picked it up hastily with a defiant glance about him, as though the desolation were trying to rob him of it; and when he rose to his feet to stagger on into the day, it was included in the pack on his back.

He bore away to the left, stopping now and again to eat muskeg berries. His ankle had stiffened, his limp was more pronounced, but the pain of it was as nothing compared with the pain of his stomach. The hunger pangs were sharp. They gnawed and gnawed until he could not keep his mind steady on the course he must pursue to gain the land of little sticks. The muskeg berries did not allay this gnawing, while they made his tongue and the roof of his mouth sore with their irritating bite.

He came upon a valley where rock ptarmigan[2] rose on whirring wings from the ledges and muskegs. Ker—ker—ker was the cry they made. He threw stones at them but could not hit them. He placed his pack on the ground and stalked them as a cat stalks a sparrow. The sharp rocks cut through his pant's legs till his knees left a trail of blood; but the hurt was lost in the hurt of his hunger. He squirmed over the wet moss, saturating his clothes and chilling his body; but he was not aware of it, so great was his fever for food. And always the ptarmigan rose, whirring, before him, till their ker—ker—ker became a mock to him, and he cursed them and cried aloud at them with their own cry.

Once he crawled upon one that must have been asleep. He did not see it till it shot up in his face from its rocky nook. He made a clutch as startled as was the rise of the ptarmigan, and there remained in his hand three tail-feathers. As he watched its flight

---

2. **ptarmigan** (tar′ mi gən): A type of grouse or game bird.

he hated it, as though it had done him some terrible wrong. Then he returned and shouldered his pack.

As the day wore along he came into valleys or swales where game was more plentiful. A band of caribou passed by, twenty and odd animals, tantalizingly within rifle range. He felt a wild desire to run after them, a certitude that he could run them down. A black fox came towards him, carrying a ptarmigan in his mouth. The man shouted. It was a fearful cry, but the fox leaping away in fright did not drop the ptarmigan.

Late in the afternoon he followed a stream, milky with lime, which ran through sparse patches of rushgrass. Grasping these rushes firmly near the root, he pulled up what resembled a young onion-sprout no larger than a shingle-nail. It was tender and his teeth sank into it with a crunch that promised deliciously of food. But its fibers were tough. It was composed of stringy filaments saturated with water, like the berries, and devoid of nourishment. But he threw off his pack and went into the rushgrass on hands and knees, crunching and munching like some bovine creature.

He was very weary and often wished to rest—to lie down and sleep; but he was continually driven on—not so much by his desire to gain the land of little sticks but by his hunger. He searched little ponds for frogs and dug up the earth with his nails for worms, though he knew in spite that neither frogs nor worms existed so far north.

He looked into every pool of water vainly, until, as the long twilight came on, he discovered a solitary fish, the size of a minnow, in such a pool. He plunged his arm in up to the shoulder, but it eluded him. He reached for it with both hands and stirred up the milky mud at the bottom. In his excitement he fell in, wetting himself to the waist. Then the water was too muddy to admit of his seeing the fish and he was compelled to wait until the sediment had settled.

The pursuit was renewed, until the water was again muddied. But he could not wait. He unstrapped the tin bucket and began to bale the pool. He baled wildly at first, splashing himself and flinging the water so short a distance that it ran back into the pool. He worked more carefully, striving to be cool, though his heart was pounding against his chest and his hands were trembling. At the end of half an hour the pool was nearly dry. Not a cupful of water remained. And there was no fish. He found a hidden crevice among the stones through which it had escaped to the adjoining and larger pool—a pool which he could not empty in a night and a day. Had he known of the crevice, he could have closed it with a rock at the beginning and the fish would have been his.

Thus he thought, and crumpled up and sank down upon the wet earth. At first he cried softly to himself, then he cried loudly to the pitiless desolation that ringed him around; and for a long time after he was shaken by great dry sobs.

He built a fire and warmed himself by drinking quarts of hot water, and made camp on a rocky ledge in the same fashion he had the night before. The last thing he did was to see that his matches were dry and to wind his watch. The blankets were wet and clammy. His ankle pulsed with pain. But he knew only that he was hungry, and through his restless sleep he dreamed of feasts and banquets and of food served and spread in all imaginable ways.

He awoke chilled and sick. There was no sun. The gray of earth and sky had become deeper, more profound. A raw wind was blowing, and the first flurries of snow were whitening the hilltops. The air about him thickened and grew white while he made a fire and boiled more water. It was wet snow, half rain, and the flakes were large and soggy. At first they melted as soon as they came in contact with the earth, but ever more fell, covering the ground, putting out the fire, spoiling his supply of moss-fuel.

This was the signal for him to strap on his pack and stumble onward he knew not where. He was not concerned with the land of little sticks, nor with Bill and the cache under the upturned canoe by the River Dease. He was mastered by the verb, "to eat." He was hunger-mad. He took no heed of the course he pursued, so long as that course led him through the swale bottoms. He felt his way through the wet snow to the watery muskeg berries, and went by feel as he pulled up the rush-grass by the roots. But it was tasteless stuff and did not satisfy. He found a weed that tasted sour and he ate all he could find of it, which was not much, for it was a creeping growth, easily hidden under the several inches of snow.

He had no fire that night nor hot water, and crawled under his blanket to sleep the broken hunger-sleep. The snow turned into a cold rain. He awakened many times to feel it falling on his upturned face. Day came—a gray day and no sun. It had ceased raining. The keenness of his hunger had departed. Sensibility, so far as concerned the yearning for food, had been exhausted. There was a dull, heavy ache in his stomach, but it did not bother him so much. He was more rational, and once more he was chiefly interested in the land of little sticks and the cache by the River Dease.

He ripped the remnant of one of his blankets into strips and bound his bleeding feet. Also, he recinched the injured ankle and prepared himself for a day of travel. When he came to his pack he paused long over the squat moose-hide sack, but in the end it went with him.

The snow had melted under the rain and only the hilltops showed white. The sun came out and he succeeded in locating the points of the compass, though he knew now that he was lost. Perhaps, in his previous days' wanderings, he had edged away too far to the left. He now bore off to the right to counteract the possible deviation from his true course.

Though the hunger pangs were no longer so exquisite, he realized that he was weak. He was compelled to pause for frequent rests when he attacked the muskeg berries and rush-grass patches. His tongue felt dry and large, as though covered with a fine hairy growth, and it tasted bitter in his mouth. His heart gave him a great deal of trouble. When he had traveled a few minutes it would begin a remorseless thump, thump, thump, and then leap up and away in a painful flutter of beats that choked him and made him go faint and dizzy.

In the middle of the day he found two minnows in a large pool. It was impossible to bale it, but he was calmer now and managed to catch them in his tin bucket. They were no longer than his little finger, but he was not particularly hungry. The dull ache in his stomach had been growing duller and fainter. It seemed almost that his stomach was dozing. He ate the fish raw, masticating with painstaking care, for the eating was an act of pure reason. While he had no desire to eat he knew that he must eat to live.

In the evening he caught three more minnows, eating two and saving the third for breakfast. The sun had dried stray shreds of moss, and he was able to warm himself with hot water. He had not covered more than ten miles that day, and the next day, traveling whenever his heart permitted him, he covered no more than five miles. But his stomach did not give him the slightest uneasiness. It had gone to sleep. He was in a strange country, too, and the caribou were growing more plentiful, also the wolves. Often their yelps drifted across the desolation, and once he saw three of them slinking away before his path.

Another night, and in the morning, being more rational, he untied the leather string that fastened the squat moose-hide sack. From its open mouth poured a yellow stream of coarse gold-dust and nuggets. He roughly divided the gold in halves, caching one half on a prominent ledge, wrapped in a piece of blanket, and returning the other half to the sack. He also began to use strips of the one remaining blanket for his feet. He still clung to his gun, for there were cartridges in that cache by the River Dease.

This was a day of fog, and this day hunger woke in him again. He was very weak and was afflicted with a giddiness which at times blinded him. It was no uncommon thing now for him to stumble and fall; and stumbling once, he fell squarely into a ptarmigan nest. There were four newly hatched chicks a day old—little specks of pulsating life no more than a mouthful; and he ate them ravenously, thrusting them alive into his mouth and crunching them like egg-shells between his teeth. The mother ptarmigan beat about him with great out-cry. He used his gun as a club with which to knock her over, but she dodged out of reach. He threw stones at her and with one chance shot broke a wing. Then she fluttered away, running, trailing the broken wing, with him in pursuit.

The little chicks had no more than whetted his appetite. He hopped and bobbed clumsily along on his injured ankle, throwing stones and screaming hoarsely at times; at other times hopping and bobbing silently along, picking himself up grimly and patiently when he fell, or rubbing his eyes with his hand when the giddiness threatened to overpower him.

The chase led him across swampy ground in the bottom of the valley, and he came upon footprints in the soggy moss. They were not his own—he could see that. They must be Bill's. But he could not stop, for the mother ptarmigan was running on. He would catch her first, then he would return and investigate.

He exhausted the mother ptarmigan; but he exhausted himself. She lay panting on her side. He lay panting on his side, a dozen feet away, unable to crawl to her. And as he recovered she recovered, fluttering out of reach as his hungry hand went out to her. The chase was resumed. Night settled down and she escaped. He stumbled from weakness and pitched head-foremost on his face, cutting his cheek, his pack upon his back. He did not move for a long while; then he rolled over on his side, wound his watch, and lay there until morning.

Another day of fog. Half of his last blanket had gone into footwrappings. He failed to pick up Bill's trail. It did not matter. His hunger was driving him too compellingly—only—only he wondered if Bill too were lost. By midday the irk of his pack became too oppressive. Again he divided the gold, this time merely spilling half of it on the ground. In the afternoon he threw the rest of it away, there remaining to him only the half-blanket, the tin bucket, and the rifle.

An hallucination began to trouble him. He felt confident that one cartridge remained to him. It was in the chamber of the rifle and he had overlooked it. On the other hand, he knew all the time that the chamber was empty. But the hallucination persisted. He fought it for hours, then threw his rifle open and was confronted with emptiness. The disappointment was as bitter as though he had really expected to find a cartridge.

He plodded on for half an hour, when the hallucination arose again. Again he fought it and still it persisted, till for very relief he opened the rifle to unconvince himself. At times his mind wandered farther afield, and he plodded on, a mere automaton, strange conceits and whimsicalities gnawing at his brain like worms. But these excursions out of the real were of brief duration, for ever the pangs of the hunger-bite called him back. He was jerked back abruptly once from such an excursion by a sight that caused him nearly to faint. He reeled and swayed, doddering like a drunken man to keep from falling. Before him stood a horse. A horse! He could not believe his eyes. A thick mist was in them, intershot with sparkling points of light. He rubbed his eyes savagely to clear his vision, and beheld not a horse but a great brown bear. The animal was studying him with bellicose curiosity.

The man had brought his gun halfway to his shoulder before he realized. He lowered it and drew his hunting-knife from its beaded sheath at his hip. Before him was meat and life. He ran his thumb along the edge of his knife. It was sharp. The point was sharp. He would fling himself upon the bear and kill it. But his heart began its warning thump, thump, thump. Then followed the wild upward leap and tattoo of flutters, the pressing as of an iron band across his forehead, the creeping of the dizziness into his brain.

His desperate courage was evicted by a great surge of fear. In his weakness, what if the animal attacked him! He drew himself up to his most imposing stature, gripping the knife and staring hard at the bear. The bear advanced clumsily a couple of steps, reared up and gave vent to a tentative growl. If the man ran he would run after him; but the man did not run. He was animated now with the courage of fear. He too, growled savagely, terribly, voicing the fear that is to life germane and that lies twisted about life's deepest roots.

The bear edged away to one side, growling menacingly, himself appalled by this mysterious creature that appeared upright and unafraid. But the man did not move. He stood like a statue till the danger was past, when he yielded to a fit of trembling and sank down into the wet moss.

He pulled himself together and went on, afraid now in a new way. It was not the fear that he should die passively from lack of food, but that he should be destroyed violently before starvation had exhausted the last particle of the endeavor in him that made toward surviving. There were the wolves. Back and forth across the desolation drifted their howls, weaving the very air into a fabric of menace that was so tangible that he found himself, arms in the air, pressing it back from him as it might be the walls of a wind-blown tent.

Now and again the wolves in packs of two or three crossed his path. But they sheered clear of him. They were not in sufficient numbers, and besides they were hunting the caribou which did not battle; while this strange creature that walked erect might scratch and bite.

In the late afternoon he came upon scattered bones where the wolves had made a kill. The debris had been a caribou calf an hour before, squawking and running and very much alive. He contemplated the bones, clean-picked and polished, pink with the cell-life in them which had not yet died.

Could it possibly be that he might be that ere the day was done! Such was life, eh? A vain and fleeting thing. It was only life that pained. There was no hurt in death. To die was to sleep. It meant cessation, rest. Then why was he not content to die?

But he did not moralize long. He was squatting in the moss, a bone in his mouth, sucking at the shreds of life that still dyed it faintly pink. The sweet meaty taste, thin and elusive almost as a memory, maddened him. He closed his jaws on the bone and crunched. Sometimes it was the bone that broke, sometimes his teeth. Then he crushed the bones between rocks, pounded them to a pulp and swallowed them. He pounded his fingers, too, in his haste, and yet found a moment in which to feel surprise at the fact that his fingers did not hurt when caught under the descending rock.

Came frightful days of snow and rain. He did not know when he made camp, when he broke camp. He traveled in the night as much as in the day. He rested whenever he fell, crawled on whenever the dying life in him flickered up and burned less dimly. He as a man no longer strove. It was the life in him, unwilling to die, that drove him on. He did not suffer. His nerves had become blunted, numb, while his mind was filled with weird visions and delicious dreams.

But ever he sucked and chewed on the crushed bones of the caribou calf, the least remnants of which he had gathered up and carried with him. He crossed no more hills or divides, but automatically followed a large stream which flowed through a wide and shallow valley. He saw nothing save visions. Soul and body walked or crawled side by side, yet apart, so slender was the thread that bound them.

He awoke in his right mind, lying on his back on a rocky ledge. The sun was shining bright and warm. Afar off he heard the squawking of caribou calves. He was aware of vague memories of rain and wind and snow, but whether he had been beaten by the storm for two days or two weeks he did not know.

For some time he lay without movement, the genial sunshine pouring upon him and saturating his miserable body with warmth. A fine day, he thought. Perhaps he could manage to locate himself. By a painful effort he rolled over on his side. Below him flowed a wide and sluggish river. Its unfamiliarity puzzled him. Slowly he followed it with his eyes, winding in wide sweeps among the bleak bare hills, bleaker and barer and lower-lying than any hills he had yet encountered. Slowly, deliberately, without excitement or more than the most casual interest, he followed the course of the strange stream toward the sky-line and saw it emptying into a bright and shining sea. He was still unexcited. Most unusual, he thought, a vision or a mirage—more likely a vision, a trick of his disordered mind. He was confirmed in this by sight of a ship lying at anchor in the midst of the shining sea. He closed his eyes for a while, then opened them. Strange how the vision persisted! Yet not strange. He knew there were no seas or ships in the heart of the barren lands, just as he had known there was no cartridge in the empty rifle.

He heard a snuffle behind him—a half-choking gasp or cough. Very slowly, because of his exceeding weakness and stiffness, he rolled over on his other side. He could see nothing near at hand, but he waited patiently. Again came the snuffle and cough, and outlined between two jagged rocks not a score of feet away he made out the gray head of a wolf. The sharp ears were not pricked so sharply as he had seen them on other wolves; the eyes were bleared and blood-shot, the head seemed to droop limply and forlornly. The animal blinked continually in the sunshine. It seemed sick. As he looked it snuffled and coughed again.

This, at least, was real, he thought, and turned on the other side so that he might see the reality of the world which had been veiled from him before by the vision. But the sea still shone in the distance and the ship's spars were plainly discernible. Was it reality after all? He closed his eyes for a long while and thought, and then it came to him. He had been making north by east, away from the Dease Divide, and into the Coppermine Valley. This wide and sluggish river was the Coppermine. That shining sea was the Arctic Ocean. That ship was a whaler, strayed east, far east, from the mouth of the Mackenzie, and it was lying at anchor at Coronation Gulf. He remembered the Hudson Bay Company chart he had seen long ago, and it was all clear and reasonable to him.

He sat up and turned his attention to immediate affairs. He had worn through the blanket-wrappings, and his feet were like shapeless lumps of raw meat. His last blanket was gone. Rifle and knife were both missing. He had lost his hat somewhere, with the bunch of matches in the band, but the matches against his chest were safe and dry inside the tobacco pouch and oil-paper. He looked at his watch. It marked eleven o'clock and was still running. Evidently he had kept it wound.

He was calm and collected. Though extremely weak he had no sensation of pain. He was not hungry. The thought of food was not even pleasant to him, and whatever he did was done by his reason alone. He ripped off his pant's legs to the knees and bound them about his feet. Somehow he had succeeded in retaining the tin bucket. He would have some hot water before he began what he foresaw was to be a terrible journey to the ship.

His movements were slow. He shook as with a palsy. When he started to collect dry moss he found he could not rise to his feet. He tried again and again, then contented himself with crawling about on hands and knees. Once he crawled near to the sick wolf. The animal dragged itself reluctantly out of his way, licking its chops with a tongue which seemed hardly to have the strength to curl. The man noticed that the tongue was not the customarily healthful red. It was a yellowish brown and seemed coated with a rough and half-dry mucus.

After he had drunk a quart of hot water the man found he was able to stand, and even to walk as well as a dying man might be supposed to walk. Every minute or so he was compelled to rest. His steps were feeble and uncertain, just as the wolf's that trailed him were feeble and uncertain; and that night, when the shining sea was blotted out by blackness, he knew he was nearer to it by no more than four miles.

Throughout the night he heard the cough of the sick wolf, and now and then the squawking of the caribou calves. There was life all around him, but it was strong life, very much alive and well, and he knew the sick wolf clung to the sick man's trail in the hope that the man would die first. In the morning, on opening his eyes, he beheld it regarding him with a wistful and hungry stare. It stood crouched, with tail between its legs, like a miserable and woebegone dog. It shivered in the chill morning wind, and grinned dispiritedly when the man spoke to it in a voice which achieved no more than a hoarse whisper.

The sun rose brightly, and all morning the man tottered and fell toward the ship on the shining sea. The weather was perfect. It was the brief Indian Summer of the high latitudes. It might last a week. To-morrow or next day it might be gone.

In the afternoon the man came upon a trail. It was of another man, who did not walk, but who dragged himself on all fours.

The man thought it might be Bill, but he thought it in a dull, uninterested way. He had no curiosity. In fact sensation and emotion had left him. He was no longer susceptible to pain. Stomach and nerves had gone to sleep. Yet the life that was in him drove him on. He was very weary, but it refused to die. It was because it refused to die that he still ate muskeg berries and minnows, drank his hot water, and kept a wary eye on the sick wolf.

He followed the trail of the other man who dragged himself along, and soon came to the end of it—a few fresh-picked bones where the soggy moss was marked by the footpads of many wolves. He saw a squat moose-hide sack, mate to his own, which had been torn by sharp teeth. He picked it up, though its weight was almost too much for his feeble fingers. Bill had carried it to the last. Ha! Ha! He would have the laugh on Bill. He would survive and carry it to the ship in the shining sea. His mirth was hoarse and ghastly, like a raven's croak, and the sick wolf joined him, howling lugubriously. The man ceased suddenly. How could he have the laugh on Bill if that were Bill; if those bones, so pinky-white and clean, were Bill!

He turned away. Well, Bill had deserted him; but he would not take the gold, nor would he suck Bill's bones. Bill would have, though, had it been the other way around, he mused as he staggered on.

He came to a pool of water. Stooping over in quest of minnows, he jerked his head back as though he had been stung. He had caught sight of his reflected face. So horrible was it that sensibility awoke long enough to be shocked. There were three minnows in the pool, which was too large to drain; and after several ineffectual attempts to catch them in the tin bucket he forbore. He was afraid, because of his great weakness, that he might fall in and drown. It was for this reason that he did not trust himself to the river astride one of the many drift-logs that lined its sand-pits.

That day he decreased the distance between him and the ship by three miles; the next day by two—for he was crawling now as Bill had crawled; and at the end of the fifth day found the ship still seven miles away and him unable to make even a mile a day. Still the Indian Summer held on, and he continued to crawl and faint, turn and turn about; and ever the sick wolf coughed and wheezed at his heels. His knees had become raw meat like his feet, and though he padded them with the shirt from his back it was a red track he left behind him on the moss and stones. Once glancing back he saw the wolf licking hungrily his bleeding trail, and he saw sharply what his own end might be—unless—unless he could get the wolf. Then began as grim a tragedy of existence as was ever played—a sick man that crawled, a sick wolf that limped, two creatures dragging their dying carcasses across the desolation and hunting each other's lives.

Had it been a well wolf, it would not have mattered so much to the man; but the thought of going to feed the maw of that loathsome and all but dead thing was repugnant to him. He was finicky. His mind had begun to wander again, and to be perplexed by hallucinations, while his lucid intervals grew rarer and shorter.

He was awakened once from a faint by a wheeze close in his ear. The wolf leaped lamely back, losing its footing and falling in its weakness. It was ludicrous, but he was not amused. Nor was he even afraid. He was far too gone for that. But his mind was for the moment clear, and he lay and considered. The ship was no more than four miles away. He could see it quite distinctly when he rubbed the mists out of his eyes, and he could see the white sail of a small boat cutting the water of the shining sea. But he could never crawl those four miles. He knew that, and was very calm in the knowledge. He knew that he could not crawl half a mile. And yet he wanted to live. It was unreasonable that he should die after all he had undergone. Fate asked too much of him. And, dying, he declined to die. It was stark madness, perhaps, but in the very grip of Death he defied Death and refused to die.

He closed his eyes and composed himself with infinite precaution. He steeled himself to keep above the suffocating languor that lapped like a rising tide through all the wells of his being. It was very like a sea, this deadly languor, that rose and rose and drowned his consciousness bit by bit. Sometimes he was all but submerged, swimming through oblivion with a faltering stroke; and again, by some strange alchemy of soul, he would find another shred of will and strike out more strongly.

Without movement he lay on his back, and he could hear slowly drawing near and nearer the wheezing intake and output of the sick wolf's breath. It drew closer, ever closer, through an infinitude of time, and he did not move. It was at his ear. The harsh dry tongue grated like sandpaper against his cheek. His hands shot out—or at least he willed them to shoot out. The fingers were curved like talons, but they closed on empty air. Swiftness and certitude require strength, and the man had not this strength.

The patience of the wolf was terrible. The man's patience was no less terrible. For half a day he lay motionless, fighting off unconsciousness and waiting for the thing that was to feed upon him and upon which he wished to feed. Sometimes the languid sea rose over him and he dreamed long dreams; but ever through it all waking and dreaming, he waited for the wheezing breath and the harsh caress of the tongue.

He did not hear the breath, and he slipped slowly from some dream to the feel of the tongue along his hand. He waited. The fangs pressed softly; the pressure increased; the wolf was exerting its last strength in an effort to sink teeth in the food for which it had waited so long. But the man had waited long, and the lacerated hand closed on the jaw. Slowly, while the wolf struggled feebly and the hand clutched feebly, the other hand crept across to a grip. Five minutes later the whole weight of the man's body was on top of the wolf. The hands had not sufficient strength to choke the animal, but the face of the man was pressed close to the throat of the wolf and the mouth was full of hair. At the end of a half hour the man was aware of a warm trickle in his throat. It was not pleasant. It was like molten lead being forced into his stomach, but it was forced by his will alone. Later the man rolled over on his back and slept.

*   *   *

There were some members of a scientific expedition on the whaleship *Bedford*. From the deck they remarked a strange object on the shore. It was moving down the beach toward the water. They were unable to classify it, and, being scientific men, they climbed into the whaleboat alongside and went ashore to see it. And they saw something that was alive but that could hardly be called a man. It was blind, unconscious. It squirmed along the ground like some monstrous worm. Most of its efforts were ineffectual, but it was persistent, and it writhed and twisted and went ahead perhaps a score of feet an hour.

Three weeks afterward the man lay in a bunk on the whaleship *Bedford*, and with tears streaming down his wasted cheeks told who he was and what he had undergone. He also babbled incoherently of his mother, of sunny Southern California, and a home among the orange groves and flowers.

The days were not many after that when he sat at table with the scientific men and ship's officers. He gloated over the spectacle of so much food, watching it anxiously as it went into the mouths of others. With the disappearance of each mouthful an expression of deep regret came into his eyes. He was quite sane, yet he hated those men at meal-time because they ate so much food. He was haunted by a fear that it would not last. He inquired of the cook, the cabin boy, the captain, concerning the food stores. They reassured him countless times; but he could not believe them, and pried cunningly about the lazarette[3] to see with his own eyes.

It was noticed that the man was getting fat. He grew stouter with each day. The scientific men shook their heads and theorized. They limited the man at his meals, but still his girth increased and his body swelled prodigiously under his shirt.

The sailors grinned. They knew. And when the scientific men set a watch on the man, they knew too. They saw him slouch for'ard after breakfast, and like a mendicant, with outstretched palm, accost a sailor. The sailor grinned and passed him a fragment of sea biscuit. He clutched it avariciously, looked at it as a miser looks at gold, and thrust it into his shirt bosom. Similar were the donations from other grinning sailors.

The scientific men were discreet. They left him alone. But they privily examined his bunk. It was lined with hardtack; every nook and cranny was filled with hardtack. Yet he was sane. He was taking precautions against another possible famine—that was all. He would recover from it, the scientific men said, and he did, ere the *Bedford's* anchor rumbled down in San Francisco Bay.

---

3. **lazarette:** Storage space below a ship's deck.

☑ Check Your Comprehension

1. Where and when does the story take place?
2. (a) What are two of the physical challenges that the main character struggles to overcome? (b) What are two mental or emotional challenges that the man faces?
3. (a) During the final days before he reaches the shore, what creature travels with the man? (b) How does this creature become the key to the man's survival?
4. On board the whaleship *Bedford,* what aftereffects does the man experience from his ordeal?

◆ Critical Thinking

1. At the opening of the story, what atmosphere or mood is created by Bill's abandonment of the main character? **[Interpret]**
2. Cite two passages from the story in which the writer's descriptions of the landscape help to increase suspense. **[Analyze]**
3. Do you agree that his ordeal comes close to turning the main character into a beast? Use details from the story to support your answer. **[Interpret]**
4. What do you think is the single most important quality in the man that enables him to survive? **[Evaluate]**
5. Does this tale of a man's struggle to survive in a primitive wilderness area have any relevance to life today, in your opinion? **[Apply]**

Jack London
Comparing and Connecting the Author's Works

◆ Literary Focus: Descriptive Writing

Jack London has been widely admired for his powers of vivid description. In **descriptive writing** an author re-creates experiences by using images that appeal to the five senses: sight, hearing, touch, taste, and smell. Careful word choice also contributes to vivid descriptive writing. For example, notice the specific nouns, vivid verbs, and graphic adjectives that are underlined in this description of the dog Buck:

His <u>furry</u> coat <u>shone</u> with the <u>sheen</u> of <u>silk</u>. Down the neck and across the shoulders, his <u>mane</u>, in <u>repose</u> as it was, half <u>bristled</u> and seemed to <u>lift</u> with every movement, as though <u>excess</u> of <u>vigor</u> made each particular hair <u>alive</u> and <u>active</u>.

1. At the climax of the excerpt from *The Call of the Wild,* in the paragraph beginning "Men gasped and began to breathe again," London uses many vivid verbs. List these verbs.

2. In "Love of Life," find the paragraph beginning "Late in the afternoon he followed a stream . . ." (page 35). List four images from this paragraph, and identify the sense to which each image appeals.

◆ Drawing Conclusions About London's Work

The American poet Carl Sandburg once wrote, "The more civilized we become, the deeper is the fear that back in barbarism is something of the beauty and joy of life we have not brought with us." In Jack London's works, the conflict between the civilized and the primitive plays a major role. London often uses physical strength or brute force to symbolize the primitive or barbaric side of life. The reader feels that London admires the primitive even as he portrays it as fearsome and ominous.

Reread the selections and look for some passages that explore this theme in London's work. Use a Herringbone Organizer like the one below to organize your thoughts. Write the central idea—civilization vs. the primitive—on the central line. Then use the diagonals to track passages in which London seems to idealize physical strength and passages in which he seems fearful or critical of the primitive.

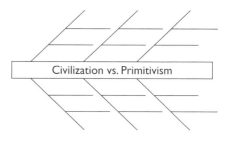

Civilization vs. Primitivism

◆ Idea Bank

Writing

1. **Timeline** Create a timeline for the principal events in "Love of Life." For each day on your timeline, include a note on the weather. Then list the challenges that the main character must confront as he struggles to survive.

2. **Descriptive Essay** Write a descriptive essay about a place in nature that has made a deep impression on you. The place may include plants, animals, or people. Before you begin, use a chart like the one at the top of page 49 to list sensory images for your description.

Sight	Sound	Touch	Smell	Taste
___	___	___	___	___
___	___	___	___	___

Speaking and Listening

3. **Panel Discussion** London's story "To Build a Fire" also focuses on a man's struggle to survive in the Klondike. Together with a small group, read "To Build a Fire," and then organize a panel discussion in which you discuss the similarities and differences between this story and "Love of Life." **[Group Activity]**

4. **Oral Report** Arctic animals adapt to the extreme conditions of their habitat in many interesting ways. Using field guides, encyclopedias, and other reference works, research the appearance, behavior, and diet of a species of mammal living in the far North. Present your results in an oral report to the class. **[Science Link]**

Researching and Representing

5. **Book Jacket** Create a book jacket for an anthology of Jack London's work. Research the titles, subject matter, and themes of some other stories and novels by London. Then create an appropriate illustration for your book jacket. On the back of the book jacket, quote some favorable reactions by your classmates to the selections they have read. **[Art Link]**

◆ **Further Reading, Listening, and Viewing**

- London, Jack. *The Sea-Wolf* (1904). This classic adventure tale features one of London's most memorable characters, the sea captain Wolf Larsen.

- London, Jack. *White Fang* (1906). Another exciting dog story, this short novel is often considered as a companion piece to *The Call of the Wild*.

- Kershaw, Alex. *Jack London: A Life* (1997). This well written biography includes critical discussion of London's major works.

- *Frontier Stories* (1993). This audiocassette includes an interpretation of "Love of Life" read by Randall James Stanton.

- *The Call of the Wild: Dog of the Yukon* (1997). This made-for-TV movie, directed by Peter Svatek, is told from Buck's point of view.

On the Web:

http://www.phschool.com/atschool/literature Go to the student edition *Silver*. Proceed to Unit 2. Then, click Hot Links to find Web sites featuring Jack London.

Toni Cade Bambara In Depth

"It's a tremendous responsibility—responsibility and honor—to be a writer, an artist, a cultural worker . . . whatever you call this vocation."

—*Toni Cade Bambara*

TONI CADE BAMBARA dedicated her career to celebrating her African American heritage and to exploring the complexities of urban life. As an educator, writer, and student of the visual and performing arts, Bambara shared her talent with a broad array of civic groups, including museums, libraries, community centers, hospitals, and prisons. In her life as an artist, her goal was nothing less than to remake readers' understanding of African Americans, and African Americans' understanding of themselves. In an interview, Bambara described her vision:" . . . I began to think that writing could be a way to engage in struggle, it could be a weapon, a real instrument for transformation. . . ."

Youth and Early Adulthood   Born Toni Cade in New York City in 1939, Bambara adopted her surname in 1970 to honor her great-grandmother, whose sketchbook she discovered in an attic trunk. After she graduated from Queens College, Bambara studied performing arts in Europe for several years: first at the University of Florence in Italy and then at a special school in Paris, France, which focused on the art of pantomime. After she returned to the United States, she undertook additional studies in dance and film, and she earned a graduate degree at City College in New York.

During the 1960's, Bambara worked as a social investigator for the New York State Department of Welfare, as a recreation director for a hospital, and as the program director for a community center. This broad range of experiences was especially helpful for Bambara's career as a writer, since she became intimately acquainted with many different aspects of urban life.

Writer and Teacher   Bambara's first important publication was *The Black Woman* (1970), an anthology of essays, poems, and short stories by African American woman writers. The following year, she published another anthology focusing on the storytelling tradition: *Tales and Stories for Black Folks*. In this collection, she included works by her students at Rutgers University, where she taught from 1969 to 1974.

In 1972, Bambara published the first collection of her own stories, entitled *Gorilla, My Love*. The anthology contained one of Bambara's best-known stories, "Raymond's Run." In this volume, the experiences of young people growing up—often humorous, but sometimes awkward or even painful—emerged as a major theme in Bambara's fiction. In praising the author, a critic for the *New York Times* noted that Bambara is "an articulate, intelligent, and sensitive writer who happens to be very funny, hip, warm, and unmistakably her own black woman."

During the 1970's, Bambara deepened her sociopolitical involvement with civil rights groups, community organizations, women's causes, and writers' collectives. She traveled widely, teaching and conducting literary readings throughout the United States. In 1977, she published a second volume of stories, entitled *The Sea Birds Are Still Alive*. Many of these tales concerned community issues. In addition to her fiction, Bambara wrote teleplays and essays.

In 1980, Bambara published an eagerly awaited first novel, *The Salt Eaters*. In this work, she traces the friendship between two women—one a community organizer and the other a faith healer—in the rural South. One reviewer praised the work as a "hymn to individual courage, a somber message of hope." Among Bambara's major themes are identity, self-worth, the opportunity for spiritual renewal, and the possibility of social change.

Last Years Among Bambara's later works were a film adaptation of Toni Morrison's novel *Tar Baby* (1984), as well as a second novel, *If Blessing Comes* (1987). She received several awards for her television documentary *The Bombing of Osage* (1986). In 1995, Bambara died of cancer in her mid-fifties. The following year, a volume of her fiction, essays, and interviews was published, entitled *Deep Sightings and Rescue Missions*.

In summing up Bambara's achievement, the critic Alice A. Deck described the writer's outlook this way:

> The basic implication of all of Toni Cade Bambara's stories is that there is an undercurrent of caring for one's neighbors that sustains black Americans. In her view the presence of those individuals who intend to do harm to people is counterbalanced by as many if not more persons who have a genuine concern for other people.

◆ Public Art

As an example of public art, the community mural in Bambara's story "The War of the Wall" is part of a long, diverse tradition. Public art can be defined as making and installing art outside conventional spaces such as museums or galleries.

Types of public art include outdoor sculpture, community murals, monuments, landscaping in public gardens, subway or bus shelter art, stamp and coin design, laser shows, and landmark symbols of cultural identity, such as the Statue of Liberty in New York Harbor or the Eiffel Tower in Paris, France. Such a wide variety of forms and styles make it difficult to generalize about public art. Nevertheless, much public art has three features in common.

First, this type of art is often created by an anonymous artist or by more than one person. Second, public art is targeted to a mass audience, not just to a small set of museum visitors, and it is often placed outdoors. Third, public art often focuses on the history, concerns, or values of a specific community.

◆ Literary Works

Short Story Collections
- *Gorilla, My Love* (1972)
- *The Sea Birds Are Still Alive: Collected Stories* (1977)

Novels
- *The Salt Eaters* (1980)
- *If Blessing Comes* (1987)

Edited Collections
- *The Black Woman: An Anthology* (1970)
- *Tales and Stories for Black Folks* (1971)
- *Southern Black Utterances Today* (1975)

$\mathcal{T}$oni Cade Bambara

The War of the Wall

Me and Lou had no time for courtesies. We were late for school. So we just flat out told the painter lady to quit messing with the wall. It was our wall, and she had no right coming into our neighborhood painting on it. Stirring in the paint bucket and not even looking at us, she mumbled something about Mr. Eubanks, the barber, giving her permission. That had nothing to do with it as far as we were concerned. We've been pitching pennies against that wall since we were little kids. Old folks have been dragging their chairs out to sit in the shade of the wall for years. Big kids have been playing handball against the wall since so-called integration when the crazies 'cross town poured cement in our pool so we couldn't use it. I'd sprained my neck one time boosting my cousin Lou up to chisel Jimmy Lyons's name into the wall when we found out he was never coming home from the war in Vietnam to take us fishing.

"If you lean close," Lou said, leaning hipshot against her beat-up car, "you'll get a whiff of bubble gum and kids' sweat. And that'll tell you something—that this wall belongs to the kids of Taliaferro Street." I thought Lou sounded very convincing. But the painter lady paid us no mind. She just snapped the brim of her straw hat down and hauled her bucket up the ladder.

"You're not even from around here," I hollered up after her. The license plates on her old piece of car said "New York." Lou dragged me away because I was about to grab hold of that ladder and shake it. And then we'd really be late for school.

When we came from school, the wall was slick with white. The painter lady was running string across the wall and taping it here and there. Me and Lou leaned against the gum ball machine outside the pool hall and watched. She had strings up and down and back and forth. Then she began chalking them with a hunk of blue chalk.

The Morris twins crossed the street, hanging back at the curb next to the beat-up car. The twin with the red ribbons was hugging a jug of cloudy lemonade. The one with yellow ribbons was holding a plate of dinner away from her dress. The painter lady began snapping the strings. The blue chalk dust measured off halves and quarters up and down and sideways too. Lou was about to say how hip it all was, but I dropped my book satchel on his toes to remind him we were at war.

Some good aromas were drifting our way from the plate leaking pot likker[1] onto the Morris girl's white socks. I could tell from where I stood that under the tinfoil was baked ham, collard greens, and candied yams. And knowing Mrs. Morris, who sometimes bakes for my mama's restaurant, a slab of buttered cornbread was probably up under there too, sopping up some of the pot likker. Me and Lou rolled our eyes, wishing somebody would send us some dinner. But the painter lady didn't even turn around. She was pulling the strings down and prying bits of tape loose.

Side Pocket came strolling out of the pool hall to see what Lou and me were studying so hard. He gave the painter lady the once-over, checking out her paint-spattered jeans, her chalky T-shirt, her floppy-brimmed straw hat. He hitched up his pants and glided over toward the painter lady, who kept right on with what she was doing.

"Watcha got there, Sweetheart?" he asked the twin with the plate.

"Suppah," she said, all soft and country-like.

"For her," the one with the jug added, jerking her chin toward the painter lady's back.

Still she didn't turn around. She was rearing back on her heels, her hands jammed into her back pockets, her face squinched up like the masterpiece she had in mind was taking shape on the wall by magic. We could have been gophers crawled up into a rotten hollow for all she cared. She didn't even say hello to anybody. Lou was muttering something about how great her concentration was. I butt him with my hip, and his elbow slid off the gum machine.

"Good evening," Side Pocket said in his best ain't-I-fine voice. But the painter lady was moving from the milk crate to the step-stool to the ladder, moving up and down fast, scribbling all over the wall like a crazy person. We looked at Side Pocket. He looked at the twins. The twins looked at us. The painter lady was giving a show. It was like those old-timey music movies where the dancer taps on the table top and then starts jumping all over the furniture, kicking chairs over and not skipping a beat. She didn't even look where she was stepping. And for a minute there, hanging on the ladder to reach a far spot, she looked like she was going to tip right over.

"Ahh," Side Pocket cleared his throat and moved fast to catch the ladder. "These young ladies here have brought you some supper."

"Ma'am?" The twins stepped forward. Finally the painter turned around, her eyes "full of sky," as my grandmama would say. Then she stepped down like she was in a trance. She wiped

---

1. **pot likker:** Or pot liquor, liquid in which food has been cooked.

her hands on her jeans as the Morris twins offered up the plate and the jug. She rolled back the tinfoil, then wagged her head as though something terrible was on the plate.

"Thank your mother very much," she said, sounding like her mouth was full of sky too. "I've brought my own dinner along." And then, without even excusing herself, she went back up the ladder, drawing on the wall in a wild way. Side Pocket whistled one of those oh-brother breathy whistles and went back into the pool hall. The Morris twins shifted their weight from one foot to the other, then crossed the street and went home. Lou had to drag me away, I was so mad. We couldn't wait to get to the firehouse to tell my daddy all about this rude woman who'd stolen our wall.

All the way back to the block to help my mama out at the restaurant, me and Lou kept asking my daddy for ways to run the painter lady out of town. But my daddy was busy talking about the trip to the country and telling Lou he could come too because Grandmama can always use an extra pair of hands on the farm.

Later that night, while me and Lou were in the back doing our chores, we found out that the painter lady was a liar. She came into the restaurant and leaned against the glass of the steam table, talking about how starved she was. I was scrubbing pots and Lou was chopping onions, but we could hear her through the service window. She was asking Mama was that a ham hock in the greens, and was that a neck bone in the pole beans, and were there any vegetables cooked without meat, especially pork.

"I don't care who your spiritual leader is," Mama said in that way of hers. "If you eat in the community, sistuh, you gonna eat pig by-and-by, one way or t'other."

Me and Lou were cracking up in the kitchen, and several customers at the counter were clearing their throats waiting for Mama to really fix her wagon for not speaking to the elders when she came in. The painter lady took a stool at the counter and went right on with her questions. Was there cheese in the baked macaroni, she wanted to know? Were there eggs in the salad? Was it honey or sugar in the iced tea? Mama was fixing Pop Johnson's plate. And every time the painter lady asked a fool question, Mama would dump another spoonful of rice on the pile. She was tapping her foot and heating up in a dangerous way. But Pop Johnson was happy as he could be. Me and Lou peeked through the service window, wondering what planet the painter lady came from. Who ever heard of baked macaroni without cheese, or potato salad without eggs?

"Do you have any bread made with unbleached flour?" the painter lady asked Mama. There was a long pause, as though everybody in the restaurant was holding their breath, wondering if Mama would dump the next spoonful on the painter lady's head. She didn't. But when she set Pop Johnson's plate down, it came down with a bang.

When Mama finally took her order, the starving lady all of a sudden couldn't make up her mind whether she wanted a vegetable plate or fish and a salad. She finally settled on the broiled trout and a tossed salad. But just when Mama reached for a plate to serve her, the painter lady leaned over the counter with her finger all up in the air.

"Excuse me," she said. "One more thing." Mama was holding the plate like a Frisbee, tapping that foot, one hand on her hip. "Can I get raw beets in that tossed salad?"

"You will get," Mama said, leaning her face close to the painter lady's, "whatever Lou back there tossed. Now sit down." And the painter lady sat back down on her stool and shut right up.

All the way to the country, me and Lou tried to get Mama to open fire on the painter lady. But Mama said that seeing as how she was from the North, you couldn't expect her to have any manners. Then Mama said she was sorry she'd been so impatient with the woman because she seemed like a decent person and was simply trying to stick to a very strict diet. Me and Lou didn't want to hear that. Who did that lady think she was, coming into our neighborhood and taking over our wall?

"Wellllll," Mama drawled, pulling into the filling station so Daddy could take the wheel, "it's hard on an artist, ya know. They can't always get people to look at their work. So she's just doing her work in the open, that's all."

Me and Lou definitely did not want to hear that. Why couldn't she set up an easel downtown or draw on the sidewalk in her own neighborhood? Mama told us to quit fussing so much; she was tired and wanted to rest. She climbed into the back seat and dropped down into the warm hollow Daddy had made in the pillow.

All weekend long, me and Lou tried to scheme up ways to recapture our wall. Daddy and Mama said they were sick of hearing about it. Grandmama turned up the TV to drown us out. On the late news was a story about the New York subways. When a train came roaring into the station all covered from top to bottom, windows too, with writings and drawings done with spray paint, me and Lou slapped five. Mama said it was too bad kids in New York had nothing better to do than spray paint all over the trains. Daddy said that in the cities, even grown-ups wrote all over the trains and buildings too. Daddy called it "graffiti." Grandmama called it a shame.

We couldn't wait to get out of school on Monday. We couldn't find any black spray paint anywhere. But in a junky hardware store downtown we found a can of white epoxy paint, the kind you touch up old refrigerators with when they get splotchy and peely. We spent out whole allowance on it. And because it was too late to use our bus passes, we had to walk all the way home lugging our book satchels and gym shoes, and the bag with the epoxy.

When we reached the corner of Taliaferro and Fifth, it looked like a block party or something. Half the neighborhood was gathered on the sidewalk in front of the wall. I looked at Lou, he looked at me. We both looked at the bag with the epoxy and wondered how we were going to work our scheme. The painter lady's car was nowhere in sight. But there were too many people standing around to do anything. Side Pocket and his buddies were leaning on their cue sticks, hunching each other. Daddy was there with a lineman he catches a ride with on Mondays. Mrs. Morris had her arms flung around the shoulders of the twins on either side of her. Mama was talking with some of her customers, many of them with napkins still at the throat. Mr. Eubanks came out of the barber shop, followed by a man in a striped poncho, half his face shaved, the other half full of foam.

"She really did it, didn't she?" Mr. Eubanks huffed out his chest. Lots of folks answered right quick that she surely did when they saw the straight razor in his hand.

Mama beckoned us over. And then we saw it. The wall. Reds, greens, figures outlined in black. Swirls of purple and orange. Storms of blues and yellows. It was something. I recognized some of the faces right off. There was Martin Luther King, Jr. And there was a man with glasses on and his mouth open like he was laying down a heavy rap. Daddy came up alongside and reminded us that he was Minister Malcolm X. The serious woman with a rifle I knew was Harriet Tubman because my grandmama has pictures of her all over the house. And I knew Mrs. Fannie Lou Hamer 'cause a signed photograph of her hangs in the restaurant next to the calendar.

Then I let my eyes follow what looked like a vine. It trailed past a man with a horn, a woman with a big white flower in her hair, a handsome dude in a tuxedo seated at a piano, and a man with a goatee holding a book. When I looked more closely, I realized that what had looked like flowers were really faces. One face with yellow petals looked just like Frieda Morris. One with red petals looked just like Hattie Morris. I could hardly believe my eyes.

"Notice," Side Pocket said, stepping close to the wall with his cue stick like a classroom pointer. "These are the flags of liberation, he said in a voice I'd never heard him use before. We all stepped closer while he pointed and spoke. "Red, black, and green," he said, his pointer falling on the leaflike flags of the vine. "Our liberation flag. And here Ghana, there Tanzania, Guinea-Bissau, Angola, Mozambique."[2] Side Pocket sounded very tall, as though he'd been waiting all his life to give this lesson.

Mama tapped us on the shoulder and pointed to a high section of the wall. There was a fierce-looking man with his arms crossed against his chest guarding a bunch of children. His muscles bulged, and he looked a lot like my daddy. One kid was looking at a row of books. Lou hunched me 'cause the kid looked like me. The one that looked like Lou was spinning a globe on the tip of his finger like a basketball. There were other kids there with microscopes and compasses. And the more I looked, the more it looked like the fierce man was not so much guarding the kids as defending their right to do what they were doing.

Then Lou gasped and dropped the paint bag and ran forward, running his hands over a rainbow. He had to tiptoe and stretch to do it, it was so high. I couldn't breathe either. The painter lady had found the chisel marks and had painted Jimmy Lyons's name in a rainbow.

"Read the inscription, honey," Mrs. Morris said, urging little Frieda forward. She didn't have to urge much. Frieda marched right up, bent down, and in a loud voice that made everybody quit oohing and ahhing and listen, she read,

To the People of Taliaferro Street
I Dedicate This Wall of Respect
Painted in Memory of My Cousin
Jimmy Lyons

---

2. **Ghana, Tanzania, Guinea-Bissau, Angola, Mozambique:** African countries.

☑ Check Your Comprehension

1. At the beginning of the story, why are Lou and the narrator angry with the painter lady?
2. (a) Where does the narrator's family go for the weekend? (b) What news story on television attracts Lou's and the narrator's attention, and why?
3. After school on Monday, why does a big crowd gather at the corner of Taliaferro and Fifth?
4. (a) Who are three of the people depicted on the wall? (b) What does Side Pocket say are the colors of the liberation flag?
5. (a) What happened to Jimmy Lyons? (b) How is the painter lady related to him? (c) How has she memorialized him?

◆ Critical Thinking

1. What are three reasons that the wall is special to the whole neighborhood?**[Interpret]**
2. What are two specific details that add humor to the restaurant scene? **[Analyze]**
3. Why do you think the painter lady didn't just explain what she was doing from the beginning? **[Speculate]**
4. From the subjects and situations depicted on the wall, how would you describe the painter lady's overall attitude toward the neighborhood and the community's heritage? **[Synthesize]**
5. Why do you think Bambara ends this story with the reading of the inscription on the wall? **[Draw Conclusions]**

Toni Cade Bambara

from Louis Massiah Interview With Toni Cade Bambara

You dedicate The Salt Eaters *to your mother for giving you the literal space to create. Could you talk about your mother as an influence in your artistic development?*

My mother had put herself through school wanting to be a journalist with the *New York Age,* but instead got married and went into civil service. I always think of her as a shadow artist in the sense that that is her take on things. I have been trying to encourage her to be a mystery writer because she really has that kind of suspicious mindset! My mother was not a house-proud woman, but she had a thing about these bookcases that she bought in Macy's basement, unfinished furniture division, and every spring she would spread the paper, get a rag, take the books out, dust them, and then she would repaint these book-cases a sparkling white. I would look at these books, and one of the books was a little, skinny, flat, black book with a little bronze insert, *Bronzeville,* by Miss Gwendolyn Brooks. It had pictures of children, so I kind of thought it was mine. I used to read it and take it to my room, but it wasn't my book, so I would bring it back and put it in the bookcase. I would hear the name Gwen Brooks because I lived in Harlem, and Harlem was a very rich, wealthy society in the sense that we had everybody. The Robesons[1] had moved back in 1936. Camilla Williams[2] was vocalizing up in the Harlem Y. Everybody in the world went to the Countee Cullen Branch,[3] and to the Arthur Schomburg Collection[4] (which is where I met John Henry Clarke). I would look at a poster of Gwen Brooks, and I liked her face. I like her name, Gwendolyn Brooks. It sounded very ordinary, and it sounded like it was possible to be a writer and to be ordinary.

Also in Mom's bookcase was Langston Hughes's *The Big Sea.* The jacket had come off, leaving only the yellow book, so I didn't see his picture, and I didn't know for years that Langston Hughes was the Mr. Langdon who used to come into the library and talk to us. When I was in the fifth grade, I was going to school in the

---

1. **the Robesons:** African American actor Paul Robeson (1898-1976) and his wife.
2. **Camilla Williams:** African American opera singer.
3. **Countee Cullen Branch:** Branch of the New York Public Libreary named for African American poet Countee Cullen.
4. **Arthur Schomburg Collection:** Library archive of materials relating to African American history, literature, and culture. Located in Harlem, the collection is now called the Schomburg Center for Research in Black Culture.

Bronx, but we lived on Morningside Avenue, and though the Mount Morris library was not the closest branch, it was the most interesting because those ladies really knew books; and they were interested in making you read. If you were taking out two books, they would recommend a third. Langston Hughes lived diagonally across the street, and he would break three rules that endeared him to me forever. First of all, he would come into the library and would not take off his hat. Not because he was rude, but because he was loaded down with a briefcase, portfolio, a satchel of books: he was coming to work. He had great hats. He had a Borsalino[5] that I would really like to have. The second violation was he would come into the children's section. As you know, in those days age borders were very strict and they were heavily patrolled. If you were little, then you went over here, and you listened to Sunday school stories; if you were a grown-up, you were over there listening to the senior choir. If you were in the movies, you were in the children's section, roped off with that lady in the white dress with the flashlight to hit you with and keep you all in check. The rest of the movie house was for the grown-ups.

It was the same thing with the library. So, Mr. Langdon (as we thought he was called) would come into the children's library, would stroll along the windowsill; looking at the sweet potato plants stuck with toothpicks hanging in the wide-mouth amber jars, and he would comment on them. We would always be looking at him thinking, Is he the stranger our parents always warned us against? What was he doing in the children's library? Then he would come and sit down with us and spread out his work. He was always very careful about space. If his book hit yours, he would say "Excuse me." I can't tell you how rare that was in those days. Nobody had respect for children or their sense of space. Well, he would be writing, reading, and pondering, and then he would look up and break the third rule—he would talk. He would ask us what we're doing. What kind of homework we have. Do we think it is intelligent homework? What was on our minds? The man was a knockout!

So, why I dedicated *The Salt Eaters* to my mom: I can remember any number of times my mother, unlike other parents, would walk around us if we were daydreaming. If she was mopping, she would mop around us. My mother had great respect for the life of the mind. Between working her two jobs, she would put one foot in her stocking and would go into this deep stare. She too had the need for daydreaming and for talking with herself. She didn't get much of an occasion with a mouthy kid like me.

I was writing stories long before I learned to spell. My father used to get the *Daily Mirror* (which my mother thought was an

---

5. **Borsalino:** (bor sa le no): Type of hat.

antilabor paper), and there were very fat margins, so I would scribble in the margins. When I had someone captive, like my mother in the bathtub, I would read this scribble-scrabble to her and she would listen. Essentially, it was my mother's respect for the life of the mind. She gave us permission to be artists. After my first aptitude test I was made aware that I was a freak in some way. In those aptitude tests they would say. "If you have a half hour to spare, would you build a wagon, take apart a clock and see how it works?" etc. They never said, "Daydream, just sit in a window and stare. Conjure up characters and plot stories." They never said that. My mother made it all very casual. My brother was something of a prodigy in terms of art and music, and so her thing was to give us access. To give us access to materials, to museums, to libraries, to parks. We figured that one of her motivations was that she had been kind of shy about going to these places, but she became emboldened as a mother. We always had equipment. We had no furniture or much in the way of wardrobes, but we had drawing paper, paints, and raffia to make mats. We had books and a piano.

☑ Check Your Comprehension

1. What does Bambara remember her mother doing every spring?
2. (a) Where did Bambara regularly see "Mr. Langdon"? (b) What three rules did "Mr. Langdon" break? (c) Who did "Mr. Langdon" turn out to be?
3. When she was a child, where did the author write her first stories?
4. What kind of access does Bambara say her mother gave her?

◆ Critical Thinking

1. (a) From the evidence in the interview, how did Bambara's mother feel about books? (b) What details in this passage show that she passed on this attitude to her daughter? [Infer]
2. What qualities in Langston Hughes impressed Bambara when she was a child? [Interpret]
3. Based on this interview, what do you think was Bambara's most important reason for dedicating her novel The Salt Eaters to her mother? [Synthesize]

Toni Cade Bambara
Comparing and Connecting the Author's Works

◆ Literary Focus: Dialect

Dialect is the form of language spoken by people in a particular region or group. Dialects differ in pronunciation, grammar, and word choice. Writers use dialect to make their characters seem realistic.

Toni Cade Bambara has been widely admired for her keen ear and her convincing mastery of colloquial speech. Novelist Anne Tyler, for example, has written about Bambara: "What pulls us along is the language of her characters, which is startlingly beautiful without once striking a false note. Everything these people say, you feel, ordinary, real-life people are saying right now on any street corner."

Rewrite the following passages in standard English. Then, as a class, discuss the advantages and disadvantages of the use of dialect in writing. Do students think the following passages were improved by being written in standard English?

1. Me and Lou had no time for courtesies. We were late for school. So we just flat out told the painter lady to quit messing with the wall.
2. The license plates on her old piece of car said "New York."
3. "If you eat in the community, sistuh, you gonna eat pig by-and-by, one way or t'other."

◆ Drawing Conclusions About Bambara's Work

"The idea of *community* is central to Bambara's fiction, and she often centers on groups, rather than individuals." How might you apply this statement to "The War of the Wall"?

To help you organize your thoughts, make a cluster diagram like the one below. Write the word *community* in the central circle. Then write plot events, dialogue, and other related details from the story that show this idea in the ovals surrounding the circle.

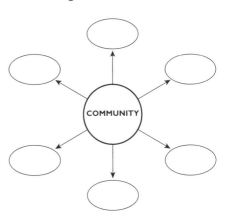

◆ Idea Bank

Writing

1. **Tribute** A tribute shows gratitude, respect, or honor for an inspiring person. Reread the passages in the Louis Massiah interview in which Toni Cade Bambara pays tribute to the influence and example of her mother. Then write a brief tribute to praise someone who has had an important influence on your life.
2. **Dialogue** Together with a partner, create a short sequel to "The War of the Wall" by writing a dialogue in which Lou and the narrator discuss their reactions to what they have learned about the painter lady and her mural. If you wish, use humor and dialect in your dialogue. When you have finished work, perform your dialogue for the class.

3. **Analysis** Use the notes you made for "Drawing Conclusions" to write a brief essay of two or three paragraphs on the importance of community in "The War of the Wall." When you have finished your essay, read it aloud to a small group of friends or classmates.

Speaking and Listening

4. **Dramatic Reading** Choose a passage from the selections for oral interpretation. Rehearse a dramatic reading of the passage, focusing on techniques such as pace, volume, emphasis, and tone of voice. When you have polished your reading, perform the passage for a small audience. **[Performing Arts Link]**

5. **Interview** Interview an older family member, relative, or neighbor for memories and anecdotes about your family history or your community. Prepare for your interview by writing some questions in advance. After the interview, write a brief summary of your results. **[Media Link]**

Researching and Representing

6. **Illustrated Report** Working with a small group of classmates, choose one of the African nations mentioned near the end of "The War of the Wall."

Using library and Internet resources, prepare an illustrated report on the location, physical features, economy, history, and culture of the country that you have chosen. **[Social Studies Link] [Group Activity]**

◆ Further Reading, Listening, and Viewing

- Bambara, Toni Cade: *Deep Sightings and Rescue Missions: Fiction, Essays, and Conversations* (1996). Edited by novelist Toni Morrison, this volume includes fiction and essays by Bambara as well as interviews with the author.

- Dash, Julie, with bell hooks and Toni Cade Bambara: *Daughters of the Dust: The Making of an African American Woman's Film* (1992). This book describes Dash's sixteen-year effort to film *Daughters of the Dust,* the first nationally distributed feature film by an African American woman.

On the Web:

http://www.phschool.com/atschool/literature
Go to the student edition *Silver*. Proceed to Unit 3. Then, click Hot Links to find Web sites featuring Toni Cade Bambara.

Jesse Stuart In Depth

> "About my writing, I do the writing and let others make the comments."
> — *Jesse Stuart*

JESSE STUART celebrated his native region of rural Appalachia in his many poems, stories, and essays.

Childhood and Youth Jesse Stuart was born in 1907 in a one-room log cabin in the tiny community of W-Hollow, Kentucky. Neither of his parents had completed elementary school. Stuart's childhood was divided between part-time schooling and farm chores. His love of literature—especially the poetry of Robert Burns, Carl Sandburg, and Walt Whitman—spurred him on through high school and then to Lincoln Memorial University in Tennessee, where he graduated in 1929.

Returning to his native region, Stuart served as a teacher and principal in a number of schools. Said critic H. Edward Richardson, "Though he made his living teaching, he was writing whenever he could, not so much because he wanted to, but because he was compelled to." In 1934, he published his first book, a volume of sonnets entitled *Man with a Bull-Tongue Plow*. The book, which contains more than 700 sonnets, received favorable reviews from several distinguished literary critics of the day.

Regional Writing and Local Color During his long career, Stuart produced an astonishing amount of writing: more than fifty-five book-length works, including 500 short stories and 2,000 poems. Stuart wrote in a literary tradition called regionalism, presenting the unique culture of a specific geographical area. For Jesse Stuart, this region was Appalachia, a mountainous, largely rural area of West Virginia and eastern Kentucky. Appalachia is rich in scenery and in local traditions, though many of its people are poor. In his literary works, Stuart often used a technique called local color, including characters, dialect, and other details that are unique to the region he knew so well.

A Writer's Themes Stuart published his best known volume of poems, *Album of Destiny,* in 1944. Two of the writer's major themes are especially prominent in this work: his admiration for his pioneer ancestors and the disturbing contrast between rural life of the past and "citified" life of the present. Stuart believed deeply in the vital link between human beings and nature. He felt that urban life of the twentieth century separated people from one of their greatest sources of strength. You will recognize echoes of this theme in Stuart's short story "Eight-one Summers," which was published in 1959.

An International Dimension In 1960-61, Stuart served as a visiting professor of English and education at the American University in Cairo, Egypt. During his career, he also worked as a lecturer for the United States Information Service, visiting Iran, Greece, Lebanon, Pakistan, the Philippines, and Korea.

Although he focused on a small, specific region in almost all his writing, Stuart's works won an international audience, and his books have been translated into many foreign languages. Writer Hal Borland commented as follows on Stuart and his work: "Early, Stuart was regarded as a regional writer. That was a superficial judgment. He always was broader than any region, and his regional accents were used for a purpose. . . . And he has come to accept and celebrate the humanity of people, even to cherish it." Stuart's vivid pictures of human life and emotions make his writing relevant to readers around the country and the world.

Later Years Stuart received many honors for his writing. In 1954, he was named Poet Laureate of the state of Kentucky, and in 1961 he was honored by the Academy of American Poets for his "distinguished service to American poetry." In the later part of his career, he published several autobiographical works; one of these, entitled *The Thread That Runs So True* (1949), was named the best book of the year by the National Education Association.

Critic Ruel E. Foster once said the following of Jesse Stuart: "He has created a place and wedged it everlastingly in the imagination of America. His stories have given a voice to the far and lost land of the Appalachians, a voice which calls us ever and delightedly into the outdoor world." Stuart died in Ironton, Ohio, in 1984.

◆ Ecology

In Jesse Stuart's story "The Blacksnake's Operation," a father teaches his daughter about the rhythms of nature. Both the blacksnake and the frog that it catches have their own special position in the environment, carrying out functions that help to keep nature in balance.

Ecology is the study of the relationships between living organisms and their environment. Although it is a relatively young science, ecology has offered many insights into the balance of nature. In the United States, for example, predators

such as wolves, mountain lions, and coyotes were often persecuted in the past as dangerous pests. We now know that these animals play an important role in their regional environments, or ecosystems, helping to keep populations of deer and other species stable.

◆ Literary Works

Short Story Collections
- *Head o' W-Hollow* (1936)
- *Men of the Mountains* (1941)
- *Tales from the Plum Grove Hills* (1946)
- *Clearing in the Sky, and Other Stories* (1950)
- *Plowshare in Heaven* (1958)
- *Save Every Lamb* (1964)
- *My Land Has a Voice* (1966)
- *Come Back to the Farm* (1971)

Novels
- *Trees of Heaven* (1940)
- *Taps for Private Tussie* (1943)
- *Foretaste of Glory* (1946)
- *Hie to the Hunters* (1950)
- *Daughter of the Legend* (1965)
- *Mister Gallion's School* (1967)

Poetry
- *Man with a Bull-Tongue Plow* (1934)
- *Album of Destiny* (1944)
- *Kentucky Is My Land* (1952)
- *The World of Jesse Stuart* (1975)

Books for Young Readers
- *Mongrel Mettle: The Autobiography of a Dog* (1944)
- *The Beatinest Boy* (1953)
- *Red Mule* (1955)
- *The Rightful Owner* (1960)
- *A Ride with Huey the Engineer* (1966)
- *Old Ben* (1970)

esse Stuart

The Blacksnake's Operation

Jane and I were sitting at the picnic table in the back yard when we heard a noise like wind in autumn leaves.

A lean bullfrog was coming down like a bowling ball, down the steep slope from the peach orchard. Each time he hit the ground, a long blacksnake tried to grab him. I'd never seen a frog run for his life as fast as this one was running. Each time he hit the ground, I thought the snake would get him. But the frog would rise into the air faster than a June bug.

"Don't let it catch the frog, Daddy!" Jane cried.

The blacksnake didn't hear Jane's screams and my shouting and hand clapping. He was determined to get the frog. He was going to chase him all the way to the creek. Just as the frog reached the foot of the steep slope and started to hop across the little bottom to the creek bank, the blacksnake caught him.

"Come on, Jane!" I shouted. "Help me and we'll save the frog."

I started running for the log that lay across the little stream. Jane was at my heels. We crossed the broad, hewn log and turned to our left. In thirty seconds more we were beside the big snake, who was lying there in the grass, swallowing the frog. We saw the frog's hind feet go in just as we got there. When the blacksnake saw us, he started crawling slowly back toward the hill. But the frog inside him made a big hump on his long, trim body. And this big hump served as a brake and slowed him down.

When he started up the hill, he found a hole in the ground made by a mole. He stuck his head inside and crawled in up to the hump on his body. But this hump again served as a brake.

"You can't get away!" Jane cried.

I caught the snake by the tail and lifted him up. He was big enough to swallow the frog easily. And he would have enjoyed swallowing him if Jane and I hadn't disturbed him.

"The poor frog was trying to get back to his home among the water lilies," Jane said. "He wanted to get back and sing in the evening when the moon comes up! What are you going to do to that snake? Aren't you going to kill him?"

"Not if I can help it," I said.

The snake squirmed. I hoped he might lose the frog, but he didn't.

"But, Daddy, he's killed the frog," Jane said.

"No, he hasn't," I said. "Not yet."

"But the frog can't breathe," she protested.

"Frogs stay under water and do without air over a minute at a time," I said. "He's not dead yet."

I laid the squirming snake upon the close-cut grass in our yard. He was, like most blacksnakes, a big friendly follow. He'd crawl away from a person any time. He didn't want any trouble with anybody. All he wanted was something to eat—a mouse, bird, frog, young rabbit, or a mole.

"Get me two forked sticks, Jane," I said. "Get them in a hurry if you want to save the frog. You can find some up there where I scythed over the peach orchard."

"How big?" she asked.

"Big enough to fit over the snake's back and fasten to the ground," I said.

Jane ran up to the top of the steep bank, where there were many little bushes with good forks scattered over the ground.

Jane came running with the two forked sticks. I put one over the snake's body near his head. I pushed it down into the ground enough to hold him. Then I placed the other fork over the snake's body on the other side of the frog.

"We'll have to have another fork, Jane," I said. "We'll have to hold the rest of his body still. Get another fork in a hurry."

By the time Jane got another fork, I had my knife out of my pocket and had figured the right place to make the incision. I put the third fork over the snake to hold the rest of his body in line. I knew he would squirm when I went to work.

My knife blade was razor-sharp. I kept it that way for farm use. When I applied the sharp blade to his tough skin, the snake flinched. I'd seen so many snake skeletons on our farm that I knew a little about the blacksnake's anatomy. I knew I'd have to cut through his ribs to get to the frog. And I had to be careful not to cut the frog. He'd already had enough punishment. Jane stood by and watched me cut through the skin, then the ribs, and slowly now I opened the snake until she could see the frog. My incision was not big enough to get the frog through, so I had to make it longer.

In a matter of seconds, I got the frog by the hind feet and carefully, slowly, I pulled him through the incision. I did as little harm to the snake as I could. He was squirming and Jane had to watch the forks carefully. Once he pushed the third one up, but Jane reset it. When I laid the frog on the close-cut grass stubble, he seemed lifeless.

"You're too late," Jane said. "The poor frog is dead."

"Maybe not," I said. "Go to the spigot and get some water and pour it over him."

Jane ran to the spigot and got a dipper of water. She poured the cool water slowly over the frog.

"He opened one eye," she shouted.

Soon the frog had both eyes open and was sitting up.

"He's going to be all right, Jane," I said. "Don't worry any more about the frog. But think of this poor, gentle blacksnake! He worked hard to get himself a meal. Now we've taken it away from him! We've got to save the snake!"

"Let 'im die, Daddy!" Jane said. "Snakes catch frogs, birds, rabbits, and moles! Snakes are killers!"

"So are frogs," I said. "So are birds and moles! They kill each other, plants, insects, flies, worms, and bugs. Each fights for survival. They play a great game. It is a rhythm in nature. They keep each other balanced. If it were not for the others, one would become a pest!"

"Not anything will kill a snake, Daddy!" she protested.

"Snakes kill each other," I said. "And chicken hawks, crows, and owls kill snakes."

Jane stood looking first at the frog, which was taking short, slow hops toward the stream. Then she looked at the incision in the writhing snake.

"You like the fireflies in the evening, don't you?" I said to Jane. "You never run and catch them and put them in a bottle like other boys and girls. You say, 'I like to watch them light their own way through a dark night-world.' Well, the frogs sit down there on the water lily leaves and leap up and catch the fireflies when they turn on their lights in the dark night. That frog was up there in the peach orchard, wasn't he? He went up where there were plenty of green flies in the hot sunlight. He was up there getting his dinner and the snake was there hunting his."

"Well, what can we do now to save the snake?"

"Run to the house and ask your mother for the turpentine bottle," I said. "Then look in my tool box and get that roll of adhesive tape."

I had to set the forks deeper into the ground. The big black-snake didn't like being held close against the ground so he could barely move.

When Jane returned, I put turpentine into the incision.

"Now, hold these forks down real tight, Jane," I said. "I want to do a good job!"

The snake writhed as if he were in much pain. I thought the turpentine might be smarting him. I unrolled the adhesive tape and cut several short strips in a hurry. Then I got down on my knees, fastened a piece of tape on one side of the incision, and drew the wound closed before I clamped the tape on the other side. I put tape on the incision from one end to the other. I had made this incision high enough so the tape wouldn't interfere with his crawling. I wanted to be sure I'd done a good job—one that would restore health to this big friendly snake so he could go into the ground after moles, mice, rats, and ground squirrels.

"Now take the forks up," I told Jane. "Let's see if he can't crawl away better than after he swallowed the frog."

Jane removed each fork and the big blacksnake crawled away very slowly at first. He held his head high in the air and stuck out his tongue.

"The frog got back to the creek and the snake is going back to the peach orchard," I said. "He's going back to live on his sunny south hillside."

"But why did we do all of this to save a snake?" Jane asked. "And, Daddy, come to think about it, after your telling me about the frogs catching my fireflies, I wonder why we saved the frog."

"They're both our friends, Jane," I said. "If it weren't for the frogs, I don't know what we'd do about bugs, flies, insects, and nests of yellow jackets. If it weren't for the blacksnakes, the moles would eat our garden. Blacksnakes catch mice, rats, and ground squirrels, and they kill the poisonous copperhead. They're friends to the farmers."

Our big blacksnake had reached the steep slope. He turned and looked back at us.

"I don't believe he holds anything against us, do you?" Jane asked.

☑ **Check Your Comprehension**

1. At the beginning of the story, what does Jane urge her father to do?
2. Why is the father confident that the frog is still alive, even though it can't breathe?
3. How does Jane's father save the frog?
4. How does the father help the snake?

◆ **Critical Thinking**

INTERPRET

1. (a) In the first part of the story, what is Jane's attitude toward the snake? (b) How does it contrast with her father's attitude toward the snake? **[Compare and Contrast]**
2. What do the father's words and actions show about his familiarity with nature and natural creatures? **[Infer]**
3. According to the father, how are the frog and the blacksnake "both our friends"? **[Interpret]**

APPLY

4. What new facts about the natural world did you learn from this story? **[Apply; Relate]**

esse Stuart

Eighty-one Summers

It was a new, strange feeling to drive my car up the winding Womack Hollow Road. It was a wonderful feeling to move up the green valley, to feel power at my finger tips, my body comfortable and cool. I loved to feel the car swerve just a little around the curves, under the shades of the tall sycamores, oaks, willows, poplars, and beeches. I'd walked over this road so many times before when there was only a path. I'd felt the sting of sweat in my eyes. But my legs were muscled then. I knew the smell of the flowers and the songs of the birds. I knew where each bird's nest was. And I knew what it was to smell the morning-fresh perfumes when dew was on the grass, leaves, and flowers. But now, I knew what it was to enjoy the comfort of a new road and a brand new automobile.

Before I reached the head of Womack Hollow, I had to make a sharp right turn. As I slowed my car I glanced up to my right and saw old Rock, the white mule I'd sold to Cass Timberlake. Rock was standing in harness, hitched to a root-cutter plow. I couldn't see the plow for the waist-high green corn, but I knew this was the only kind of a plow that could be used on this steep, new-ground slope. And between the handles of the plow stood Cass. He wasn't wearing his old black felt hat today and his hair was as white as the mule. My father told me three or four times that Cass had told him he wanted me to stop, so I slammed on the brakes, pulled over to one side of the road among the wilted rag-weeds, and stopped the car.

"You want to see me, Cass?" I shouted up the hill.

"Yep, I do, Shan," he said. "Wait just a minute until I go down to the house!"

Cass Timberlake's shack was down in the little valley between two high hills. This little valley was the first and only one on the right side of the road that dented the western wall of Womack Hollow. The shack was made of rough boards, with strips of batting[1] to cover the cracks. His wife, Bridget, had painted the boards white and the strips of batting brown. It was a pretty little shack, with morning-glories vining up the porch posts and sun-flowers in the front yard growing along the palings.[2] There were four hives of honeybees between the shack and the garden. There

---

1. **batting:** Wadded cotton or wool used to plug cracks.
2. **palings:** Fence posts.

was a box for martins[3] on a long pole in the front yard and a dinner bell between the forks of a tall locust post in the back yard.

I watched Cass go down the hill at a fast pace, dodging the stalks of stalwart corn as he hurried down to his shack. And, as I looked at him, his white head was against a white cloud. Behind him, a little higher up the steep hill, was the white mule standing just the way Cass had left him. He was bearing his weight on three legs and resting the other, while the rope lines, wrapped around the plow handles, sagged with limpness in the sultry July air.

Sweat ran from my forehead into my eyebrows and dropped down between my eyes. I didn't like to wait in this hot car, parked over the smelly, wilted ragweeds. I wanted to be going. I wanted to feel power at my finger tips and have the cool wind blow through the windows. I was restless to get started. I didn't have long to wait. I saw Cass coming around a corn row from the shack and he was carrying a feed sack in his hand.

"Oh, so that's what you wanted, Cass," I said. I had to laugh. "Why didn't you keep that old sack? I didn't want it back! I intended for you to keep it."

"But the sack don't belong to me," he said. "It's your sack. Since I'm so busy with my corn, terbacker, and potatoes, I hated to make a trip, Shan, to your place to return the sack. Not when you passed here most every day in your car. I told your dad to tell you to stop so I could return the sack to you! It's a busy season for me right now!"

"I see it is," I said. "It must be pretty hot up there on the hill plowing."

"Not so hot, Shan, as you might think," he said. "Not hot enough to notice after you get used to it!"

I looked at Cass Timberlake's blue eyes in their wrinkled sockets. His blue eyes were laughing at me. And the white beard stuck to his face, for the sweat had dampened it. Cass Timberlake wasn't a big man. He never in his lifetime could have lifted the end of a small saw log upon a log wagon, as I had seen my Grandpa Shelton do. He didn't have shoulders broad as a corncrib door like Grandpa. He didn't have big arms and hands like my Grandpa either. But Cass was nearly six feet tall and he had bright eyes, a good smile, and a few of his natural teeth. The hair on his head was as thick and white as clean sheep's wool. His eyebrows were as white as frosted ragweeds over a winter cliff.

"When I get so I can't plow, I don't know what I'll do," he said. "I love to plow and smell the dirt. I love to smell pussley,[4]

---

3. **martins:** Birds of the swallow family.
4. **pussley:** Purslane, a weed with small, yellow flowers.

careless, smartweeds, and ragweeds when the July sun is at its best. Love to watch the lizards sunning on the stumps and rocks. There's something about plowing, too, that means corn in my crib when the snows and the rains fall and the season's done. Corn in my crib, Shan, means bread for Bridget and me. Yep," he talked on, "this summer makes eighty-one summers I've plowed!"

I was stunned. I looked again at Cass Timberlake. I didn't say anything. He smiled as he looked at me.

"You don't believe me, Shan?" he said. "I was born in 1868 and this is 1959. So you figure it up. Today is my birthday and Bridget is making me a cake."

"You mean to tell me that you're ninety-one?" I asked.

"I'm ninety-one, Shan," he said. "I've plowed since I was ten years old. I used to plow cattle on the Elliott County hills! I traveled down to this country when I was twenty years old, found Bridget and married her, a girl of sixteen then. And we raised seven children and they raised thirty-five children and these thirty-five children are about all married and are raising children! Bridget and I got the place all to ourselves again!"

My memory flashed back to last year when the state built this road. They had sawed down a giant elm, too big to push down with a big bulldozer. It grew across the road in front of Cass Timberlake's shack. When they sawed the tree down, they left it lay to rot on the ground. But Cass Timberlake didn't let it lay and rot. Bridget, a large, white-haired, beautiful, elderly woman, with a smile on her lips and a sparkle in her eye, helped Cass pull a big crosscut saw through the big trunk. She helped him saw the big body into sections as big around as barrels, but not as tall. The first one sawed from the tree would have been big enough for a small round table. A meal for two could have been served on the top of it.

I passed by one morning and stopped my car while they were sawing. Bridget and Cass were quarreling. He said Bridget was riding the saw and she accused him of riding it. I listened a minute to their quarreling, then they both broke out in explosive laughter. They changed their minds about each other's riding the saw. They agreed that the saw was dull and Cass decided to file it. He was ninety then, and she was eighty-six. Cass Timberlake split the big pieces of wood with a wedge, sledge, and double-bitted ax. He chopped the branches of its bushy top. He cut enough wood from this tree to fill a woodshed.

"When Bridget and I got married," Cass continued, "we built a log house on a farm we rented and moved into it. It was a one-room shack. But in three years we bought the farm. And we added to the shack as our youngins were born. By the time we had our seven we had a pretty good-sized house. We lived on that farm for fifty years. I cleared the farm, made pasture fields and meadows. I loved that farm where we just had a little wagon road up Straight Creek. But after the automobiles got here and everybody started gettin' 'em, and big steel monsters started tearing down hillsides to build a road up Straight Creek and through my farm, I started wondering whether I'd live on there. When the automobiles drove by and clouds of dust blew over our way, Bridget and I agreed to get away soon as we could. We didn't have any more new ground. We'd conquered the hundred acres of wilderness we'd bought. That's why we come up Womack Hollow and bought this fifty-acre farm. There was only a little crooked wagon road leading to it. There was fresh spring water here and plenty of new ground. We never dreamed the big steel monsters would ever come up this narrow valley and build a road for the automobiles to give us their dust. But it's happened here. Shan, it's getting so there's no place to go. Not a place left. Do you know of one where there's plenty of new ground, good ankle-deep leaf-rot loam on top of the soil?"

"No, I don't," I said. "I can't think of one just now!"

"I love to grow corn in it," Cass said. "Corn has strength that's grown in leaf-rot loam. I don't care what people say about it. And the taste of tomatoes grown there is sweeter and better. Shan, new ground has strength, but now it's about all gone! But it is new ground I'm after. That hillslope there I'm plowing is new ground! Look at my dark green corn. Pretty corn, ain't it?"

"It certainly is," I said. I looked up the hillslope at the tall green corn. Old Rock, Cass's mule, was standing quietly resting another leg. Once he stomped at a biting fly and swished him with the brush of his shorn[5] tail. Cass looked at his corn too. His eagle eyes surveyed his clean field that seemed to reach up to the sky on the ridge line above. His tall corn near the ridge line was etched against a white cloud. It was beautiful to see.

"I'm one of the last new-ground farmers[6] left here, Shan," Cass said as he turned from looking at his field to look at me. "This country has changed. When I first come to Womack Hollow twenty years go, everybody around here made his living from new ground. They plowed these steep hills, the little bottoms and the valleys. Now, who will plow a steep hillside? The young men don't. They don't even plow the slopes. They don't walk between the handles of a plow any more in this hilly country. They plow the creek and river bottoms and they ride when they plow. If they don't ride, they don't plow! There's only one farmer left around here with me. That's Fred Doore! Old Fred's still farming his hills

---

5. **shorn:** Cut or clipped.
6. **new-ground farmers:** Farmers who work soil that has never been cultivated before.

and growing the best cane and corn in this county! But he's a young man, Shan. He's only sixty-five."

Cass stood behind the palings, resting one hand on the fence and holding the sack in the other.

"I'm about to forget your sack, Shan," he said, handing it to me.

I reached from the window and got the sack that was worth a dime. I threw it over onto the back seat. He had worried more about getting the old sack back to me than I worried about making the payments on my car. But that was the way he lived.

Cass Timberlake didn't have a smile on his face now. He had a faraway look in his eyes.

"I don't understand it all, Shan," Cass said. "So many of the people who worked, farmed, thought, and believed in the way of livin' that Bridget and I do are gone. I couldn't go down there and take that state handout like my children tried to get Bridget and me to do. My oldest boy, Lew, said we'd been eligible for it for the last twenty-five years. I don't want it as long as I can plow old Rock!"

The sweat ran down my face in little streams and soaked my shirt collar. I looked at Cass Timberlake's sun-tanned face and he wasn't sweating. I couldn't mop any more sweat from my face with my bandanna; it was already soaked. The sun's rays, slanting down over the growing green waves of corn, heated the steel and glass that enclosed me. Even the springy new seat of my car was wet with perspiration. Honeybees zoomed past us and fussed with each other over the nectar in the white blossoms of Queen Anne's lace and the purple blossoms of ironweed.

"But Bridget and I are holding out on all this stuff," Cass said. "We're not goin' to let it swallow us. And when we find a farm with a lot of good new ground on it, away from a road and automobile dust, we're sellin' this farm and buyin' that one. She feels just like I do about it. We loved this place until the steel monsters come up this hollow, cutting down the slopes with their big blades and rooting up the poor helpless trees! We'll go to new ground where we can raise what we eat and eat about all we raise from that good earth. It'll give us strength. It always has. You can't beat the fertilizer made by the earth itself and tempered by the rain that falls on earth. You can't beat it, Shan. I'll never be a-takin' these pills that give you this and that and have some other kind of strength shot into me with a long needle! When I go, I'll go as the leaf from the tree the frost has nipped."

I fidgeted in my car for I was hot. Cass had held me too long over a ten-cent feed sack. I had helped to get this road. I'd written to the Governor of Kentucky about it. I knew the Governor personally and I got it. The road had softened my legs a bit, put a little weight around my middle, where I sat bent over so much in

the car. And I couldn't smell like I did when I walked up and
down the little path that was the Womack Hollow Road. I didn't
know where the birds' nests were and where the patches of
snow-white percoon grew and bloomed in late March and early
April. I never had time to find it now and fondle the snow-white
blossoms and smell their pleasant perfumes of spring. And I
wondered how I ever got around without my car and a good road.
My world had changed, too, but I didn't tell Cass. I didn't want to
talk any longer. I'd lost all this time because he wanted to return
a feed sack.

"It's a hot contraption you're in, Shan," Cass said. "You ought
to get out so the wind can blow over you!"

"I guess it would be cooler," I said.

"Shan, you've got to go and I've got work to do," Cass said as
he watched me fidget restlessly. "And I've got to get back up there
to old Rock. He's had time to rest all four legs now and dream
about the big ears of white and yellow corn we'll have in the crib
this winter when the cold November rain falls and the snows
come! Corn for old Rock and the cows, and corn to make the
finest new-ground corn meal in the land! Talk about good hot
corn bread with strength and yellow butter to go with it!"

"You make me hungry, Cass," I said. "Come to see me. Bring
Bridget!"

"I'll do that," he said. "Stop again and see me!"

I looked once from the side windows as I got started. Cass was
walking up the slope across the corn rows toward his mule and
plow.

☑ Check Your Comprehension

1. (a) Why does Shan feel happy at the beginning of the story? (b) Why does he stop the car?
2. (a) How old is Cass Timberlake? (b) Why did Cass and his wife Bridget decide to leave Straight Creek and come to Womack Hollow?
3. Why do Cass Timberlake's comments about the road and the "steel monsters" make Shan nervous and impatient?

◆ Critical Thinking

INTERPRET

1. This story revolves around a contrast between past and present, between two ways of life. What detail in the first paragraph foreshadows or hints at this contrast? [Analyze]
2. How would you describe Cass Timberlake's relationship to the land? [Interpret]
3. How does Cass's outlook toward the land contrast with Shan's attitude? [Compare and Contrast]

APPLY

4. Do you think change and progress are inevitable, or would the world be better off if people lived more simply, in harmony with nature? Explain your opinion. [Apply]

Jesse Stuart

Too Many Roads

We stand here idle, half afraid to stir.
We cannot even find the path to take.
Too many roads are leading everywhere,
Through pasture field, cornfields, and brushy brake.[1]
5   Here are the skies, the good clean wind to breathe,
The deep rich loamy[2] earth beneath our feet;
And here are many roads to take or leave,
Earth for the bed, the clean wind for a sheet.
It does not matter much the way we go,
10   Or where we go, or when, or how, or why.
For we must keep our feet upon the earth
And we must live in wind beneath the sky.
The road lies here before us; if I lose
It is my fault. No certain road I choose.

---

1. **brake:** Thicket.
2. **loamy:** Rich in organic matter.

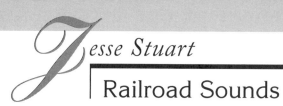

Jesse Stuart

Railroad Sounds

I have heard mean groans of heavy engines
Striking the emptiness of night.
And I have heard the drive wheels slipping
At Black Mountain when the track was sanded.
5   Those sounds I have heard and loved.

I have heard the lonesome whistle screaming
When a bright light was leading,
A red light trailing,
And the naked train moaned with the wind.

10   I have heard the oozing steam from slick pistons,
The swinging and banging of box car doors.
And I have heard the winter winds
Whip the frozen wiring
And tear across the bitter sky.
15   These sounds I have loved.

Their Eyes Have Seen

He sees them walking slowly by the stream,
Their small hands holding book and dinner pail.
They are awake to life and do not dream;
They shout to wind and mock the calling quail
5   With laughter ringing through the thin blue air,
As boys run for the old persimmon[1] grove
To pick up mellowed fruit frost-ripened there,
To share with little rose-lipped girls they love.
This wakes the old man's dreams and memories
10   Of life that goes back fifty years and more
When coming home from school he pillaged[2] these
Wild groves for the lady by him in the door,
Whose hair, like his, is white as moonlit snow.
Each morn and afternoon they watch them pass,
15   Remembering youth carefree as winds that blow
And steps once light as raindrops on the grass.

---

1. persimmon (pər sim´ ən): Tree of the ebony family that produces orange-red, plumlike fruit.
2. pillaged (pil´ ij'd): Robbed.

Jesse Stuart

Invitation

If you should chance to wander lost someday
On paths that lead through mountains near about
And see briar-tangled banks of yellow clay
And have a time of finding your way out;
5   If you should chance to see upon that hill
Not far from cone-shaped hills, green-clad in pines,
A house with burdock[1] growing at the sill
And in the front a trellis[2] with rose vines,
Come up and say you are a stranger, friend!
10   Say you are lost on paths in vine-clad space
And you have failed to find your journey's end.
Stay here with us; we shall not fear your face.
We high-hill people squeeze the stranger's hand
And welcome him, a duty that we must.
15   Stop here when you are lost upon this land.
We'll know if you are worthy of our trust!

---

1. burdock: Large plant with purple-flowered heads.
2. trellis: Wooden lattice structure on which vines are trained to grow.

How Can One Sleep?

Restless is this night with a soft moon hanging
Red as a sliced beet under lichen stone;
Wind and the leaves are cymbals softly clanging
Music for him who loves to walk alone.

5   Night has no barrier for a man whose brain
Grows wild with her realms of poetic moods;
He feels and hears the wind and tastes the rain
When it drips from the leaves in poplar woods.
Night is godsend to man when it is full

10   Of darkness, mud, and blowing wind and cloud—
Night is a joyous mood that's beautiful;
Night is a whispering ghost in velvet shroud.
How can one sleep when wind and darkness stir?
How can one let his active brain be dead?

15   How can he lie awake night-long to hear
A million words of facts that should be said?

☑ **Check Your Comprehension**

1. What choice confronts the speaker in "Too Many Roads"?
2. In "Railroad Sounds," name three specific noises that the speaker says he has heard.
3. In "Their Eyes Have Seen," what sight reminds the old couple of their youth?
4. Whom does the speaker address in "Invitation"?
5. According to lines 9-11 of "How Can One Sleep?" how does the speaker feel about a night full of darkness, mud, blowing wind, and cloud?

◆ **Critical Thinking**

INTERPRET

1. In "Too Many Roads," how would you describe the speaker's mood? **[Interpret]**

2. Why do you think the speaker in "Railroad Sounds" loves the sounds of trains? What might trains represent or symbolize for the speaker? **[Infer]**
3. In the last two lines of "Their Eyes Have Seen," what two similes does Stuart use to describe youth? **[Analyze]**
4. From the evidence in "Invitation," what values do you think are held dear by the "high-hill people"? **[Interpret]**

COMPARE LITERARY WORKS

5. Which poem in this group did you like best? Briefly explain your answer. **[Evaluate]**

Jesse Stuart

Comparing and Connecting the Author's Works

◆ Literary Focus: Narrator and Point of View

The **narrator** of a story is the speaker or character who tells the tale. A third-person narrator is someone who stands outside the action and speaks about it. A first-person narrator is one who tells a story and participates in its action. This type of narrator, who uses the pronouns *I, me, my,* and *we,* is said to use the first-person **point of view.**

First-person point of view has the advantage of making a story seem direct and immediate. In "The Blacksnake's Operation," for example, the father plunges us directly into the action in the first sentence of the story: "Jane and I were sitting at the picnic table in the back yard when we heard a noise like wind in autumn leaves."

When you read a story with first-person point of view, keep in mind that the narrator is a character in the story and does not necessarily represent the opinions or outlook of the author. In "The Blacksnake's Operation," the father's lessons about the balance of nature probably reflect Jesse Stuart's own opinions, since Stuart stresses the link between human beings and nature in many of his works. In "Eighty-one Summers," however, it is Cass Timberlake, not the narrator, who cherishes the land ethic that Stuart admired.

1. In "Eighty-one Summers," what do the narrator's thoughts about the feed sack reveal about his personality?

2. Near the end of "Eighty-one Summers," the narrator realizes that his life has changed since the new road was built. How is this realization linked to the theme of the story as a whole?

◆ Drawing Conclusions About Stuart's Work

In an essay on Jesse Stuart, critic Jim Wayne Miller singled out the relationship between human beings and nature as a key theme in Stuart's writing. Miller wrote that Stuart created "a living world in which the connection between people and the land is close and organic, in which people are aware of their dependence on the land."

In a brief essay, apply this statement to "The Blacksnake's Operation," "Eighty-one Summers," and one of the poems by Jesse Stuart that you have read. Find opinions, examples, details, and facts that support Miller's view. You may want to use a chart like the one below to organize your examples and details.

Purpose: To explore the connection between people and the land in the works of Jesse Stuart	
OPINIONS	
EXAMPLES	
SENSORY DETAILS	
FACTS	

◆ Idea Bank

Writing

1. **Anecdote** Retell "The Blacksnake's Operation," using the first-person point of view of Jane. Feel free to condense the story so that it is shorter, but try to include all the major incidents in your retelling.

2. **Poem** In Stuart's poem "Railroad Sounds," the speaker loves the sounds of trains. Write a short poem, with or without rhyme, in which you feature the sounds of another means of transport, such as an automobile, a bus, a ship, or an airplane. When you finish, read your poem aloud for a small audience of classmates, friends, or family members.

3. **Regional Film** Together with a small group, create an outline for a short film that features distinctive sights, characters, customs, or events in the life of your region of the country. You can use made-up events, or your film can be a nonfictional, documentary-style treatment of the region. When you finish, post your outline on the class bulletin board. **[Media Link; Group Activity]**

Speaking and Listening

4. **Oral Interpretation** Practice reading aloud your favorite poem by Jesse Stuart. In order to bring out the meaning of the poem as well as its sound effects, concentrate on rhythm, rhyme, sentence structure, tone, and volume. When you have polished your interpretation, perform your reading for the class. **[Performing Arts Link]**

5. **Debate** Ever since ancient times, people have debated whether city life is to be preferred to country life, or vice versa. Together with a partner, plan and perform a debate in which you list the advantages and disadvantages of each position. Agree in advance on the rules for the debate: for example, which speaker is to go first, how many minutes each side will have for its presentation, and whether or not each side can directly question the other. **[Social Studies Link]**

Researching and Representing

6. **Emergency Care** Jane's father calls the blacksnake, which is nonpoisonous, a big friendly fellow. In some parts of the country, however, poisonous snakes can be dangerous. What species are the most common poisonous snakes in the United States? How can they be identified from their size and markings? What should be done at once if a person is bitten? Using Internet and library resources, research these questions. Write up your findings in an illustrated report. **[Science Link; Health Link]**

◆ Further Reading, Listening, and Viewing

- Stuart, Jesse: *Album of Destiny* (1944). This is one of Stuart's highly regarded collections of poems.

- Stuart, Jesse: *Dawn of Remembered Spring* (1972). "The Blacksnake's Operation" is taken from this collection of stories.

- Stuart, Jesse: *The Best-Loved Short Stories of Jesse Stuart* (1982).

- LeMaster, J. R. and Mary Washington Clarke: *Jesse Stuart: Essays on His Work* (1977).

- Copland, Aaron: *Appalachian Spring* (1944). This orchestral music memorably evokes the region of Appalachia.

On the Web:

http://www.phschool.com/atschool/literature
Go to the student edition Silver. Proceed to Unit 4. Then, click Hot Links to find Web sites featuring Jesse Stuart.

Arthur Conan Doyle In Depth

> "Come, Watson, come! The game is afoot."
> —*Holmes to Watson in* **The Return of Sherlock Holmes**

SIR **A**RTHUR **C**ONAN **D**OYLE'S unforgettable creations—Sherlock Holmes and Dr. Watson and their adventures—continue to shape detective fiction more than a century after they first appeared.

Medical Studies Arthur Conan Doyle was born in 1859 in Edinburgh, Scotland, into a family descended on both sides from painters, cartoonists, and illustrators. Educated at Stonyhurst College in England, Doyle prepared for a career in medicine at Edinburgh University. One of his professors, Dr. Joseph Bell, had an uncanny ability to deduce the occupations of his patients from their physical appearance. Bell became the model for Sherlock Holmes.

Doyle received his medical degree in 1885, and his first medical posts were as a ship's surgeon on voyages to the Arctic and to the west coast of Africa. He then set up a medical practice in the small city of Portsmouth in England, where he remained for eight years.

A Second Career When his medical practice failed to produce enough money, Doyle turned to writing. Later in his career, he recalled that he was disappointed in the detective fiction he read for entertainment, since the solution to the mystery nearly always depended on chance. Doyle decided that he would try to "reduce this fascinating but unorganized business to something nearer to an exact science." With the publication of *A Study in Scarlet* in 1887, Sherlock Holmes was born.

National Fame Sherlock Holmes and Dr. Watson quickly caught the public's imagination and brought fame to their creator. In the same year that *A Study in Scarlet* was published, Doyle started work on a historical novel, *Micah Clarke,* set in seventeenth-century England. Publication of a series of Holmes tales in an illustrated monthly magazine called the *Strand* brought Doyle a handsome income, and soon after his move to London in 1891 he abandoned his medical practice to become a full-time writer.

Ironically, however, Doyle soon grew tired of writing the Holmes stories. By 1893, he had written and published two more historical novels, and he felt that this type of writing was far more serious and important than detective fiction. In 1893, in a story entitled "The Final Problem," Doyle killed his most famous creation by having Holmes and the detective's arch-enemy, Professor Moriarty, fall off a cliff.

Readers were furious. Twenty thousand subscribers to the *Strand* canceled their subscriptions, and one reader denounced Doyle in a letter as "You brute!"

Middle Years Although Doyle had stopped writing about Sherlock Holmes, he continued to write prolifically, producing stories, novels, and plays. In 1900, he served as a physician in South Africa during the Boer War. When he returned to England, he compiled a history of the conflict and defended the actions of the British in a lengthy pamphlet. In 1902, he received a knighthood from King Edward VII.

Around this time, Doyle brought his famous detective back to life after an absence of ten years. Legions of Holmes fans were ecstatic. It was then that he wrote one of his most famous Holmes tales, *The Hound of the Baskervilles* (1902). More stories followed, and the demand for them was so great that by the 1920's Doyle was the most highly-paid writer in the world.

Final Years Doyle's personal life brought him a mixture of happiness and misfortune. Following his wife's death in 1906, he remarried in 1907. However, the death of his brother and oldest son in World War I dealt him a grievous blow.

Despite heart disease, Doyle continued to work until his death in July 1930 in Crowborough, Sussex, England.

◆ Detective Fiction

In a detective story (sometimes called a "whodunit"), a crime is committed by one of a group of suspects, and an expert detective solves the puzzle of the criminal's identity. The American writer Edgar Allan Poe (1809-1849) is widely acknowledged as the inventor of the modern detective story. Poe probably based his character C. Auguste Dupin, the detective in three of his best-known stories, on the memoirs of a French detective named Eugène-François Vidocq.

Many features found in detective fiction today may be traced back to Poe, including the super-intelligent detective, the police who are stumped by the crime, and the detective's friend who serves as the narrator. All these characteristics are prominent in the Sherlock Holmes stories of Sir Arthur Conan Doyle.

Detective fiction is an extremely popular, international literary genre. One measure of Sherlock Holmes's popularity is the large number of film and television adaptations of Doyle's stories about the detective.

◆ Literary Works

Sherlock Holmes Fiction

Novels
- *A Study in Scarlet* (1887)
- *The Sign of Four* (1890)
- *The Hound of the Baskervilles* (1901–1902)
- *The Valley of Fear* (1914–1915)

Short Story Collections
- *The Adventures of Sherlock Holmes* (1892)
- *The Memoirs of Sherlock Holmes* (1893)
- *The Return of Sherlock Holmes* (1905)
- *His Last Bow: Some Reminiscences of Sherlock Holmes* (1917)
- *The Case-Book of Sherlock Holmes* (1927)

Other Fiction
- ***The White Company*** (1891)
- ***The Great Shadow*** (1892)
- ***The Lost World*** (1912)
- ***The Poison Belt*** (1913)

Nonfiction
- ***The Great Boer War*** (1900)
- ***The War in South Africa: Its Cause and Conduct*** (1902)
- ***The British Campaign in France and Flanders*** (1916–1920)

Mr. Sherlock Holmes
from A Study in Scarlet

In the year 1878 I took my degree of Doctor of Medicine of the University of London, and proceeded to Netley to go through the course prescribed for surgeons in the Army. Having completed my studies there, I was duly attached to the Fifth Northumberland Fusiliers[1] as assistant surgeon. The regiment was stationed in India at the time, and before I could join it, the second Afghan war had broken out. On landing at Bombay, I learned that my corps had advanced through the passes, and was already deep in the enemy's country. I followed, however, with many other officers who were in the same situation as myself, and succeeded in reaching Candahar in safety, where I found my regiment, and at once entered upon my new duties.

The campaign brought honours and promotion to many, but for me it had nothing but misfortune and disaster. I was removed from my brigade and attached to the Berkshires,[2] with whom I served at the fatal battle of Maiwand. There I was struck on the shoulder by a Jezail bullet, which shattered the bone and grazed the subclavian artery. I should have fallen into the hands of the murderous Ghazis had it not been for the devotion and courage shown by Murray, my orderly, who threw me across a pack-horse, and succeeded in bringing me safely to the British lines.

Worn with pain, and weak from the prolonged hardships which I had undergone, I was removed, with a great train of wounded sufferers, to the base hospital at Peshawar. Here I rallied, and had already improved so far as to be able to walk about the wards, and even to bask a little upon the veranda, when I was struck down by enteric fever, that curse of our Indian possessions. For months my life was despaired of, and when at last I came to myself and became convalescent, I was so weak and emaciated that a medical board determined that not a day should be lost in sending me back to England. I was despatched, accordingly, in the troopship *Orontes*, and landed a month later on Portsmouth jetty, with my health irretrievably ruined, but with permission from a paternal government to spend the next nine months in attempting to improve it.

I had neither kith nor kin in England, and was therefore as free as air—or as free as an income of eleven shillings and sixpence a day will permit a man to be. Under such circumstances I

---

1. **Fifth Northumberland Fusiliers:** A military regiment.
2. **the Berkshire:** Another regiment.

naturally gravitated to London, that great cesspool into which all the loungers and idlers of the Empire are irresistibly drained. There I stayed for some time at a private hotel in the Strand, leading a comfortless, meaningless existence, and spending such money as I had, considerably more freely than I ought. So alarming did the state of my finances become, that I soon realized that I must either leave the metropolis and rusticate[3] somewhere in the country, or that I must make a complete alteration in my style of living. Choosing the latter alternative, I began by making up my mind to leave the hotel, and take up my quarters in some less pretentious and less expensive domicile.

On the very day that I had come to this conclusion, I was standing at the Criterion Bar, when someone tapped me on the shoulder, and turning round I recognized young Stamford, who had been a dresser under me at Bart's. The sight of a friendly face in the great wilderness of London is a pleasant thing indeed to a lonely man. In old days Stamford had never been a particular crony of mine, but now I hailed him with enthusiasm, and he, in his turn, appeared to be delighted to see me. In the exuberance of my joy, I asked him to lunch with me at the Holborn, and we started off together in a hansom.

"Whatever have you been doing with yourself, Watson?" he asked in undisguised wonder, as we rattled through the crowded London streets. "You are as thin as a lath and as brown as a nut."

I gave him a short sketch of my adventures, and had hardly concluded it by the time that we reached our destination.

"Poor devil!" he said, commiseratingly, after he had listened to my misfortunes. "What are you up to now?"

"Looking for lodgings," I answered. "Trying to solve the problem as to whether it is possible to get comfortable rooms at a reasonable price."

"That 's a strange thing," remarked my companion; "you are the second man to-day that has used that expression to me."

"And who was the first?" I asked.

"A fellow who is working at the chemical laboratory up at the hospital. He was bemoaning himself this morning because he could not get someone to go halves with him in some nice rooms which he had found, and which were too much for his purse."

"By Jove!" I cried; "if he really wants someone to share the rooms and the expense, I am the very man for him. I should prefer having a partner to being alone."

Young Stamford looked rather strangely at me over his wine-glass. "You don't know Sherlock Holmes yet," he said; "perhaps you would not care for him as a constant companion."

---

3. **rusticate:** Be exiled to a rustic, rural area.

"Why, what is there against him?"

"Oh, I didn't say there was anything against him. He is a little queer in his ideas—an enthusiast in some branches of science. As far as I know he is a decent fellow enough."

"A medical student, I suppose?" said I.

"No—I have no idea what he intends to go in for. I believe he is well up in anatomy, and he is a first-class chemist; but, as far as I know, he has never taken out any systematic medical classes. His studies are very desultory[4] and eccentric, but he has amassed a lot of out-of-the-way knowledge which would astonish his professors."

"Did you never ask him what he was going in for?" I asked.

"No; he is not a man that it is easy to draw out, though he can be communicative enough when the fancy seizes him."

"I should like to meet him," I said. "If I am to lodge with anyone, I should prefer a man of studious and quiet habits. I am not strong enough yet to stand much noise or excitement. I had enough of both in Afghanistan to last me for the remainder of my natural existence. How could I meet this friend of yours?"

"He is sure to be at the laboratory," returned my companion. "He either avoids the place for weeks, or else he works there from morning till night. If you like, we will drive round together after luncheon."

"Certainly," I answered, and the conversation drifted away into other channels.

As we made our way to the hospital after leaving the Holborn, Stamford gave me a few more particulars about the gentleman whom I proposed to take as a fellow-lodger.

"You mustn't blame me if you don't get on with him," he said; "I know nothing more of him than I have learned from meeting him occasionally in the laboratory. You proposed this arrangement, so you must not hold me responsible."

"If we don't get on it will be easy to part company," I answered. "It seems to me, Stamford," I added, looking hard at my companion, "that you have some reason for washing your hands of the matter. Is this fellow's temper so formidable, or what is it? Don't be mealymouthed about it."

"It is not easy to express the inexpressible," he answered with a laugh. "Holmes is a little too scientific for my tastes—it approaches to cold-bloodedness. I could imagine his giving a friend a little pinch of the latest vegetable alkaloid[5], not out of malevolence, you understand, but simply out of a spirit of inquiry in order to have an accurate idea of the effects. To do him justice, I think that he would take it himself with the same readiness. He appears to have a passion for definite and exact knowledge."

---

4. **desultory:** Irregularly engaged in.
5. **alkaloid:** A chemical extract, often extremely poisonous.

"Very right too."

"Yes, but it may be pushed to excess. When it comes to beating the subjects in the dissecting-rooms with a stick, it is certainly taking rather a bizarre shape."

"Beating the subjects!"

"Yes, to verify how far bruises may be produced after death. I saw him at it with my own eyes."

"And yet you say he is not a medical student?"

"No. Heaven knows what the objects of his studies are. But here we are, and you must form your own impressions about him." As he spoke, we turned down a narrow lane and passed through a small side-door, which opened into a wing of the great hospital. It was familiar ground to me, and I needed no guiding as we ascended the bleak stone staircase and made our way down the long corridor with its vista of whitewashed wall and dun-coloured doors. Near the farther end a low arched passage branched away from it and led to the chemical laboratory.

This was a lofty chamber, lined and littered with countless bottles. Broad, low tables were scattered about, which bristled with retorts, test-tubes, and little Bunsen lamps, with their blue flickering flames. There was only one student in the room, who was bending over a distant table absorbed in his work. At the sound of our steps he glanced round and sprang to his feet with a cry of pleasure. "I've found it! I've found it," he shouted to my companion, running towards us with a test-tube in his hand. "I have found a re-agent which is precipitated by hæmoglobin, and by nothing else." Had he discovered a gold mine, greater delight could not have shone upon his features.

"Dr. Watson, Mr. Sherlock Holmes," said Stamford, introducing us.

"How are you?" he said cordially, gripping my hand with a strength for which I should hardly have given him credit. "You have been in Afghanistan, I perceive."

"How on earth did you know that?" I asked in astonishment.

"Never mind," said he, chuckling to himself. "The question now is about hemoglobin. No doubt you see the significance of this discovery of mine?"

"It is interesting, chemically, no doubt," I answered, "but practically—"

"Why, man, it is the most practical medico-legal discovery for years. Don't you see that it gives us an infallible test for blood stains? Come over here now!" He seized me by the coat-sleeve in his eagerness, and drew me over to the table at which he had been working. "Let us have some fresh blood," he said, digging a long bodkin into his finger, and drawing off the resulting drop of blood in a chemical pipette. "Now, I add this small quantity of blood to a litre of water. You perceive that the resulting mixture has the appearance of pure water. The proportion of blood cannot be more than one in a million. I have no doubt, however, that we shall be able to obtain the characteristic reaction." As he spoke, he threw into the vessel a few white crystals, and then added some drops of a transparent fluid. In an instant the contents assumed a dull mahogany colour, and a brownish dust was precipitated to the bottom of the glass jar.

"Ha! ha!" he cried, clapping his hands, and looking as delighted as a child with a new toy. "What do you think of that?"

"It seems to be a very delicate test," I remarked.

"Beautiful! beautiful! The old guaiacum test was very clumsy and uncertain. So is the microscopic examination for blood corpuscles. The latter is valueless if the stains are a few hours old. Now, this appears to act as well whether the blood is old or new. Had this test been invented, there are hundreds of men now walking the earth who would long ago have paid the penalty of their crimes."

"Indeed!" I murmured.

"Criminal cases are continually hinging upon that one point. A man is suspected of a crime months perhaps after it has been committed. His linen or clothes are examined and brownish stains discovered upon them. Are they blood stains, or mud stains, or rust stains, or fruit stains, or what are they? That is a question which has puzzled many an expert, and why? Because there was no reliable test. Now we have Sherlock Holmes's test, and there will no longer be any difficulty."

His eyes fairly glittered as he spoke, and he put his hand over his heart and bowed as if to some applauding crowd conjured up by his imagination.

"You are to be congratulated," I remarked, considerably surprised at his enthusiasm.

"There was the case of Von Bischoff at Frankfort last year. He would certainly have been hung had this test been in existence. Then there was Mason of Bradford, and the notorious Muller, and Lefevre of Montpellier, and Samson of New Orleans. I could name a score of cases in which it would have been decisive."

"You seem to be a walking calendar of crime," said Stamford with a laugh. "You might start a paper on those lines. Call it the 'Police News of the Past.' "

"Very interesting reading it might be made, too," remarked Sherlock Holmes, sticking a small piece of plaster over the prick on his finger. "I have to be careful," he continued, turning to me with a smile, "for I dabble with poisons a good deal." He held out his hand as he spoke, and I noticed that it was all mottled over with similar pieces of plaster, and discoloured with strong acids.

"We came here on business," said Stamford, sitting down on a high three-legged stool, and pushing another one in my direction with his foot. "My friend here wants to take diggings[6]; and as you were complaining that you could get no one to go halves with you, I thought that I had better bring you together."

Sherlock Holmes seemed delighted at the idea of sharing his rooms with me. "I have my eye on a suite in Baker Street," he said, "which would suit us down to the ground. You don't mind the smell of strong tobacco, I hope?"

"I always smoke 'ship's' myself," I answered.

"That's good enough. I generally have chemicals about, and occasionally do experiments. Would that annoy you?"

"By no means."

"Let me see—what are my other shortcomings? I get in the dumps at times, and don't open my mouth for days on end. You must not think I am sulky when I do that. Just let me alone, and I'll soon be right. What have you to confess now? It's just as well for two fellows to know the worst of one another before they begin to live together."

I laughed at this cross-examination. "I keep a bull pup," I said, "and I object to rows because my nerves are shaken, and I get up at all sorts of ungodly hours, and I am extremely lazy. I have another set of vices when I'm well, but those are the principal ones at present."

"Do you include violin playing in your category of rows?" he asked, anxiously.

"It depends on the player," I answered. "A well-played violin is a treat for the gods—a badly played one—"

"Oh, that's all right," he cried, with a merry laugh. "I think we may consider the thing as settled—that is, if the rooms are agreeable to you."

"When shall we see them?"

"Call for me here at noon to-morrow, and we'll go together and settle everything," he answered.

"All right—noon exactly," said I, shaking his hand.

We left him working among his chemicals, and we walked together towards my hotel.

"By the way," I asked suddenly, stopping and turning upon Stamford, "how the deuce did he know that I had come from Afghanistan?"

My companion smiled an enigmatical smile. "That's just his little peculiarity," he said. "A good many people have wanted to know how he finds things out."

---

6. **take diggings:** Find a place to live.

"Oh! a mystery is it?" I cried, rubbing my hands. "This is very piquant.[7] I am much obliged to you for bringing us together. 'The proper study of mankind is man,' you know."

"You must study him, then," Stamford said, as he bade me good-bye. "You'll find him a knotty problem, though. I'll wager he learns more about you than you about him. Good-bye."

"Good-bye," I answered, and strolled on to my hotel, considerably interested in my new acquaintance.

---

7. **piquant** (pē kant′): Intriguing.

☑ **Check Your Comprehension**

1. What happened to Watson when he served in the second Afghan War?
2. Where does Watson first meet Sherlock Holmes?
3. What discovery has Holmes just made?
4. What does Stamford predict to Watson about Holmes?

◆ **Critical Thinking**

1. What does Watson's account of his military service and his habits suggest about his personality? **[Infer]**

2. What details support Stamford's judgment that Sherlock Holmes is eccentric? **[Support]**
3. Why do you think Holmes is reluctant to tell Watson how he deduced that Watson had been in Afghanistan? **[Infer]**
4. Do you agree that two people should tell each other about their shortcomings before they begin a friendship? Explain why or why not. **[Apply]**

The Recollections of Captain Wilkie

'Who can he be?' thought I, as I watched my companion in the second-class carriage of the London and Dover Railway.

I had been so full of the fact that my long-expected holiday had come at last, and that for a few days at least the gaieties of Paris were about to supersede the dull routine of the hospital wards, that we were well out of London before I observed that I was not alone in the compartment. In these days we have all pretty well agreed that 'Three is company and two is none' upon the railway. At the time I write of, however, people were not so morbidly sensitive about their travelling companions. It was rather an agreeable surprise to me to find that there was some chance of whiling away the hours of a tedious journey. I therefore pulled my cap down over my eyes, took a good look from beneath it at my vis-à-vis, and repeated to myself, 'Who can he be?'

I used rather to pride myself on being able to spot a man's trade or profession by a good look at his exterior. I had the advantage of studying under a Professor at Edinburgh[1] who was a master of the art, and used to electrify both his patients and his clinical classes by long shots, sometimes at the most unlikely of pursuits, and never very far from the mark. 'Well, my man,' I have heard him say, 'I can see by your fingers that you play some musical instrument for your livelihood, but it is a rather curious one—something quite out of my line.' The man afterwards informed us that he earned a few coppers by blowing *Rule Britannia*[2] on a coffee-pot, the spout of which was pierced to form a rough flute. Though a novice in the art compared to the shrewd Professor, I was still able to astonish my ward companions on occasion, and I never lost an opportunity of practising myself. It was not mere curiosity, then, which led me to lean back on the cushions and analyse the quiet middle-aged man in front of me.

I used to do the thing systematically and my train of reflections ran somewhat in this wise: 'General appearance vulgar, fairly opulent, and extremely self-possessed—looks like a man who could outchaff a bargee,[3] and yet be at his ease in the best middle-class society. Eyes well set together, and nose rather prominent—would be a good long-range marksman. Cheeks flabby, but the softness of expression redeemed by a square-cut jaw and a well-set lower lip. On the whole, a powerful type. Now for

---

1. Edinburgh: Capital city of Scotland.
2. *Rule Britannia*: Patriotic British song.
3. bargee: Bargeman.

the hands—rather disappointed there. Thought he was a self-made man by the look of him, but there is no callus in the palm, and no thickening at the joints. Has never been engaged in any real physical work, I should think. No tanning on the backs of the hands; on the contrary, they are very white, with blue projecting veins and long delicate fingers. Couldn't be an artist with that face, and yet he has the hands of a man engaged in delicate manipulations. No red acid spots upon his clothes, no ink-stains, no nitrate-of-silver marks upon the hands (this helps to negative my half-formed opinion that he was a photographer). Clothes not worn in any particular part. Coat made of tweed, and fairly old; but the left elbow, as far as I can see it, has as much of the fluff left on as the right, which is seldom the case with men who do much writing. Might be a commercial traveller, but the little pocket-book in the waistcoat is wanting, nor has he any of those handy valises suggestive of samples.'

I give these brief headings of my ideas merely to demonstrate my method of arriving at a conclusion. As yet I had obtained nothing but negative results; but now, to use a chemical metaphor, I was in a position to pour off this solution of dissolved possibilities and examine the residue. I found myself reduced to a very limited number of occupations. He was neither a lawyer nor a clergyman, in spite of a soft felt hat, and a somewhat clerical cut about the necktie. I was wavering now between pawnbroker and horse-dealer; but there was too much character about his face for the former; and he lacked that extraordinary equine atmosphere which hangs about the latter even in his hours of relaxation; so I formed a provisional diagnosis of betting man of methodistical proclivities[4], the latter clause being inserted in deference to his hat and necktie.

Pray, do not think that I reasoned it out like this in my own mind. It is only now, sitting down with pen and paper, that I can see the successive steps. As it was, I had formed my conclusion within sixty seconds of the time when I drew my hat down over my eyes and uttered the mental ejaculation with which my narrative begins.

I did not feel quite satisfied even then with my deduction. However, as a leading question would—to pursue my chemical analogy—act as my litmus paper, I determined to try one. There was a *Times* lying by my companion, and I thought the opportunity too good to be neglected.

'Do you mind my looking at your paper?' I asked.

'Certainly, sir, certainly,' said he most urbanely, handing it across.

---

4. **methodistical proclivities:** Orderly habits.

I glanced down its columns until my eye rested upon the list of the latest betting.

'Hullo!' I said, 'they are laying odds upon the favorite for the Cambridgeshire.[5]—But perhaps,' I added, looking up, 'you are not interested in these matters?'

'Snares, sir!' said he violently, 'wiles of the enemy! Mortals are but given a few years to live; how can they squander[6] them so!— They have not even an eye to their poor worldly interests,' he added in a quieter tone, 'or they would never back a single horse at such short odds with a field of thirty.'

There was something in this speech of his which tickled me immensely. I suppose it was the odd way in which he blended religious intolerance with worldly wisdom. I laid the *Times* aside with the conviction that I should be able to spend the next two hours to better purpose than in its perusal.

'You speak as if you understood the matter, at any rate,' I remarked.

'Yes, sir,' he answered; 'few men in England understood these things better in the old days before I changed my profession. But that is all over now.'

'Changed your profession!' said I interrogatively.

'Yes; I changed my name too.'

'Indeed?' said I.

'Yes; you see, a man wants a real fresh start when his eyes become opened, so he has a new deal all round, so to speak. Then he gets a fair chance.'

There was a short pause here, as I seemed to be on delicate ground in touching on my companion's antecedents, and he did not volunteer any information. I broke the silence by offering him a cheroot.

'No; thanks,' said he; 'I have given up tobacco. It was the hardest wrench of all, was that. It does me good to smell the whiff of your weed.—Tell me,' he added suddenly, looking hard at me with his shrewd gray eyes, 'why did you take stock of me so carefully before you spoke?'

'It is a habit of mine,' said I. 'I am a medical man, and observation is everything in my profession. I had no idea you were looking.'

'I can see without looking,' he answered. 'I thought you were a detective, at first; but I couldn't recall your face at the time I knew the force.'

'Were you a detective, then?' said I.

'No,' he answered with a laugh; 'I was the other thing—the detected, you know. Old scores are wiped out now, and the law

---

5. the Cambridgeshire: A horse race.
6. squander: Waste.

cannot touch me, so I don't mind confessing to a gentleman like yourself what a scoundrel I have been in my time.'

'We are none of us perfect,' said I.

'No; but I was a real out-and-outer. A "fake," you know, to start with, and afterwards a "cracksman."[7] It is easy to talk of these things now, for I've changed my spirit. It's as if I was talking of some other man, you see.'

'Exactly so,' said I. Being a medical man I had none of that shrinking from crime and criminals which many men possess. I could make all allowances for congenital influence[8] and the force of circumstances. No company, therefore, could have been more acceptable to me than that of the old malefactor; and as I sat puffing at my cigar, I was delighted to observe that my air of interest was gradually loosening his tongue.

'Yes; I'm a changed man now,' he continued, 'and of course I am a happier man for that. And yet,' he added wistfully, 'there are times when I long for the old trade again, and fancy myself strolling out on a cloudy night with my jemmy[9] in my pocket. I left a name behind me in my profession, sir. I was one of the old school, you know. It was very seldom that we bungled a job. We used to begin at the foot of the ladder, in my younger days, and then work our way up through the successive grades, so that we were what you might call good men all round.'

'I see,' said I.

'I was always reckoned a hard-working, conscientious man, and had talent too—the very cleverest of them allowed that. I began as a blacksmith, and then did a little engineering and carpentering, and then I took to sleight-of-hand tricks, and then to picking pockets. I remember, when I was home on a visit, how my poor old father used to wonder why I was always hovering around him. He little knew that I used to clear everything out of his pockets a dozen times a day, and then replace them, just to keep my hand in. He believes to this day that I am in an office in the City. There are few of them could touch me in that particular line of business, though.'

'I suppose it is a matter of practice?' I remarked.

'To a great extent. Still, a man never quite loses it, if he has once been an adept.—Excuse me; you have dropped some cigar ash on your coat,' and he waved his hand politely in front of my breast, as if to brush it off.—'There,' he said, handing me my gold scarf pin, 'you see I have not forgot my old cunning yet.'

He had done it so quickly that I hardly saw the hand whisk over my bosom, nor did I feel his fingers touch me, and yet there

---

7. a "fake," a "cracksman": Kinds of thieves.
8. congenital influence: Heredity.
9. jemmy: A short crowbar used by burglars.

was the pin glittering in his hand. 'It is wonderful!' I said as I fixed it again in its place.

'Oh, that's nothing! But I have been in some really smart jobs. I was in the gang that picked the new patent safe. You remember the case. It was guaranteed to resist anything; and we managed to open the first that was ever issued, within a week of its appearance. It was done with graduated wedges, sir, the first so small that you could hardly see it against the light, and the last strong enough to prise it open. It was a cleverly managed affair.'

'I remember it,' said I. 'But surely some one was convicted for that?'

'Yes, one was nabbed. But he didn't split, nor even let on how it was done. It would have been as much as his life was worth.— Perhaps I am boring you, talking about these old wicked days of mine?'

'On the contrary,' I said, 'you interest me extremely.'

'I like to get a listener I can trust. It's a sort of blow-off, you know, and I feel lighter after it. When I am among my new and highly respectable acquaintances, I dare hardly think of what has gone before.—Now, I'll tell you about another job I was in. To this day, I cannot think about it without laughing.'

I lit another cigar, and composed myself to listen.

'It was when I was a youngster,' said he. 'There was a big City man in those days who was known to have a very valuable gold watch. I followed him about for several days before I could get a chance; but when I did get one, you may be sure I did not throw it away. He found to his disgust, when he got home that day, that there was nothing in his fob.[10] I hurried off with my prize, and got it stowed away in safety, intending to have it melted down next day. Now, it happened that this watch possessed a special value in the owner's eyes because it was a sort of ancestral possession—present to his father on coming of age, or something of that sort. I remember there was a long inscription on the back. He was determined not to lose it if he could help it, and accordingly he put an advertisement in an evening paper offering thirty pounds reward for its return, and promising that no questions should be asked. He gave the address of his house, 31 Caroline Square, at the end of the advertisement. The thing sounded good enough, so I set off for Caroline Square, leaving the watch in a parcel at a public-house which I passed on the way. When I got there, the gentleman was at dinner; but he came out quick enough when he heard that a young man wanted to see him. I suppose he guessed who the young man would prove to be. He was a genial-looking old fellow, and he led me away with him into his study.

---

10. **fob:** A small pocket for carrying a watch.

"Well, my lad," said he, "what is it?"

"I've come about that watch of yours," said I. "I think I can lay my hands on it."

"Oh, it was you that took it!" said he.

"No," I answered; "I know nothing whatever about how you lost it. I have been sent by another party to see you about it. Even if you have me arrested, you will not find out anything."

"Well," he said, "I don't want to be hard on you. Hand it over, and here is my cheque for the amount."

"Cheques won't do," said I; "I must have it in gold."

"It will take me an hour or so to collect it in gold," said he.

"That will just suit," I answered, "for I have not got the watch with me. I'll go back and fetch it, while you raise the money."

'I started off, and got the watch where I had left it. When I came back, the old gentleman was sitting behind his study table, with the little heap of gold in front of him.

"Here is your money," he said, and pushed it over.

"Here is your watch," said I.

'He was evidently delighted to get it back; and after examining it carefully, and assuring himself that it was none the worse, he put it into the watch-pocket of his coat with a grunt of satisfaction.

"Now, my lad," he said, "I know it was you that took the watch. Tell me how you did it, and I don't mind giving you an extra five-pound note."

"I wouldn't tell you in any case," said I; "but especially I wouldn't tell you when you have a witness hid behind that curtain." You see, I had all my wits about me, and it didn't escape me that the curtain was drawn tighter than it had been before.

"You are too sharp for us," said he good-humouredly. "Well you have got your money, and that's an end of it. I'll take precious good care you don't get hold of my watch again in a hurry.—Goodnight.—No; not that door," he added as I marched towards a cupboard. "This is the door," and he stood up and opened it. I brushed past him, opened the hall door, and was round the corner of the square in no time. I don't know how long the old gentleman took to find it out, but in passing him at the door, I managed to pick his pocket for the second time, and next morning the family heirloom was in the melting pot after all.— That wasn't bad, was it?"

The old war-horse was evidently getting his blood up now. There was a tone of triumph in the conclusion of his anecdote which showed that, sometimes at least, his pride in his smartness surpassed his repentance of his misdeeds. He seemed pleased at the astonishment and amusement I expressed at his adroitness.

'Yes,' he continued with a laugh, 'it was a capital joke. But sometimes the fun lies all the other way. Even the sharpest of us comes to grief at times. There was one rather curious incident which occurred in my career. You may possibly have seen the anecdote, for it got into print at the time.'

'Pray, let me hear it,' said I.

'Well, it is hard lines telling stories against one's self, but this was how it happened. I had made a rather good haul, and invested some of the swag in buying a very fine diamond ring. I thought it would be something to fall back upon when all the ready[11] was gone and times were hard. I had just purchased it, and was going back to my lodgings in the omnibus, when, as luck would have it, a very stylishly dressed young lady came in and took her seat beside me. I didn't pay much attention to her at first; but after a time something hard in her dress knocked up against my hand, which my experienced touch soon made out to be a purse. It struck me that I could not pass the time more profitably or agreeably than by making this purse my own. I had to do it very carefully; but I managed at last to wriggle my hand into her rather tight pocket, and I thought the job was over. Just at this moment she rose abruptly to leave the 'bus, and I had hardly time to get my hand with the purse in it out of her pocket without detection. It was not until she had been gone some time that I found out that, in drawing out my hand in that hurried manner, the new and ill-fitting ring I wore had slipped over my finger and remained in the young lady's pocket. I sprang out, and ran in the direction in which she had gone, with the intention of picking her pocket once again. She had disappeared, however; and from that day till this I have never set eyes on her. To make the matter worse, there was only fourpence-halfpenny in coppers inside the purse. Serve me right for trying to rob such a pretty girl; still, if I had that two hundred quid[12] now, I should not be reduced to—Good Heavens, forgive me! What am I saying?'

He seemed inclined to relapse into silence after this; but I was determined to draw him out a little more, if I could possibly manage it. 'There is less personal risk in the branch you have been talking of,' I remarked, 'than there is in burglary.'

'Ah!' he said, warming to his subject once again, 'it is the higher game which is best worth aiming at.—Talk about sport, sir, talk about fishing or hunting! why, it is tame in comparison! Think of the great country-house with its men-servants and its dogs and its firearms, and you with only your jemmy and your centre-bit,[13] and your mother-wit, which is best of all. It is the

---

11. **the ready:** Ready money or cash in hand.
12. **quid:** Slang term for pounds sterling, a unit of British currency.
13. **centre-bit:** Another burglar's tool.

triumph of intellect over brute-force, sir, as represented by bolts and bars.'

'People generally look upon it as quite the reverse,' I remarked.

'I was never one of those blundering life-preserver fellows,' said my companion. 'I did try my hand at garrotting once; but it was against my principles, and I gave it up. I have tried everything. I have been a bedridden widow with three young children; but I do object to physical force.'

'You have been what?' said I.

'A bedridden widow. Advertising, you know, and getting subscriptions. I have tried them all.—You seem interested in these experiences,' he continued; 'so I will tell you another anecdote. It was the narrowest escape from penal servitude that ever I had in my life. A pal and I had gone down on a country beat—it doesn't signify where it was—and taken up our headquarters in a little provincial town. Somehow it got noised abroad that we were there and householders were warned to be careful, as suspicious characters had been seen in the neighbourhood. We should have changed our plans when we saw the game was up; but my chum was a plucky fellow, and wouldn't consent to back down. Poor little Jim! He was only thirty-four round the chest, and about twelve at the biceps; but there is not a measuring tape in England could have given the size of his heart. He said we were in for it, and we must stick to it; so I agreed to stay, and we chose Morley Hall, the country-house of a certain Colonel Morley, to begin with.

'Now, this Colonel Morley was about the last man in the world that we should have meddled with. He was a shrewd, cool-headed fellow, who had knocked about and seen the world, and it seems that he took a special pride in the detection of criminals. However, we knew nothing of all this at that time; so we set forth hopefully to have a try at the house.

'The reason that made us pick him out among the rest was that he had a good-for-nothing groom,[14] who was a tool in our hands. This fellow had drawn up a rough plan of the premises for us. The place was pretty well locked up and guarded, and the only weak point we could see was a certain trap-door, the padlock of which was broken, and which opened from the roof into one of the lumber-rooms. If we could only find any method of reaching the roof, we might force a way securely from above. We both thought the plan rather a good one, and it had a spice of originality about it which pleased us. It is not the mere jewels or plate, you know, that a good cracksman thinks about. The neatness of the job, and his reputation for smartness, are almost as important in his eyes.

---

14. **groom:** Servant.

'We had been very quiet for a day or two, just to let suspicion die away. Then we set out one dark night, Jim and I, and got over the avenue railings and up to the house without meeting a soul. It was blowing hard, I remember, and the clouds hurrying across the sky. We had a good look at the front of the house, and then Jim went round to the garden side. He came running back in a minute or two in a great state of delight. "Why, Bill," he said, gripping me by the arm, "there never was such a bit of luck! They've been repairing the roof or something, and they've left the ladder standing." We went round together, and there, sure enough, was the ladder towering above our heads, and one or two labourers' hods[15] lying about, which showed that some work had been going on during the day. We had a good look round, to see that everything was quiet, and then we climbed up, Jim first, and I after him. We got to the top, and were sitting on the slates, having a bit of a breather, before beginning business, when you can fancy our feelings to see the ladder that we came up by suddenly stand straight up in the air, and then slowly descend until it rested in the garden below! At first, we hoped it might have slipped, though that was bad enough; but we soon had that idea put out of our head.

"Hullo, up there!" cried a voice from below.

We craned our heads over the edge, and there was a man, dressed, as far as we could make out, in evening dress, and standing in the middle of the grass plot. We kept quiet.

"Hullo!" he shouted again. "How do you feel yourselves? Pretty comfortable, eh? Ha! ha! You London rogues thought we were green in the country. What's your opinion now?"

'We both lay still, though feeling pretty considerably small, as you may imagine.

"It's all right; I see you," he continued. "Why, I have been waiting behind that lilac bush every night for the last week, expecting to see you. I knew you couldn't resist going up that ladder, when you found the windows were too much for you.—Joe! Joe!"

"Yes, sir," said a voice, and another man came from among the bushes.

"Just you keep your eye on the roof, will you, while I ride down to the station and fetch up a couple of constables?—*Au revoir*, gentlemen! You don't mind waiting, I suppose?" And Colonel Morley—for it was the owner of the house himself—strode off; and in a few minutes we heard the rattle of his horse's hoofs going down the avenue.

'Well, sir, we felt precious silly, as you may imagine. It wasn't so much having been nabbed that bothered us, as the feeling of being caught in such a simple trap. We looked at each other in

---

15. hods: Trays or troughs mounted on a handle, for carrying mortar or brick.

blank disgust, and then, to save our lives, we couldn't help bursting into laughter at our own fix. However, it was no laughing matter; so we set to work going round the roof, and seeing if there was a likely water-pipe or anything that might give us a chance of escape. We had to give it up as a bad job; so we sat down again, and made up our minds to the worst. Suddenly an idea flashed into my head, and I groped my way over the roof until I felt wood under my feet. I bent down, and found that the Colonel had actually forgotten to secure the padlock! You will often notice, as you go through life, that it is the shrewdest and most cunning man who falls into the most absurd mistakes; and this was an example of it. You may guess that we did not lose much time, for we expected to hear the constables every moment. We dropped through into the lumber-room, slipped down-stairs, tore open the library shutters, and were out and away before the astonished groom could make out what had happened. There wasn't time enough to take any little souvenir with us, worse luck. I should have liked to have seen the Colonel's face when he came back with the constables and found that the birds were flown.'

'Did you ever come across the Colonel again?' I asked.

'Yes; we skinned him of every bit of plate he had, down to the salt-spoons, a few years later. It was partly out of revenge, you see, that we did it. It was a very well-managed and daring thing, one of the best I ever saw, and all done in open daylight too.'

'How in the world did you do it?' I asked.

'Well, there were three of us in it—Jim was one; and we set about it in this way. We wanted to begin by getting the Colonel out of the way, so I wrote him a note purporting to come from Squire Brotherwick, who lived about ten miles away, and was not always on the best of terms with the master of Morley Hall. I dressed myself up as a groom and delivered the note myself. It was to the effect that the Squire thought he was able to lay his hands on the scoundrels who had escaped from the Colonel a couple of years before, and that if the Colonel would ride over, they would have little difficulty in securing them. I was sure that this would have the desired effect; so, after handing it in, and remarking that I was the Squire's groom, I walked off again, as if on the way back to my master's.

'After getting out of sight of the house, I crouched down behind a hedge; and, as I expected, in less than a quarter of an hour the Colonel came swinging past me on his chestnut mare. Now, there is another accomplishment I possess which I have not mentioned to you yet, and that is, that I can copy any handwriting that I see. It is a very easy trick to pick up, if you only give your mind to it. I happened to have come across one of Colonel

Morley's letters some days before, and I can write so that even now I defy an expert to detect a difference between the hands. This was a great assistance to me now, for I tore a leaf out of my pocket-book and wrote something to this effect:

"As Squire Brotherwick has seen some suspicious characters about, and the house may be attempted again, I have sent down to the bank, and ordered them to send up their bank-cart to convey the whole of the plate to a place of safety. It will save us a good deal of anxiety to know that it is in absolute security. Have it packed up and ready, and give the bearer a glass of beer."

'Having composed this precious epistle,[16] I addressed it to the butler, and carried it back to the Hall, saying that their master had overtaken me on the way and asked me to deliver it. I was taken in and made much of down-stairs; while a great packing-case was dragged into the hall, and the plate stowed away among cotton-wool and stuffing. It was nearly ready, when I heard the sound of wheels upon the gravel, and sauntered round just in time to see a businesslike closed car drive up to the door. One of my pals was sitting very demurely on the box; while Jim, with an official-looking hat, sprang out and bustled into the hall.

"Now, then," I heard him say, "look sharp! What's for the bank? Come on!"

"Wait a minute, sir," said the butler.

"Can't wait. There's a panic all over the country, and they are clamouring for us everywhere. Must drive on to Lord Blackbury's place, unless you are ready."

"Don't go, sir!" pleaded the butler. "There's only this one rope to tie.—There; it is ready now. You'll look after it, won't you?"

"That we will. You'll never have any more trouble with it now," said Jim, helping to push the great case into the car.

"I think I had better go with you and see it stowed away in the bank," said the butler.

"All right!" said Jim, nothing abashed.[17] "You can't come in the car, though, for Lord Blackbury's box will take up all the spare room.—Let's see—it's twelve o'clock now. Well, you be waiting at the bank door at half-past one, and you will just catch us."

"All right—half-past one," said the butler.

"Good-day!" cried my chum; and away went the car, while I made a bit of a short cut and caught it round a turn of the road. We drove right off into the next county, got a down-train to London; and before midnight, the Colonel's silver was fused into a solid lump.'

I could not help laughing at the versatility of the old scoundrel. 'It was a daring game to play,' I said.

---

16. epistle: Letter.
17. nothing abashed: Not embarrassed or upset.

'It is always the daring game which succeeds best,' he answered.

At this point the train began to show symptoms of slowing down, and my companion put on his overcoat and gave other signs of being near the end of his journey. 'You are going on to Dover?' he said.

'Yes.'

'For the Continent?'

'Yes.'

'How long do you intend to travel?'

'Only for a week or so.'

'Well, I must leave you here. You will remember my name, won't you? John Wilkie, I am pleased to have met you.—Is my umbrella behind you?' he added, stretching across.—'No; I beg your pardon. Here it is in the corner;' and with an affable smile, the ex-cracksman stepped out, bowed, and disappeared among the crowd upon the platform.

I lit another cigar, laughed as I thought of my late companion, and lifted up the *Times*, which he had left behind him. The bell had rung, the wheels were already revolving, when, to my astonishment, a pallid face looked in at me through the window. It was so contorted and agitated, that I hardly recognised the features which I had been gazing upon during the last couple of hours. 'Here, take it,' he said—'take it. It's hardly worth my while to rob you of seven pounds four shillings; but I couldn't resist once more trying my hand;' and he flung something into the carriage and disappeared.

It was my old leather purse, with my return ticket, and the whole of my travelling expenses. How he had taken it he knows best himself; I suppose it was while he was bending over in search of an imaginary umbrella. His newly re-awakened conscience had then pricked him, so that he had been driven to instant restitution.

☑ Check Your Comprehension

1. (a) Where is the narrator as the selection begins? (b) What puzzle is he trying to solve?

2. In the first story that Wilkie tells, what trick does he play on the old gentleman to earn the reward money?

3. In the second anecdote, how does Wilkie turn out to be too clever for his own good?

4. (a) In the third story, how does Colonel Morley attempt to trap Wilkie and Jim? (b) How do the two thieves take their revenge on Morley?

◆ Critical Thinking

1. In your opinion, what qualities would Doyle say enable Wilkie to be a successful criminal? **[Interpret]**

2. Doyle includes many touches of humor in the story. Identify two humorous events, situations, or statements. **[Analyze]**

3. Does the reader end up liking Wilkie, despite his inclination for crime? If so, why? **[Evaluate]**

4. Wilkie says, "It is always the daring game which succeeds best." How might you apply this statement to situations in your everyday life? **[Apply]**

Arthur Conan Doyle
Comparing and Connecting the Author's Works

◆ Literary Focus: Irony

Irony is the name given to literary techniques that involve surprising, interesting, or amusing contradictions. In verbal irony, words are used to suggest the opposite of their usual meanings. In irony of situation, an event occurs that directly contradicts the expectations of the characters, the reader, or the audience.

1. In "The Recollections of Captain Wilkie," Wilkie describes the letter he forges from Colonel Morley to the butler as a "precious epistle." Why is this phrase verbally ironic? You may wish to check the multiple definitions of the word *epistle* in a dictionary.

2. How does Wilkie's anecdote about robbing the stylish young lady on the omnibus illustrate irony of situation?

◆ Drawing Conclusions About Doyle's Work

Arthur Conan Doyle has been singled out for the following four areas of strength in his writing:

- a clear, readable style
- vivid description
- memorable characters
- ingenious plots and suspenseful storytelling

Together with a partner, apply these standards to the selections you have read by Arthur Conan Doyle. Draw up two charts like the one below: one for the excerpt from *A Study in Scarlet* and one for "The Recollections of Captain Wilkie." In the left-hand column, list Doyle's strengths as a writer. In the right-hand column, identify specific examples of these strengths from each work.

Title of Work

Doyle's Strengths	Examples
1. clear style	
2. vivid description	
3. striking characters	
4. suspenseful plot	

◆ Idea Bank

Writing

1. **Postcard** Assume that you are Dr. Watson and that you have shared lodgings with the mysterious, eccentric Sherlock Holmes for a month after your first meeting. Write a postcard to Stamford telling him your impressions of Holmes.

2. **Casting Notes** Write some detailed notes for a film adaptation of "The Recollections of Captain Wilkie." Begin by making a list of all the characters in the story, together with notes about their physical appearance and personality traits. Then write some suggestions for casting the roles, either using your favorite movie and television performers or assigning the parts to suitable classmates or friends.

3. **Report** Research one of Arthur Conan Doyle's historical or science fiction novels: for example: *The White Company* or *The Lost World*. Write up your results in an informative report in which you describe the setting, the main characters, and the major events of the plot.

Speaking and Listening

4. Opinion Poll Hold a series of interviews with a cross-section of your classmates to explore their opinions about detective and mystery stories. Then interview the same number of adult family members or neighbors to identify their opinions on the same subject. Write up your results in a brief report. **[Social Studies Link]**

5. Dramatic Reading Practice an oral interpretation of one of the stories told by Captain Wilkie. When you have polished your performance, present your dramatic reading to a small audience of classmates or friends.
[Performing Arts Link]

Researching and Representing

6. Ad Campaign Together with a small group, research some of the many film adaptations of Arthur Conan Doyle's Sherlock Holmes tales. Then plan a Holmes film festival for your school or community. Design an ad campaign for the festival, including posters, newspaper ads, and newspaper ads. When you have finished work, present your campaign to the class as a whole. **[Media Link] [Group Activity]**

◆ Further Reading, Listening, and Viewing

- Carr, John Dickson. *The Life of Sir Arthur Conan Doyle* (1949). This standard biography emphasizes Doyle as the creator of Sherlock Holmes.

- Booth, Martin: *The Doctor, the Detective, and Arthur Conan Doyle: A Biography of Arthur Conan Doyle* (1997). This updated biography presents a broader view of Doyle and his work.

- *The Lost World* (1997). Audiocassettes dramatize this science fiction tale about discovering a land of dinosaurs.

- *The Hound of the Baskervilles* (1939). This classic film introduces Basil Rathbone as Holmes and Nigel Bruce as Watson.

On the Web:

http://www.phschool.com/atschool/literature
Go to the student edition *Silver.* Proceed to Unit 5. Then, click on Hot Links to find Web sites featuring Sir Arthur Conan Doyle.

Yoshiko Uchida In Depth

"It seems to me I've been interested in books and writing for as long as I can remember."

—Yoshiko Uchida

The author of many books for readers of all ages, **YOSHIKO UCHIDA** was especially noted for her graceful, inspiring celebration of Japanese culture and of her Japanese American heritage.

Childhood of a Nisei Yoshiko Uchida was born in 1921 in Alameda, California, and grew up in the nearby city of Berkeley. Uchida's parents had been born in Japan and had immigrated to the United States some years before. Thus Yoshiko was a *nisei*—a second-generation Japanese American. Her father was a businessman, and her mother was a homemaker and a poet. Uchida's mother often read Japanese folktales to Yoshiko and her older sister Keiko. Uchida later included many of these stories in her first book, *The Dancing Kettle* (1949).

The Shock of Internment After attending local schools, Uchida enrolled at the University of California at Berkeley. As she was studying for her final exams on Sunday, December 7, 1941, news came over the radio that Japanese forces had attacked the United States naval base at Pearl Harbor in Hawaii. The United States immediately entered World War II against Japan and Germany.

Less than three months later, the federal government issued an order requiring that Japanese Americans be evacuated from their homes and imprisoned indefinitely at "Wartime Relocation Agency (WRA) camps." This policy was known as internment. In early May 1942, the Uchida family was uprooted to a makeshift barracks surrounded by barbed wire at a racetrack. After five

months there, they were sent to Topaz, a WRA camp in the Utah desert.

Yoshiko Uchida later recorded in a number of works her family's experiences. In May 1943, she was released from Topaz in order to begin a graduate fellowship at Smith College in Massachusetts. Shortly afterwards, her parents were also released. Forty years later, in 1983, a government commission concluded that a "grave injustice" had been done to Japanese Americans, who were overwhelmingly loyal to their adopted land. The commission declared that the causes of internment were race prejudice, war hysteria, and a failure of political leadership.

Early Career Uchida, who had taught elementary school while she was living at the camp in Utah, earned a master's degree in education at Smith College. Moving to New York City shortly after the war ended in 1945, Uchida worked at a variety of secretarial jobs, which gave her more time than teaching did to write. During the early 1950's, she produced a steady stream of children's tales. In 1952, she won a fellowship from the Ford Foundation for study in Japan. For two years she collected folk tales there and became deeply interested in Japanese arts and crafts. Uchida recalls, "I came home aware of a new dimension to myself as a Japanese American and with new respect and admiration for the culture that had made my parents what they were."

Later Years In addition to her stories for children, Uchida authored a number of nonfiction works for adults. In *We Do Not Work Alone: The Thoughts of Kanjiro Kawai* (1953), she explored Japanese folk art. In 1982, she published her memoirs of wartime imprisonment in *Desert Exile: The Uprooting of a Japanese-American Family*. In 1987, Uchida published her first novel for adults, *Picture Bride*, which focused on the courage and strength of early Japanese women immigrants.

A Writer's Philosophy Yoshiko Uchida died in 1992. In her final years, she worked steadily, producing two especially notable tales for children, *The Magic Purse* (1993) and *The Bracelet* (1993). Commenting in 1984 on her life and goals as a writer for young people, Uchida remarked: "I feel that children need the sense of community that comes through knowing about the past. All of us must understand our own past in order to move ahead into the future. I feel it's so important for Japanese American—and all Asian American—children to be aware of their history and culture, and to understand some of the traditions, hopes, and values of the early immigrants. At the same time, I write for *all* children, and I try to write about values and feelings that are universal."

◆ San Francisco and the Bay Area

Yoshiko Uchida grew up in northern California on the eastern edges of the San Francisco Bay, and much of her fiction is set in the Bay Area. Built on a hilly peninsula, San Francisco is a large port, a cultural center, and one of the nation's most picturesque cities. Its many landmarks, such as the Golden Gate Bridge, Telegraph Hill, Fisherman's Wharf, and Chinatown draw countless tourists annually. The University of California at Berkeley continues to set standards of excellence in education nationwide.

The population of San Francisco and the Bay Area includes one of the largest Chinese communities in North America. The region is also home to many Japanese Americans. From 1910 to 1940, Angel Island, the largest island in San Francisco Bay, was the entry point for Asian immigrants to the United States.

◆ Literary Works

Fiction
- *The Dancing Kettle and Other Japanese Folk Tales* (1949)
- *The Magic Listening Cap—More Folk Tales from Japan* (1955)
- *The Forever Christmas Tree* (1963)
- *A Jar of Dreams* (1981)
- *The Best Bad Thing* (1983)
- *The Happiest Ending* (1985)
- *Picture Bride* (1987)
- *The Magic Purse* (1993)
- *The Bracelet* (1993)
- *The Wise Old Woman* (1994)

Nonfiction
- *We Do Not Work Alone: The Thoughts of Kanjiro Kawai* (1953)
- *Journey to Topaz: A Story of the Japanese-American Evacuation* (1971)
- *Journey Home* (1978)
- *Desert Exile: The Uprooting of a Japanese-American Family* (1982)
- *The Invisible Thread* (1991)

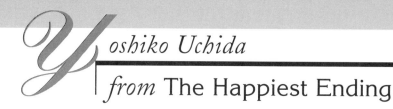

Yoshiko Uchida

from The Happiest Ending

Chapter 1

How did I ever let Mama talk me into this, I wondered. How could I have been so stupid?

Here I had a nice free Saturday afternoon with no school to worry about, I'd finished my chores and helped Mama do the wash in the home laundry she runs in our basement. After that, if I'd had any brains at all, I would have been going to the five and ten to browse around or start shopping for Christmas presents.

But no, dumb me. I was rattling down to Oakland[1] on the #3 streetcar because of an agreement I'd made with Mama. I was going for my first private Japanese-language lesson with Mama's friend, Mrs. Sugino, whom I didn't even know and whom I already didn't like.

The reason I got into this terrible predicament was because the school nurse told Mama last year that I was too skinny and looked anemic. She thought I shouldn't have to go learn Japanese every day after regular school because I had enough homework to do for my sixth-grade class.

Of course, I was absolutely ecstatic when Mama listened to the nurse, because I hate going to Japanese Language School.

"It makes me feel like a foreigner," I told Mama, "and I'm not!"

It's bad enough that I have this Japanese face, with stick-straight black hair and eyes that aren't even as pretty as my big brother Cal's. And having a name like Rinko Tsujimura, which my teachers can't pronounce, (instead of a nice simple one like Mary Smith) is another burden I have to put up with.

But Mama doesn't seem to understand. She insists my two brothers and I learn Japanese because she says it's part of our heritage.

"You're Japanese as well as American, you know," she always says. "Someday you'll be glad you learned how to read and write Japanese."

Deep down, I know she's right, and I know I should be more proud of being Japanese.

But just the same, I answer, "No, I won't. I just want to be like any other American."

---

1. **Oakland:** City on the east side of San Francisco Bay.

But Mama goes on and on, giving me a dozen other reasons why I should study Japanese, and then I just tune her out, as I often do.

All last year I'd gloated over my kid brother, Joji (aged ten and a half), who of course had to keep on studying Japanese every day after school, since he is so plump and healthy.

"It ain't fair," he'd complained to Mama.

But she'd just told him, "Be glad you're strong and healthy, Joji," and she warned him to stop playing hooky, which he did whenever he had the chance.

"Tough luck, kiddo," I'd say to him when I saw him gather up his books and go off to learn Japanese. "I'm *really* sorry for you," I'd say, sitting at the kitchen table munching on leftover toast covered with butter and strawberry jam. I usually grinned when I said this, looking about as sorry as a dog that just found a nice bone.

"Aw, go soak your head, Rink," Joji would say, scowling.

But today the shoe was on the other foot. It was Joji's turn to gloat.

"Have a *wonderful* time studying all afternoon," he yelled, as he banged out the back door with a football under his arm.

"Thanks, Joji, I will," I said, trying to sound lofty. And I used one of the new words I'd just learned even though I knew he wouldn't understand it.

"I know it's going to be an *edifying*² experience," I yelled at him.

But what I really thought was, edifying, my foot! The only reason I was going was because Mama had given me an ultimatum.

"Either you have Mrs. Sugino tutor you, Rinko, or you start over again with the third and fourth-graders when you go back to Japanese Language School next spring."

What could I do with a choice like that? I chose Mrs. Sugino, of course.

I slouched down on the streetcar seat and was so busy feeling sorry for myself I missed the 7th Street stop where I was supposed to get off and had to walk back two long blocks.

Mrs. Sugino lived just on the edge of Oakland's Chinatown, and I poked along past dingy little grocery stores with crates of mustard greens and long white radishes and onions spilling out onto the sidewalk. I passed the shop that sold roast duck and slabs of barbecued pork and tried not to look at the skinned rabbits hanging upside down in the window. They looked so pathetic, I couldn't stand the thought of anybody eating them. I even have trouble eating the chickens we raise in our backyard, espe-

---

2. **edifying** (ed´ i fi ing): Enlightening, educational.

cially since I am the one who has to feed them and collect their eggs. I feel like such a traitor, when they've been trusting us and laying eggs for us every day.

When I finally got to Mrs. Sugino's house, I saw that it was an old two-storied Victorian one, and I wondered if she had a big family to fill all the rooms upstairs. Mama hadn't told me much about her. Only that she was an excellent teacher who taught Japanese at the Buddhist Church. Mama also informed me that Mrs. Sugino was taking me on as a private pupil only as a special favor. I was prepared not to like her at all.

Gloom and doom, I thought as I rang the doorbell. And I tried hard to think of a way to get out of coming again next Saturday.

When the door opened there was a little boy staring at me, holding a half-eaten piece of bread smeared with jelly.

"Whachew want?" he asked, licking all the jelly off his bread.

He was small but solid, (like a miniature *sumo* wrestler), with hair clipped close to his skull and narrow eyes that stared at me. I noticed he had his right shoe on his left foot and vice versa, so his feet looked like they were trying to walk away from each other.

"I'm here to see your mama," I said, and squeezed my way inside before he could slam the door in my face. I went into the parlor, and he followed right behind me.

"Go call your mama," I said, and sat down on the sofa, which was about the only place there was any space to sit. The room was so jammed with furniture and knickknacks and cartons and plants and books and magazines, it looked more like somebody's attic than a parlor.

The little boy just stood there, inspecting me like a new specimen in his bug collection, so I decided I'd better get friendly.

"What's your name?" I asked, figuring that was a good place to start.

"Everybody calls me Boku."

I knew enough Japanese to know that's what little boys call themselves. "That's the word for *me*, isn't it?"

"Yup," he nodded. "I'm me."

Then he suddenly threw the rest of his sticky bread on my lap and went racing out the room yelling for his mama.

Good grief, I thought. Not only was I going to have to study Japanese every Saturday afternoon, I was going to have to put up with that little monster as well.

I looked around the cluttered room while I waited for Mrs. S. (which is what I began calling her in my head), and knew right away that she was a saver.

Mama is a saver too. She saves everything, from old string and paper bags to empty jars and cardboard cartons. She's also saved every picture I have ever drawn since the age of two.

About the strings and jars, she says, "You never know when you're going to need them." And about my old drawings, she says, "You certainly don't expect me to throw those away in the garbage can, do you?" She also keeps every Valentine and birthday card that my two brothers and I have ever given her. She has two cartons full. But at least she keeps everything in our basement and not in the parlor, thank goodness.

I got up to look at a table piled with old copies of the *National Geographic* and saw that some were even dated back to 1930, which meant they'd been sitting there for six years. There were lots of magazines from Japan too, but of course I couldn't read those.

It wasn't the magazines I was interested in though, it was the tablecloth under them. It was made out of dozens and dozens of old cards—Christmas cards and birthday cards, and even some wedding invitations and picture post cards. They were all crocheted[3] together with double strands of pink embroidery thread, and I thought it was just about the most fascinating tablecloth I'd ever seen. If Mama had something like that on our dining room table, I thought, Joji and I would at least have something interesting to look at during Sunday dinners when the adult conversation gets boring.

Mama likes to crochet too, but so far she hasn't thought of crocheting all her cards together. In fact, she doesn't embroider or crochet at all any more because her hands are too rough and chapped from all the washing she has to do. She says the silk threads catch on her hands now, and she can't do the kind of handiwork she did before Papa's bills got too high and she started our home laundry to help him out.

I was twisting my head and trying to read the greetings on one of the birthday cards. "May your days be filled with . . ." Then I heard a rustle behind me, and someone said. "Ah, so you're Mrs. Tsujimura's daughter."

I turned around and there was Mrs. Sugino. She turned out to be a total surprise.

---

3. **crocheted** (krō shād´); Sewn together in a special kind of needlework.

Chapter 2

Since I was planning to dislike her, I was expecting Mrs. S. to be plain or ugly or even mean-looking. But she wasn't any of those things. She looked about the same age as Mama, who is thirty-eight, and I was surprised at how pretty she was. She had a thin friendly face and hair that was pulled back into a bun like Mama's, only there were little curls that escaped around her forehead.

She was wearing an apron over a long-sleeved pongee blouse[4] with a row of tiny mother-of-pearl buttons that came right up to her throat. I thought it might have been her Sunday blouse once, but now it looked sort of tired and faded.

"Yes, I'm Rinko," I said. And I handed her the jar of pickled long radishes that Mama had sent over to her. Mama can never go see anybody without taking something, and she makes me do the same. (Of course I'd made sure the lid was screwed on good and tight so nobody would smell it on the streetcar.) I also gave her Boku's hunk of sticky bread because I didn't know what to do with it.

She thanked me for both and then said, "I see you've already met Boku. That's not his real name, of course. It's Kanzaburo, but that's too much name for a little boy, don't you think?"

Before I could answer, she asked me how old I was. When I told her, she said, "Well, how do you like being twelve and a half?" She made it sound like a place and was asking me how I liked being there.

"It's OK, but I'd rather be fifteen," I said, "or even sixteen would be nice. My big brother, Cal, is always telling me to grow up, but since he's already a sophomore in college, I'll never catch up with him."

Mrs. S. patted me on the shoulder. "Well, never mind, Rinko," she said. "Before you know it you will be twenty-three and then thirty-three and wishing you were twelve again."

I knew I wouldn't, but I didn't have a chance to tell her because she was leading the way to her kitchen. It was much bigger than ours with a black pot-bellied stove at one end and a long table covered with yellow oilcloth in the middle.

"This is where we have all our meals," she explained, and Boku immediately told me who sat at each place.

"Mr. Kinjo sits here, Papa sits here, Mr. Higa here, Johnny Ochi here, Mama here, and me here."

"We have three boarders," Mrs. S. explained, "since we have so much room and we . . ." She stopped suddenly, as though she'd decided not to say something that had almost slipped out.

---

4. **pongee** (pän´jē) **blouse:** A blouse made of soft, thin silk.

Then she took off her apron to show that she'd stopped being Boku's mama and was about to become my teacher. She had several Japanese text books on the table, and I saw that they were readers for grades three, four, and five.

I got a sick feeling in my stomach just looking at those readers with their gray covers and Japanese writing. I'd gotten up to the fifth grade reader once, but now I'd forgotten everything. It was as though I'd pulled out a stopper inside my head and all the Japanese words I'd learned had gone flowing right out. I didn't think there was even one left inside my head.

"Which book do you think you can read, Rinko?" Mrs. S. asked.

"Well . . . I guess maybe I'd better start with grade three."

"Grade three!" Boku exploded, settling into the chair next to me. "I can read Book Three and I'm only barely six!"

If his mama hadn't been sitting right there, I probably would have told him to go soak his head. Fortunately, Mrs. S. knew exactly how to deal with her smart-aleck son.

"Run out and get some wood for the stove, will you, Boku?" she asked. "It's getting a little chilly."

Boku looked out the window and didn't budge. "It's raining," he said. "I'll get wet."

Mrs. S. and I both looked out the window and sure enough it had begun to rain.

But Mrs. S. gave Boku a little nudge and said, "It's only polite rain, Boku. You'll hardly get wet at all. Go on now."

"Polite rain?" I asked.

"Yes, you know, it's not blowing or splashing. It's just coming down soft and gentle—politely."

"Oh."

I found myself smiling at Mrs. S. She smiled back, and I noticed she had a dimple in her right cheek.

"Well then, Rinko, let's start with Book Three. Now if you'll just begin here, I'll . . ."

"Mama! Help!"

It was Boku bellowing like a bull, as he dropped the wood he was carrying. We both heard it racketing down the back steps.

"Oh dear." Mrs. S. sighed. "He can be such a bother sometimes." Then she added as an afterthought, "But he *is* a good boy."

I wanted to ask her why she had only one little boy, but I know you aren't supposed to ask questions like that or ask some people why they don't have any children at all. Mama says things like that are none of my business.

I watched Mrs. S. pull on a heavy white sweater and hurry out the back door. She hadn't been gone a minute when I heard her cry out, and then there was a bumping thud.

Good grief, I thought. Now what?

I rushed to the back door and when I looked out, I saw Mrs. S. lying in a heap at the foot of the steps. Her hair had come undone and was hanging loose because all her big hairpins had fallen out. The rain had stopped being polite, and she was getting soaked.

"Oh, my gosh!" I yelled. "Are you all right, Mrs. Sugino?"

"I'm not sure," she said in a weak voice. "I slipped on the wet steps. I . . . oh . . ." She cried out again. "I think I may have broken my wrist."

Boku and I helped her get up, and she leaned on me to go back up the steps and into the house. I could tell she was in a lot of pain, but she just gritted her teeth and didn't complain.

"I'll call Papa," I said.

But Mrs. S. shook her head. "No, I'm afraid this is something your papa can't fix, even in his repair shop. Do you think you could call Dr. Kita for me?"

Boku ran to the phone in the hall and came back waving a small black book. "Here, the doctor's in here," he said.

I was so flustered, I kept looking under *D* for doctor, until Mrs. S. told me to try looking under the *K*s. I was wishing Papa or Mama or Cal or somebody was there to help me when I heard a truck pull into the driveway.

Then a man wearing old gardening clothes came in the back door. He wasn't too tall—about like Papa—and I thought probably about his age too. He was heavy-set and solid-looking, with a wide nose and thick lips. He wore horn-rimmed glasses and had a lot of thick black hair that was combed straight back and was wet from the rain.

The minute I saw him I thought of him as a St. Bernard—solid and helpful, but not at all handsome. This is something I like to do whenever I meet somebody new. I try to think what kind of animal that person would be. I'd already decided that if Mrs. S. were a bird, she'd probably be a sparrow—friendly and cheerful. Or maybe even a hummingbird—dainty and quite beautiful.

"Oh, Mr. Kinjo. I'm so glad to see you," she said.

He took one look at her wrist, which was swelling up like a balloon, and knew exactly what to do.

"Come with me," he said, taking her good arm. "I'm taking you to see Dr. Kita."

Then he turned to me and said, "Rinko, can you stay here and look after Boku? And you'd better call your mama and tell her you'll be late."

"Sure," I answered.

Then they were gone, and Boku and I sat at the kitchen table looking at each other. He jiggled a loose front tooth with his tongue and said, "Pretty soon I ain't gonna have no teeth left in my whole mouth."

But I wasn't listening because I was thinking about something very strange.

"Say," I said. "How come Mr. Kinjo knew who I was when I've never laid eyes on him before?"

Boku sat with his elbows on the table and his chin propped in his hands. He looked up at the ceiling and said, "I dunno. Why donchew ask him?"

"You know something," I said. "That's exactly what I'm going to do."

I could hardly wait for Mrs. S. and Mr. Kinjo to get back.

☑ **Check Your Comprehension**

1. At the beginning of the story, why is Rinko unhappy?
2. At Mrs. Sugino's house, whom does Rinko first meet?
3. According to Rinko, what personality trait does Mrs. Sugino share with Rinko's mother?
4. What does Mrs. Sugino mean by "polite rain"?
5. (a) What happens to Mrs. Sugino when she goes outdoors to help collect wood for the stove? (b) How does Mr. Kinjo help?

◆ **Critical Thinking**

INTERPRET

1. (a) What does Mama's insistence that her children learn Japanese suggest about her attitude toward the family's heritage? (b) Why does this outlook lead to conflict with Rinko? **[Infer; Connect]**
2. (a) While Rinko waits to meet Mrs. Sugino for the first time, what conclusions does she draw about her new teacher? (b) How do these conclusions foreshadow a change in Rinko's attitude? **[Interpret]**
3. When Mrs. Sugino explains to Rinko that the family has three boarders, why do you think she stops suddenly? **[Speculate]**
4. What does Rinko's habit of comparing new people she meets to an animal or bird suggest about her personality? **[Analyze]**

oshiko Uchida

Of Dry Goods and Black Bow Ties

Long after reaching the age of sixty, when my father was persuaded at last to wear a conservative four-in-hand tie,[1] it was not because of his family's urging, but because Mr. Shimada (I shall call him that) had died. Until then, for some forty years, my father had always worn a plain black bow tie, a formality which was required on his first job in America and which he had continued to observe as faithfully as his father before him had worn his samurai sword.

My father came to America in 1906 when he was not yet twenty-one. Sailing from Japan on a small six-thousand-ton ship which was buffeted all the way by rough seas, he landed in Seattle on a bleak January day. He revived himself with the first solid meal he had enjoyed in many days, and then allowed himself one day of rest to restore his sagging spirits. Early on the second morning, wearing a stiff new bowler,[2] he went to see Mr. Shozo Shimada to whom he carried a letter of introduction.

At that time, Shozo Shimada was Seattle's most successful Japanese business man. He owned a chain of dry goods stores which extended not only from Vancouver to Portland, but to cities in Japan as well. He had come to America in 1880, penniless but enterprising, and sought to work as a laborer. It wasn't long, however, before he saw the futility in trying to compete with American laborers whose bodies were twice his in muscle and bulk. He knew he would never go far as a laborer, but he did possess another skill that could give him a start toward better things. He knew how to sew. It was a matter of expediency over masculine pride. He set aside his shovel, and hung a dressmaker's sign in his window. He was in business.

In those days, there were some Japanese women in Seattle who had neither homes nor sewing machines, and were delighted to find a friendly Japanese person to do some sewing for them. They flocked to Mr. Shimada with bolts of cloth, elated to discover a dressmaker who could speak their native tongue and, although a male, sew western-styled dresses for them.

Mr. Shimada acquainted himself with the fine points of turning a seam, fitting sleeves, and coping with the slippery folds of silk, and soon the women told their friends and gave him enough

---

1. **four-in-hand tie:** A necktie tied in a slipknot with the ends left hanging.
2. **bowler:** A type of hat.

business to keep him thriving and able to establish a healthy bank account. He became a trusted friend and confidant to many of them and soon they began to bring him what money they earned for safekeeping.

"Keep our money for us, Shimada-san," they urged, refusing to go to American banks whose tellers spoke in a language they could not understand.

At first the money accumulated slowly and Mr. Shimada used a pair of old socks as a repository,[3] stuffing them into a far corner of his drawer beneath his union suits. But after a time, Mr. Shimada's private bank began to overflow and he soon found it necessary to replenish his supply of socks.

He went to a small dry goods store downtown, and as he glanced about at the buttons, threads, needles, and laces, it occurred to him that he owed it to the women to invest their savings in a business venture with more future than the dark recesses of his bureau drawer. That night he called a group of them together.

"Think, ladies," he began. "What are the two basic needs of the Japanese living in Seattle? Clothes to wear and food to eat," he answered himself. "Is that not right? Every man must buy a shirt to put on his back and pickles and rice for his stomach."

The women marveled at Mr. Shimada's cleverness as he spread before them his fine plans for a Japanese dry goods store that would not only carry everything available in an American dry goods store, but Japanese foodstuff as well. That was the beginning of the first Shimada Dry Goods Store on State Street.

By the time my father appeared, Mr. Shimada had long since abandoned his sewing machine and was well on his way to becoming a business tycoon. Although he had opened cautiously with such stock items as ginghams, flannel, handkerchiefs, socks, shirts, overalls, umbrellas, and ladies' silk and cotton stockings, he now carried tins of salt rice crackers, bottles of soy sauce, vinegar, ginger root, fish-paste cakes, bean paste, Japanese pickles, dried mushrooms, salt fish, red beans, and just about every item of canned food that could be shipped from Japan. In addition, his was the first Japanese store to install a U.S. Post Office Station, and he thereby attained the right to fly an American flag in front of the large sign that bore the name of his shop.

When my father first saw the big American flag fluttering in front of Mr. Shimada's shop, he was overcome with admiration and awe. He expected that Mr. Shozo Shimada would be the finest of Americanized Japanese gentlemen, and when he met him, he was not disappointed.

---

3. **repository** (ri päz´ ə tôr ē): A storage place for safekeeping.

Although Mr. Shimada was not very tall, he gave the illusion of height because of his erect carriage. He wore a spotless black alpaca suit, an immaculate white shirt and a white collar so stiff it might have overcome a lesser man. He also wore a black bow tie, black shoes that buttoned up the side, and a gold watch whose thick chain looped grandly on his vest. He was probably in his fifties then, a ruddy-faced man whose hair, already turning white, was parted carefully in the center. He was an imposing figure to confront a young man fresh from Japan with scarcely a future to look forward to. My father bowed, summoned as much dignity as he could muster, and presented the letter of introduction he carried to him.

Mr. Shimada was quick to sense his need. "Do you know anything about bookkeeping?" he inquired.

"I intend to go to night school to learn this very skill," my father answered.

Mr. Shimada could assess a man's qualities in a very few minutes. He looked my father straight in the eye and said, "Consider yourself hired." Then he added, "I have a few basic rules. My employees must at all times wear a clean white shirt and a black bow tie. They must answer the telephone promptly with the words, 'Good morning or good afternoon, Shimada's Dry Goods,' and they must always treat each customer with respect. It never hurts to be polite," he said thoughtfully. "One never knows when one might be indebted to even the lowliest of beggars."

My father was impressed with these modest words from a man of such success. He accepted them with a sense of mission and from that day was committed to white shirts and black bow ties, and treated every customer, no matter how humble, with respect and courtesy. When, in later years, he had his own home, he never failed to answer the phone before it could ring twice if at all possible.

My father worked with Mr. Shimada for ten years, becoming first the buyer for his Seattle store and later, manager of the Portland branch. During this time Mr. Shimada continued on a course of exhilarated expansion. He established two Japanese banks in Seattle, bought a fifteen-room house outside the dreary confines of the Japanese community, and dressed his wife and daughter in velvets and ostrich feathers. When his daughter became eighteen, he sent her to study in Paris, and the party he gave on the eve of her departure, hiring musicians, as well as caterers to serve roast turkey, venison, baked ham, and champagne, seemed to verify rumors that he had become one of the first Japanese millionaires of America.

In spite of his phenomenal success, however, Mr. Shimada never forgot his early friends nor lost any of his generosity, and this, ironically enough, was his undoing. Many of the women for whom he had once sewn dresses were now well established, and they came to him requesting loans with which they and their husbands might open grocery stores and laundries and shoe repair shops. Mr. Shimada helped them all and never demanded any collateral.[4] He operated his banks on faith and trust and gave no thought to such common prudence as maintaining a reserve.

When my father was called to a new position with a large Japanese firm in San Francisco, Mr. Shimada came down to Portland to extend personally his good wishes. He took Father to a Chinese dinner and told him over the peanut duck and chow mein that he would like always to be considered a friend.

"If I can ever be of assistance to you," he said, "don't ever hesitate to call." And with a firm shake of the hand, he wished my father well.

That was in 1916. My father wrote regularly to Mr. Shimada telling him of his new job, of his bride, and later, of his two children. Mr. Shimada did not write often, but each Christmas he sent a box of Oregon apples and pears, and at New Year's a slab of heavy white rice paste from his Seattle shop.

In 1929 the letters and gifts stopped coming, and Father learned from friends in Seattle that both of Mr. Shimada's banks had failed. He immediately dispatched a letter to Mr. Shimada, but it was returned unopened. The next news he had was that Mr. Shimada had had to sell all of his shops. My father was now manager of the San Francisco branch of his firm. He wrote once more asking Mr. Shimada if there was anything he could do to help. The letter did not come back, but there was no reply, and my father did not write again. After all, how do you offer help to the head of a fallen empire? It seemed almost irreverent.[5]

It was many years later that Mr. Shimada appeared one night at our home in Berkeley. In the dim light of the front porch my mother was startled to see an elderly gentleman wearing striped pants, a morning coat, and a shabby black hat. In his hand he carried a small black satchel. When she invited him inside, she saw that the morning coat was faded, and his shoes badly in need of a shine.

"I am Shimada," he announced with a courtly bow, and it was my mother who felt inadequate to the occasion. She hurriedly pulled off her apron and went to call my father. When he heard who was in the living room, he put on his coat and tie before going out to greet his old friend.

---

4. **collateral:** Property or other assets securing a loan.
5. **irreverent** (ir rev' ər ənt): disrespectful

Mr. Shimada spoke to them about Father's friends in Seattle and about his daughter who was now married and living in Denver. He spoke of a typhoon that had recently swept over Japan, and he drank the tea my mother served and ate a piece of her chocolate cake. Only then did he open his black satchel.

"I thought your girls might enjoy these books," he said, as he drew out a brochure describing *The Book of Knowledge.*

"Fourteen volumes that will tell them of the wonders of this world." He spread his arms in a magnificent gesture that recalled his eloquence of the past. "I wish I could give them to your children as a personal gift," he added softly.

Without asking the price of the set, my father wrote a check for one hundred dollars and gave it to Mr. Shimada.

Mr. Shimada glanced at the check and said, "You have given me fifty dollars too much." He seemed troubled for only a moment, however, and quickly added, "Ah, the balance is for a deposit, is it? Very well, yours will be the first deposit in my next bank."

"Is your home still in Seattle then?" Father asked cautiously.

"I am living there, yes," Mr. Shimada answered.

And then, suddenly overcome with memories of the past, he spoke in a voice so low he could scarcely be heard.

"I paid back every cent," he murmured. "It took ten years, but I paid it back. All of it. I owe nothing."

"You are a true gentleman, Shimada-san," Father said. "You always will be." Then he pointed to the black tie he wore, saying, "You see, I am still one of the Shimada men."

That was the last time my father saw Shozo Shimada. Some time later he heard that he had returned to Japan as penniless as the day he set out for America.

It wasn't until the Christmas after we heard of Mr. Shimada's death that I ventured to give my father a silk four-in-hand tie. It was charcoal gray and flecked with threads of silver. My father looked at it for a long time before he tried it on, and then fingering it gently, he said, "Well, perhaps it is time now that I put away my black bow ties."

☑ Check Your Comprehension

1. (a) How old was the narrator's father when he came to America? (b) Where and when did he land?
2. (a) Describe how Mr. Shimada became a highly successful businessman. (b) What three rules does Mr. Shimada have for his employees?
3. What causes Mr. Shimada's undoing in business?
4. During Mr. Shimada's visit to the family many years later, what compliment does the narrator's father pay to his former boss?

◆ Critical Thinking

INTERPRET

1. What qualities in Mr. Shimada helped to make him a successful businessman? **[Infer]**
2. Ironic situations or events contain unexpected, surprising reversals. Explain two ways in which the second half of this story is ironic. **[Analyze]**
3. (a) What significance does the bow tie have in the story? (b) At the end, how might the bow tie be considered a symbol, and what might it symbolize? **[Interpret]**

EVALUATE

4. (a) What ethical code or set of values guides Mr. Shimada in life? (b) Do you think he remains loyal to this code? **[Evaluate]**

oshiko Uchida

from Journey to Topaz

Prologue

When war broke out between the United States and Japan in December 1941, I was one of several thousand Japanese living in California. Almost immediately, our lives were transformed. Our parents, who had come to America from Japan and by law were never permitted to become American citizens, suddenly became "enemy aliens." Those of us who were American citizens of Japanese ancestry were also looked upon with suspicion. Wild rumors, such as those of sabotage by the Japanese in Hawaii (later proved to be completely untrue), helped create an atmosphere of hatred and fear all along the West Coast of the United States.

On February 19, 1942, President Franklin D. Roosevelt issued an executive order which authorized the Secretary of War "to prescribe areas from which any or all persons may be excluded."

This order cleared the way for the indiscriminate removal of 110,000 persons of Japanese ancestry, without hearings of any kind, from the entire West Coast. All Japanese were uprooted from their homes and sent to inland camps to be held behind barbed wire. Two-thirds of these people were American citizens, and I was one of them. We went because, at the time, it was the only way in which we could prove our loyalty to the United States, and this we were determined to do.

Journey to Topaz is the story of one Japanese family and what happened to them as a result of the evacuation orders. Although the characters are fictitious, the events are based on actual fact, and much that happened to the Sakane family also happened to my own.

Chapter 1: Strangers at the Door

It was only the first week in December, but already Yuki could feel the tingling excitement of Christmas in the air. There was, of course, no sign of snow, for it never snowed in Berkeley except for the winter when she was six and a thin flurry of flakes had surprised them all. Yuki remembered how she had run outside, stretched her arms wide and opened her mouth, thrusting out her tongue so she could feel the snow and taste it and gather it to her in any way she could before the flakes reached the ground and disappeared. Today looked like snow weather for the sky was gray and murky, but only with fog that blew in cold and damp from San Francisco Bay.

Yuki stood close to the fireplace with its burning oak logs and lifted her skirt to feel the warmth as she waited for Mother to fix lunch. On such a cold gloomy Sunday, it felt especially good to be close to a fire and think glowing thoughts about Christmas. It wouldn't be long before a tall fir tree with its fresh green forest smell would be standing in the corner of the living room and the kitchen would be filled with the wonderful scent of Mother's butter cookies.

Yuki thought happily of the presents that would soon gather under the tree. She had already decided to get Mother a soft blue chiffon scarf to go with her Sunday church coat, some wool socks for Father and maybe a tie or a record for her older brother, Ken. It was hardest to find something good for Ken. Now that he was going to the university, he seemed to live in a changed world and to be almost a different person. He was eighteen and suddenly it was no longer football and baseball and basketball alone that fascinated him. He liked girls.

"I'm a girl," Yuki reminded him periodically. "Why don't you take me to the movies?"

But Ken only laughed. "I like girls over sixteen," he explained. "You've still got five years to go, and besides that, you're my sister. That makes you an entirely different specimen altogether!"

Yuki sometimes looked at herself in the mirror, wrinkling her nose at the round full face and the straight black hair that fell to her shoulders. She would push aside her bangs and contemplate the possibilities. How would she look when she was sixteen anyway? Not very good, she decided, but she wasn't going to let that bother her, at least for now.

"Yuki Chan!" Mother roused Yuki from her reveries about Christmas and her older brother. "Lunch is ready. Will you go outside and call your father?"

Yuki hurried toward the back door, stopping on the way to get some dog biscuits for Pepper. Father was out in the yard tying up the last of the white chrysanthemums and burning old leaves. He hadn't been home from church an hour and already he was hard at work outdoors where he loved to be.

Father went to church each Sunday because he believed it was the proper thing to do. He didn't read the Bible each day as Mother did, and Yuki wasn't even sure he said his prayers every night before going to sleep. In fact, she suspected that if he had his way, he would have preferred working in his garden on Sundays to sitting in the small dark Japanese church in Oakland listening to Reverend Wada, their minister from Japan, and hearing the drone of the reed organ wheezing out the seemingly endless hymns. "You know," he had once said to Mother, "sometimes God seems closer out there in the fresh air with the flowers and trees than in that sanctuary." But when he talked like that, Mother wouldn't even dignify his comment with an answer.

As Yuki went out the back door, Pepper came bounding up the steps to meet her, barking and wagging his tail and running in circles around her. He knew Yuki had some biscuits for him, just as he knew that Mother or Father or Ken would. They all spoiled Pepper terribly, but in return, Pepper gave them every ounce of love that he had stored in his lively black body.

"Down Pepper!" Yuki commanded, and then, still playing with Pepper, she shouted to her father. "Come on in, Papa. Lunch is ready."

Father raised his shears to show that he had heard, but he quickly disappeared again behind the chrysanthemums. Yuki knew she'd have to call him at least two more times before he'd even begin to think about coming inside. She took her time, stopping to peer into the fishpond, stirring the water to see if the big gray carp would rise to the surface, his mouth open wide expecting some food. It was a shabby trick, but one that Yuki couldn't resist occasionally just to see if the old carp was alive and alert.

As Yuki studied the murky depths of the fishpond, she heard Mother ringing her small black bell. Mother didn't like shouting to people, so instead she rang her bell and when she did, it meant that everyone should hurry.

Yuki called once more to Father, and then ran inside to wash up and set the table with chopsticks, rice bowls, and tea cups. Sunday dinners were usually Japanese meals and Mother would cook a pot of rice in the morning before church and leave it bundled in a quilt on her bed to keep warm. If guests were coming, she would prepare the night before some chicken *teriyaki* and vegetables cooked Japanese style with soy sauce and sugar and ginger. Today, however, there were no guests and Yuki was glad. She wasn't terribly fond of the Japanese students from the seminary who seemed to cluster under Mother's protective wing.

"They're lonely and miss their families in Japan," Mother would explain. But Yuki didn't like the smell of camellia oil that lingered on their thick glossy hair, and she didn't much care for their conversations about the Old Testament or the Sunday sermon. Today, they all had other places to go for Sunday dinner and Ken had gone off to study at the library, so there were only the three of them for dinner.

"Good, no company today," Yuki said cheerfully to her canary, Old Salt. Yuki knew that was not the most appropriate name for a canary, but she had given him that name for Mrs. Jamieson's sake.

Mrs. Jamieson was the widow who lived across the street. When her parrot, Old Salt, had died, she had been so disconsolate[1] that Yuki had been moved to name her own new canary after the parrot.

"Why that's a lovely idea, Yuki dear," Mrs. Jamieson had said brightly, and then quickly added, "Now you'll have a Salt and a Pepper," and she laughed so at her own small joke that she got a stitch in her side and had to sit down.

When Father came in from the garden he turned on the radio before sitting down at the table. Then he gave a short quick grace that fit in nicely just before the voice from the radio filled the room.

"This is a repeat of the news bulletin," a newscaster said harshly, his voice trembling with urgency. "Japanese planes have attacked Pearl Harbor[2] . . . The United States Fleet has been heavily damaged . . . Fires are raging over the waterfront . . ."

Father put down his chopsticks and listened intently. Mother brushed away a piece of hair that had strayed from her bun and pinned it back into place. A frown swept across her pleasant face and she didn't even attempt to eat her lunch. Only Yuki had a mouthful of chicken and sat chewing silently, looking first at Father and then at Mother, trying to understand what had happened.

"It's a terrible mistake, of course," Father said at last. "It must be the work of a fanatic. That is, if it really happened."

Mother agreed. "Of course," she said. "It must be a mistake. Why would Japan ever do such a foolish thing?"

They sat in silence, listening in disbelief as the newscaster continued to tell of the attack. Yuki shuddered. The news was like a burden of darkness suddenly blotting out the light of day.

Father turned from the radio and saw the frightened look on Yuki's face. He saw Mother's hands tremble as she picked up her cup of tea, and rising abruptly, he switched off the radio.

"Maybe it is only a drama," he suggested. "Maybe it is not really news at all. In any case, let's not let it spoil our dinner," he said, trying to smile. And pushing his glasses up on his nose, he turned his attention to the food on the table.

Yuki knew, however, that Father was more than a little upset. He always pushed up his glasses when he was disturbed about something, and she knew by his silence that the program had already spoiled his dinner.

---

1. **disconsolate** (dis kän´ sə lit): Very upset.
2. **Pearl Harbor:** United States naval base in Honolulu, Hawaii.

It wasn't long before the telephone rang and Father got up to answer it. It was Mr. Toda, one of the men who lived upstairs in the building behind their Japanese church which served as a bachelors' dormitory. Mr. Toda was a frequent Sunday dinner guest too because Mother said he was old and lonely and needed their friendship. He hadn't come today because he thought he was catching a cold.

Yuki liked Mr. Toda better than the seminary students because he was more open about his feelings. If he liked you, he let you know, and if he didn't, he was equally frank. Yuki liked people like that. She knew that the old man liked her too. They were both fond of dogs and birds and fish, and he always had especially pleasant ways of showing his friendship. Whenever he came, he usually brought her small bags of pastel-colored candy that oozed sweet mouthfuls of fruit-flavored juices. Yuki loved the purple grape flavor best and saved those for the last.

Father told Mr. Toda the same thing he'd told Yuki and Mother. It had to be a mistake, he said over and over. And yes, he would surely keep him informed if he heard anything further.

As soon as dinner was over, Father went back to his garden and Mother went to the kitchen to bake a cake. Mother usually baked when she was going to have company or when she was too nervous to settle down to do anything else. Yuki didn't care what prompted her to bake as long as she did it. She made the best cream puffs and chocolate cakes of anyone she knew, Mrs. Jamieson included.

When the doorbell rang, Yuki was sure it must be Michelle Nelson who lived next door. Mimi usually came over on Sunday afternoons to see if she and Yuki could find something interesting to do together.

Yuki ran to the door and flung it open only to find three strange men standing on the porch. They were not Japanese and looked as though they might be business associates of Father's from San Francisco. "Is your father home?" one of them asked. He was not unfriendly, but he did not smile.

Yuki nodded. Then she saw two uniformed policemen come up the stairs behind them.

"Just a minute," she said unsteadily, and leaving the screen door latched, she ran to tell Mother and then rushed outside to call her father.

Father hurried inside and let the men in. He spoke quietly to them and then told Yuki to call Mother.

"These gentlemen are from the FBI," he explained calmly. "It seems the news on the radio was true after all. Japan has attacked Pearl Harbor. They would like me to go with them to answer a few questions. They would also like to search . . . to look around the house," Father said. His voice was strained and the color had drained from his face.

"But why?" Mother asked nervously. "You have done nothing."

"We have orders to apprehend certain men who work for Japanese firms in this area," one of the men answered briefly. "Your husband, Mr. Sakane, is employed by one of Japan's largest business firms."

"I see," Mother said. She was pale and tense.

Yuki could hear the men opening bureau drawers and closet doors. What in the world were they looking for? What did they think Father had hidden?

Soon the men led Father toward the front door. "I am in my gardening clothes," Father explained. "Permit me to change to my business suit."

The men shook their heads. "There isn't time, Mr. Sakane," they said, and they just gave him time to put on a jacket. Father looked small and frail beside the two large FBI men and one took a firm grip on his arm as they went down the steps.

"I'll be back soon," Father said, trying to sound casual. "Don't worry." And then he was gone.

Two of the FBI men went with Father and the third stayed behind, sitting down beside the telephone. The two policemen stayed too. One stood at the front door and the other at the back door.

"We won't try to leave," Mother assured them.

But the policemen told Mother they weren't worried about that. "We have orders not to let anyone in," he explained.

Although the FBI man and the policemen tried to make polite conversation with her, Yuki didn't feel the least bit friendly. When they asked her name and how old she was, she replied tersely, "Yuki" and "eleven." They had taken Father off like a common criminal and Yuki didn't like it at all.

"Can I go see Mimi?" Yuki asked, looking at Mother but knowing it was the FBI man who would decide.

"Sorry," he said gently, "but you'll have to stay home awhile."

As things turned out, they not only had to stay home, no one could come in or even talk to them by phone. Yuki looked out the window and saw Mimi standing in front of their house, trying to see inside and waving frantically when she caught a glimpse of Yuki's face. She also saw Mrs. Jamieson standing on her front porch peering anxiously in their direction. The telephone rang several times, but to each caller the FBI men simply answered that the Sakanes were indisposed and could not come to the phone.

It was a strange feeling to be a prisoner in one's own home. Still, Yuki felt no fear, for at the time she had no way of knowing that this was only the beginning of a terrible war and that her small comfortable world would soon be turned upside down.

Yoshiko Uchida

Letter From a Concentration Camp

Mailing Address: Barrack 16, Apartment 40
Tanforan Assembly Center
San Bruno, California
Actual Address: Stable 16, Horse stall 40
Tanforan Racetrack

May 6, 1942

Dear Hermie:

Here I am sitting on an army cot in a smelly old horse stall, where Mama, Bud, and I have to live for who knows how long. It's pouring rain, the wind's blowing in through all the cracks, and Mama looks like she wants to cry. I guess she misses Papa. Or maybe what got her down was that long, muddy walk along the racetrack to get to the mess hall for supper.

Anyway, now I know how it feels to stand in line at a soup kitchen with hundreds of hungry people. And that cold potato and weiner they gave me sure didn't make me feel much better. I'm still hungry, and I'd give you my last nickel if you appeared this minute with a big fat hamburger and a bagful of cookies.

You know what? It's like being in jail here—not being free to live in your own house, do what you want, or eat what you want. They've got barbed wire all around this racetrack and guard towers at each corner to make sure we can't get out. Doesn't that sound like a prison? It sure feels like one!

What I want to know is, What am I doing here anyway? *Me*—a genuine born-in-California citizen of the United States of America stuck behind barbed wire, just because I *look* like the enemy in Japan. And how come you're not in here too, with that German blood in your veins and a name like Herman Schnabel. We're at war with Germany too, aren't we? And with Italy? What about the people at Napoli Grocers?

My brother, Bud, says the US government made a terrible mistake that they'll regret someday. He says our leaders betrayed us and ignored the Constitution. But you know what I think? I think war makes people crazy. Why else would a smart man like President Franklin D. Roosevelt sign an executive order to force us Japanese Americans out of our homes and lock us up in concentration camps? Why else would the FBI take Papa off to a

POW camp just because he worked for a Japanese company? Papa—who loves America just as much as they do.

Hey, ask Mrs. Wilford what that was all about. I mean that stuff she taught us in sixth grade about the Bill of Rights and due process of law. If that means everybody can have a hearing before being thrown in prison, how come nobody gave us a hearing? I guess President Roosevelt forgot about the Constitution when he ordered us into concentration camps. I told you war makes people crazy!

Well, Hermie, I gotta go now. Mama says we should get to the showers before the hot water runs out like it did when she went to do the laundry. Tomorrow she's getting up at 4:00 A.M. to beat the crowd. Can you imagine having to get up in the middle of the night and stand in line to wash your sheets and towels? By hand too! No luxuries like washing machines in this dump!

Hey, do me a favor? Go pet my dog, Rascal, for me. He's probably wondering why I had to leave him with Mrs. Harper next door. Tell him I'll be back to get him for sure. It's just that I don't know when. There's a rumor we're getting shipped to some desert—probably in Utah. But don't worry, when this stupid war is over, I'm coming home to California and nobody's ever going to kick me out again! You just wait and see! So long, Hermie.

Your pal,
Jimbo Kurasaki

Note: In 1942, shortly after the outbreak of war with Japan, the United States government uprooted and imprisoned, without trial or hearing, 120,000 Americans of Japanese ancestry. They were sent first to "assembly centers" located in abandoned racetracks and fairgrounds. From there they were sent to ten bleak concentration camps located in remote areas of the country.

In 1976 President Gerald R. Ford stated, "not only was that evacuation wrong, but Japanese Americans were and are loyal Americans." In 1983 a commission established by the Congress of the United States concluded that a grave injustice had been done to Americans of Japanese descent. It also stated that the causes of the uprooting were race prejudice, war hysteria, and a failure of political leadership.

☑ Check Your Comprehension

1. As the passage from *Journey to Topaz* opens, what is the Sakane family preparing to do?
2. (a) What news does the family hear over the radio? (b) How do Yuki's parents react to this news?
3. Soon afterwards, what visitors arrive at the Sakanes' house, and why have they come?
4. In "Letter From a Concentration Camp," what favor does Jimbo ask Hermie to do for him?

◆ Critical Thinking

INTERPRET

1. In *Journey to Topaz*, what impressions about the Sakane family's life does the opening description help to create? **[Interpret]**
2. How do Yuki's parents attempt to conceal their concern when they hear the news about Pearl Harbor? **[Analyze]**
3. In "Letter From a Concentration Camp," how does the contrast between the "mailing address" and the "actual address" suggest the real conditions at the camp? **[Compare and Contrast]**
4. How does the note at the end of the letter show that Jimbo's brother Bud was right when he said the government made a terrible mistake? **[Support]**

COMPARE LITERARY WORKS

5. Uchida uses two different formats—a narrative and a letter—to reveal the shock and horror felt by Japanese Americans when they were uprooted from their homes. Which selection do you think is more vivid and compelling? Explain your answer. **[Evaluate]**

Yoshiko Uchida
Comparing and Connecting the Author's Works

◆ Literary Focus: Conflict

A **conflict** is a struggle between opposing forces. Conflict is the mainspring for the plot in stories, novels, and plays because it motivates the action.

Conflict in a literary work may be external or internal. In an **external conflict,** the struggle may be between two characters: For example, Rinko in *The Happiest Ending* experiences conflicts with her mother and her brother. Another type of external conflict may take place between a character and a force of nature or between a character and society: for example, the conflict between the Sakane family and the government in *Journey to Topaz.*

Finally, an **internal conflict** takes place within the mind of a character.

1. (a) What internal conflict bothers Rinko at the beginning of the passage from *The Happiest Ending?* (b) By the end of the passage, what change do you think has occurred in Rinko's feelings?

2. Sometimes writers hint at conflicts instead of portraying them directly. In "Of Dry Goods and Bow Ties," what types of conflict do you think Mr. Shimada experienced after his business failed?

3. In the excerpt from *Journey to Topaz,* how does a broader conflict in the world at large shatter a family's sense of peace and well-being?

◆ Drawing Conclusions About Uchida's Work

Yoshiko Uchida once described her goals as a writer this way:

"Although all my books have been about the Japanese people, my hope is that they will enlarge and enrich the reader's understanding, not only of the Japanese and the Japanese Americans, but of the *human condition.* I think it's important for each of us to take pride in our special heritage, but we must never lose our sense of connection with the community of man. And I hope our young people will, through the enriching diversity of the books they read, learn to celebrate our common humanity and the universality of the human spirit."

In your opinion, do the selections by Uchida address universal themes and issues, as well as specifically Japanese American concerns? Evaluate Uchida's success in achieving her goals by developing a chart such as the one below for two of the four selections in this group. In the left-hand column of your chart, list details that specifically relate to Japanese American culture. In the right-hand column, list ideas, conflicts, passages of dialogue, or themes that reflect what Uchida calls "our common humanity."

Title of Selection:

_____

_____

Japanese American Concerns	Universal Concerns
_____	_____
_____	_____
_____	_____

◆ Idea Bank

Writing

1. **Sequel** Write a brief sequel to the excerpt from *The Happiest Ending* in which you continue Rinko's story. How did Mr. Kinjo know her name?

How successful are Rinko's lessons with Mrs. Sugino? What happens to Rinko's relationship with her mother? When you have finished writing, share your sequel with a partner or a small group.

2. **News Article** Use the information in *Journey to Topaz,* as well as research sources in the library, to write a news article about the Japanese attack on Pearl Harbor in December 1941. When you have finished writing, post a copy of your article on the class bulletin board. **[Social Studies Link]**

3. **Character Sketch** In "Of Dry Goods and Bow Ties," Uchida recalls the strong impression left by Mr. Shozo Shimada on her family. Write a character sketch of an older person who has strongly impressed your own family. In your sketch, emphasize the personality traits that you and other family members admire in this person.

Speaking and Listening

4. **Storytelling** Imagine that you are Rinko and that you must entertain Little Boku while Mrs. Sugino goes to the doctor. What folk tale or fairy tale might you choose to read aloud to Boku? Choose a suitable story and then practice reading it with a pace, tone, and emphasis appropriate for a young child. When you have polished your performance, tell the story to an audience of younger children. **[Performing Arts Link]**

5. **Radio Commentary** Using the selections by Uchida as a springboard, carry out some research on the internment of Japanese Americans during World War II. Then, write a two-minute radio commentary in which you state your opinions about the situation, and support them with reasons and examples. **[Media Link; Social Studies Link]**

Researching and Representing

6. **Illustrated Report** Uchida was highly interested in Japanese folk arts and crafts. With a small group, investigate traditional folk art in Japan. Using Internet and library resources, compile a small collection of photographs, drawings, fabric samples, toys, and other artifacts. Group members can take turns presenting these materials to the class in an illustrated report. **[Art Link; Group Activity]**

◆ Further Reading, Listening, and Viewing

* Uchida, Yoshiko. *Picture Bride* (1987). Uchida's novel tells of the challenges faced by early Japanese women immigrants to America.

* Uchida, Yoshiko. *The Invisible Thread: An Autobiography* (1995). This autobiography describes the childhood experiences of a young Japanese American girl.

* Chang, Catherine E. Studier. "Profile: Yoshiko Uchida," *Language Arts* (February 1984).

* Uchida, Yoshiko. *The Two Foolish Cats* (1977). This children's tale is presented in filmstrip format, together with an audiocassette.

* *America Goes to War: World War II* (1998). These four videocassettes cover the battle fronts and the home front, including the internment of Japanese Americans.

On the Web:

http://www.phschool.com/atschool/literature
Go to the student edition *Silver.* Proceed to Unit 6. Then, click Hot Links to find Web sites featuring Yoshiko Uchida.

*M*artin Luther King, Jr., In Depth

"I have a dream that one day this nation will rise up and live out the true meaning of its creed: 'We hold these truths to be self-evident, that all men are created equal.'"

—Martin Luther King, Jr.

As the most influential leader of the civil rights movement during the 1950's and 1960's, DR. MARTIN LUTHER KING, JR., inspired millions of Americans. King's philosophy of nonviolence, his persuasive speaking style, and his personal example resulted in sweeping social change.

Youthful Studies Martin Luther King, Jr., was born on January 15, 1929, in Atlanta, Georgia, the son and grandson of Baptist ministers. King was ordained a minister in his father's church at the age of eighteen. After graduating from Morehouse College in 1948, he attended Crozer Theological Seminary in Pennsylvania for three years. It was during this period that King was first exposed to the philosophy of nonviolent resistance promoted by the Indian social and political leader Mohandas K. Gandhi. India had won independence from Great Britain in 1947, largely thanks to Gandhi's leadership. King's adoption of Gandhi's principles was a landmark in his development as a great leader. In 1953, King married Coretta Scott, and in time they became the parents of four children.

Turning Point in Montgomery King capped his education by earning a doctorate at Boston University in 1955. That same year, as pastor of the Dexter Avenue Baptist Church in Montgomery, Alabama, he took up the cause of Rosa Parks, an African American woman who had been arrested for refusing to give up her seat to a white passenger on a public bus. King organized a year-long bus boycott to protest the policy of segregation in public accommodations. Although King was arrested and his life was threatened, the boycott ultimately prevailed. Montgomery's bus segregation law was struck down by the United States Supreme Court.

Strides Toward Freedom King recounted the story of the bus boycott in his first book, *Stride Toward Freedom* (1958). A gifted writer as well as one of the most talented orators in American history, he produced a series of important books. In 1957, he was elected president of the Southern Christian Leadership Conference. Increasingly acknowledged as a national spokesman for civil rights, King returned to Atlanta in 1960 and became co-pastor, together with his father, of the Ebenezer Baptist Church.

In 1962, King began to work for civil rights in Birmingham, Alabama, one of the most rigidly segregated cities in America. The following year, he helped to organize an enormous march on Washington, D.C. King's speech on that occasion, delivered to 250,000 people gathered in front of the Lincoln Memorial, has often been called his most eloquent address. In his ringing conclusion, he repeated the phrase "I have a dream" to emphasize his confidence that America would achieve liberty and justice for all people.

A Leader in Action In early 1964, King was the first African American to be named "Man of the Year" by *Time* magazine. Later that year, he was awarded the Nobel Peace Prize. In a book entitled *Why We Can't Wait* (1964), he persuasively addressed the claims of some of his critics, who argued for a more gradual pace of social change. Also in 1964, President Lyndon B. Johnson signed a major Civil Rights Act into law.

In 1965, King led a march in Selma, Alabama, on behalf of voting rights. At that time, African Americans faced many obstacles to voting, including poll taxes and complex literacy tests. Outbreaks of violence in Selma and Montgomery led to vigorous action by President Johnson, who demanded that Congress pass a strong Voting Rights Bill. This measure was enacted into law later in 1965.

Throughout his career, King championed the ideal of nonviolent resistance. Within the Civil Rights Movement, however, other leaders felt that King's approach was too tame. In 1967, King published his next book, *Where Do We Go From Here: Chaos or Community?* In this work he responded to the arguments of these leaders, condemning any acceptance or approval of violence.

Final Years In the last years of his life, King aspired to even more ambitious goals: expanding his nonviolent demonstrations for civil rights to northern cities, as well as speaking out for peace in Vietnam and in favor of antipoverty legislation. On April 3, 1968, while he was organizing a labor action in Memphis, Tennessee, King delivered a speech in which he spoke of having "been to the mountaintop" and "seen the promised land." The following day, he was assassinated. Since 1986, the nation has observed a public holiday in mid-January to honor the memory of Martin Luther King, Jr.

◆ The Civil Rights Movement

The civil rights movement in the 1950's and 1960's challenged the public laws that segregated whites from people of color in the South. These laws, known as Jim Crow laws, specified that certain places, such as schools, restaurants, and public transport vehicles, be segregated according to race.

In 1954, the United States Supreme Court held that separate educational facilities were unequal and therefore unconstitutional. Racial tensions began to rise. In 1955, Rosa Parks's refusal to give up her seat to a white passenger spurred a bus boycott in Montgomery, Alabama; in 1957, black students, accompanied by federal troops, integrated schools in Little Rock, Arkansas. Other challenges to segregation sprang from these acts of courage. Voter registration drives were mounted in the rural counties of Alabama, Georgia, and Mississippi, where as few as one percent of eligible African Americans were registered to vote.

Martin Luther King, Jr., became a national figure and led thousands of Americans in the famous March on Washington in August 1963, when he delivered his inspiring "I Have a Dream" speech. In 1964, Congress passed the Civil Rights Act, which prohibited discrimination in education and employment, as well as segregation in public places.

◆ Literary Works

- *Stride Toward Freedom: The Montgomery Story* (1958)

- *Letter From Birmingham Jail* (1963)

- *Why We Can't Wait* (1964)

- *Where Do We Go From Here: Chaos or Community?* (1967)

- *The Trumpet of Conscience* (1968)

Martin Luther King, Jr.

from Letter From Birmingham City Jail

Dr. King wrote this famous essay (written in the form of an open letter) on 16 April 1963 while in jail. He was serving a sentence for participating in civil rights demonstrations in Birmingham, Alabama. He rarely took time to defend himself against his opponents. But eight prominent "liberal" Alabama clergymen, all white, published an open letter earlier in January that called on King to allow the battle for integration to continue in the local and federal courts, and warned that King's nonviolent resistance would have the effect of inciting civil disturbances. Dr. King wanted Christian ministers to see that the meaning of Christian discipleship was at the heart of the African American struggle for freedom, justice, and equality.

My dear Fellow Clergymen,

While confined here in the Birmingham city jail, I came across your recent statement calling our present activities "unwise and untimely." Seldom, if ever, do I pause to answer criticism of my work and ideas. If I sought to answer all of the criticisms that cross my desk, my secretaries would be engaged in little else in the course of the day, and I would have no time for constructive work. But since I feel that you are men of genuine good will and your criticisms are sincerely set forth, I would like to answer your statement in what I hope will be patient and reasonable terms.

I think I should give the reason for my being in Birmingham, since you have been influenced by the argument of "outsiders coming in." I have the honor of serving as president of the Southern Christian Leadership Conference, an organization operating in every southern state, with headquarters in Atlanta, Georgia. We have some eight-five affiliate organizations all across the South—one being the Alabama Christian Movement for Human Rights. Whenever necessary and possible we share staff, educational, and financial resources with our affiliates. Several months ago our local affiliate here in Birmingham invited us to be on call to engage in a nonviolent direct-action program if such were deemed necessary. We readily consented and when the hour came we lived up to our promises. So I am here, along with several members of my staff, because we were invited here. I am here because I have basic organizational ties here.

Beyond this, I am in Birmingham because injustice is here. Just as the eighth century prophets left their little villages and carried their "thus saith the Lord" far beyond the boundaries of their hometowns; and just as the Apostle Paul left his little village of Tarsus and carried the gospel of Jesus Christ to practically every hamlet and city of the Graeco-Roman world, I too am compelled to carry the gospel of freedom beyond my particular hometown. Like Paul, I must constantly respond to the Macedonian call for aid.

Moreover, I am cognizant[1] of the interrelatedness of all communities and states. I cannot sit idly by in Atlanta and not be concerned about what happens in Birmingham. Injustice anywhere is a threat to justice everywhere. We are caught in an inescapable network of mutuality, tied in a single garment of destiny. Whatever affects one directly affects all indirectly. Never again can we afford to live with the narrow, provincial "outside agitator"[2] idea. Anyone who lives in the United States can never be considered an outsider anywhere in this country.

You deplore[3] the demonstrations that are presently taking place in Birmingham. But I am sorry that your statement did not express a similar concern for the conditions that brought the demonstrations into being. I am sure that each of you would want to go beyond the superficial social analyst who looks merely at effects, and does not grapple with underlying causes. I would not hesitate to say that it is unfortunate that so-called demonstrations are taking place in Birmingham at this time, but I would say in more emphatic terms that it is even more unfortunate that the white power structure of this city left the Negro community with no other alternative.

In any nonviolent campaign there are four basic steps: (1) collection of the facts to determine whether injustices are alive, (2) negotiation, (3) self-purification, and (4) direct action. We have gone through all of these steps in Birmingham. There can be no gainsaying[4] of the fact that racial injustice engulfs this community.

Birmingham is probably the most thoroughly segregated city in the United States. Its ugly record of police brutality is known in every section of this country. Its injust treatment of Negroes in the courts is a notorious reality. There have been more unsolved bombings of Negro homes and churches in Birmingham than any city in this nation. These are the hard, brutal, and unbelievable facts. On the basis of these conditions Negro leaders sought to negotiate with the city fathers. But the political leaders consistently refused to engage in good faith negotiation.

---

1. **cognizant** (käg′ nə zənt): Aware.
2. **agitator:** One who tries to stir up others in support of a political or social cause; often used in an unfavorable sense.
3. **deplore:** Strongly criticize.
4. **gainsaying:** Denying.

Then came the opportunity last September to talk with some of the leaders of the economic community. In these negotiating sessions certain promises were made by the merchants—such as the promise to remove the humiliating racial signs from the stores. On the basis of these promises Rev. Shuttlesworth and the leaders of the Alabama Christian Movement for Human Rights agreed to call a moratorium[5] on any type of demonstrations. As the weeks and months unfolded we realized that we were the victims of a broken promise. The signs remained. Like so many experiences of the past we were confronted with blasted hopes, and the dark shadow of a deep disappointment settled upon us. So we had no alternative except that of preparing for direct action, whereby we would present our very bodies as a means of laying our case before the conscience of the local and national community. We were not unmindful of the difficulties involved. So we decided to go through a process of self-purification. We started having workshops on nonviolence and repeatedly asked ourselves the questions, "Are you able to accept blows without retaliating?" "Are you able to endure the ordeals of jail?" We decided to set our direct-action program around the Easter season, realizing that with the exception of Christmas, this was the largest shopping period of the year. Knowing that a strong economic withdrawal program would be the by-product of direct action, we felt that this was the best time to bring pressure on the merchants for the needed changes. Then it occurred to us that the March election was ahead and so we speedily decided to postpone action until after election day. When we discovered that Mr. Connor[6] was in the run-off, we decided again to postpone action so that the demonstrations could not be used to cloud the issues. At this time we agreed to begin our nonviolent witness the day after the run-off.

This reveals that we did not move irresponsibly into direct action. We too wanted to see Mr. Connor defeated; so we went through postponement after postponement to aid in this community need. After this we felt that direct action could be delayed no longer.

You may well ask, "Why direct action? Why sit-ins, marches, etc.? Isn't negotiation a better path?" You are exactly right in your call for negotiation. Indeed, this is the purpose of direct action. Nonviolent direct action seeks to create such a crisis and establish such creative tension that a community that has constantly refused to negotiate is forced to confront the issue. It seeks so to dramatize the issue that it can no longer be ignored. I just referred to the creation of tension as a part of the work of

---

5. **moratorium:** Delay or suspension of an activity.
6. **Mr. Connor:** Birmingham police chief and mayoral candidate.

the nonviolent resister. This may sound rather shocking. But I must confess that I am not afraid of the word tension. I have earnestly worked and preached against violent tension, but there is a type of constructive nonviolent tension that is necessary for growth. Just as Socrates felt that it was necessary to create a tension in the mind so that individuals could arise from the bondage of myths and half-truths to the unfettered realm of creative analysis and objective appraisal, we must see the need of having nonviolent gadflies to create the kind of tension in society that will help men to rise from the dark depths of prejudice and racism to the majestic heights of understanding and brotherhood. So the purpose of the direct action is to create a situation so crisis-packed that it will inevitably open the door to negotiation. We, therefore, concur with you in your call for negotiation. Too long has our beloved Southland been bogged down in the tragic attempt to live in monologue rather than dialogue.

One of the basic points in your statement is that our acts are untimely. Some have asked, "Why didn't you give the new administration time to act?" The only answer that I can give to this inquiry is that the new administration must be prodded about as much as the outgoing one before it acts. We will be sadly mistaken if we feel that the election of Mr. Boutwell[7] will bring the millennium to Birmingham. While Mr. Boutwell is much more articulate and gentle than Mr. Connor, they are both segregationists, dedicated to the task of maintaining the status quo. The hope I see in Mr. Boutwell is that he will be reasonable enough to see the futility of massive resistance to desegregation. But he will not see this without pressure from the devotees of civil rights. My friends, I must say to you that we have not made a single gain in civil rights without determined legal and nonviolent pressure. History is the long and tragic story of the fact that privileged groups seldom give up their privileges voluntarily. Individuals may see the moral light and voluntarily give up their unjust posture; but as Reinhold Niebuhr[8] has reminded us, groups are more immoral than individuals.

We know through painful experience that freedom is never voluntarily given by the oppressor; it must be demanded by the oppressed. Frankly, I have never yet engaged in a direct action movement that was "well-timed," according to the timetable of those who have not suffered unduly from the disease of segregation. For years now I have heard the words "Wait!" It rings in the ear of every Negro with a piercing familiarity. This "Wait" has almost always meant "Never." It has been a tranquilizing

---

7. **Mr. Boutwell:** Mayor of Birmingham.
8. **Reinhold Niebuhr** (1892–1971): American religious and social thinker.

thalidomide,[9] relieving the emotional stress for a moment, only to give birth to an ill-formed infant of frustration. We must come to see with the distinguished jurist of yesterday that "justice too long delayed is justice denied." We have waited for more than 340 years for our constitutional and God-given rights. The nations of Asia and Africa are moving with jetlike speed toward the goal of political independence, and we still creep at horse and buggy pace toward the gaining of a cup of coffee at a lunch counter. I guess it is easy for those who have never felt the stinging darts of segregation to say, "Wait." But when you have seen vicious mobs lynch your mothers and fathers at will and drown your sisters and brothers at whim; when you have seen hate-filled policemen curse, kick, brutalize, and even kill your black brothers and sisters with impunity; when you see the vast majority of your twenty million Negro brothers smothering in an airtight cage of poverty in the midst of an affluent society; when you suddenly find your tongue twisted and your speech stammering as you seek to explain to your six-year-old daughter why she can't go to the public amusement park that has just been advertised on television, and see tears welling up in her little eyes when she is told that Funtown is closed to colored children, and see the depressing clouds of inferiority begin to form in her little mental sky, and see her begin to distort her little personality by unconsciously developing a bitterness toward white people; when you have to concoct an answer for a five-year-old son asking in agonizing pathos: "Daddy, why do white people treat colored people so mean?"; when you take a cross-country drive and find it necessary to sleep night after night in the uncomfortable corners of your automobile because no motel will accept you; when you are humiliated day in and day out by nagging signs reading "white" and "colored"; when your first names becomes "nigger" and your middle name becomes "boy" (however old you are) and your last name becomes "John," and when your wife and mother are never given the respected title "Mrs."; when you are harried by day and haunted by night by the fact that you are a Negro, living constantly at tiptoe stance never quite knowing what to expect next, and plagued with inner fears and outer resentments; when you are forever fighting a degenerating sense of "nobodiness"; then you will understand why we find it difficult to wait. There comes a time when the cup of endurance runs over, and men are no longer willing to be plunged into an abyss of injustice where they experience the blackness of corroding despair. I hope, sirs, you can understand our legitimate and unavoidable impatience.

---

9. **thalidomide** (thə lid′ ə mĭd): Drug found to be responsible for severe birth deformities.

☑ Check Your Comprehension

1. What two reasons does King give for his being in Birmingham?
2. According to King, what are the four basic steps in any nonviolent campaign?
3. What contrast does King draw between the United States and the nations of Asia and Africa?
4. Identify three examples of racial injustice that King lists in the last paragraph of this excerpt.

◆ Critical Thinking

INTERPRET

1. According to King, why can we never afford to live with the narrow "outside agitator" idea? **[Analyze]**
2. What facts does King cite to support his claim about segregation in Birmingham? **[Support]**
3. Why do you think the civil rights leaders held workshops on nonviolence for their followers? **[Infer]**
4. What does King mean by establishing "creative tension" in a community? **[Interpret]**

Martin Luther King, Jr.

from Kenneth B. Clark Interview

Kenneth Clark was himself deeply involved in Dr. King's struggle. As a noted black child psychologist and educator, he used his skills to provide psychological data to support the civil rights activists' claim that segregated education was psychologically debilitating for black youth, and made white youth culturally parochial and socially isolated. His own headnote to his interview with Dr. King provides a helpful insight into the setting for this conversation. Dr. Clark was quite adept in this interview at getting Dr. King to talk about his own feelings about facing death-threatening situations. He unfortunately did not state when this interview took place. But it appears to have been prior to the 28 August 1963 March on Washington.

Martin Luther King was interviewed on a day when he had already spent three hours taping another television program. When we called for him at his hotel, he seemed weary, but desirous of hiding this fact. On the way to the studio, we talked generally about developments on the various civil rights fronts. He seemed particularly optimistic that a solid and workable agreement was going to be implemented in Birmingham. His tone before the interview was the same as his tone during the interview—a calm, quiet, confident belief in the future.

This observer has no doubts that Martin Luther King's philosophy of love for the oppressor is a genuine aspect of his being. He personally does not differentiate between this philosophy and the effectiveness of the nonviolent direct-action approach to the attainment of racial justice, which he personifies and leads. For him, the philosophy is not just a strategy; it is a truth, it is his assertion of the philosophical position that one cannot differentiate means from ends. The quiet, contemplative, at times exasperatingly academic style is truly King. He is the paradox of the scholar and the effective man of social action.

Martin Luther King is a quietly pleasant young man. There is little about his personal appearance that suggests the firm, courageous leader of public demonstrations. There is no way that one could tell by looking at him that he has exposed himself repeatedly to death, and that by sheer force of his personality and the depth of his convictions, has moved the South and the North. He is the embodiment of that dignity which is essential for every man.

CLARK: Now, if we could shift a little from the education within the academic halls to your education in the community. I look at our newspapers and see that you have not only engaged in and led many of these demonstrations, but have paid for this by seeing the inside of many jails. I've wondered—how many jails have you been to as a result of your involvement in this direct-action, nonviolent insistence upon the rights of Negroes?

KING: Well, I've been arrested fourteen times since we started out in Montgomery. Some have been in the same jail, that is, I've been in some jails more than once. I haven't calculated the number of different jails. I would say about eight of them were different jails. I remember once within eight days I transferred to three different jails within the state of Georgia. I think I've been to about eight different jails and I've been arrested about fourteen times.

CLARK: Have you attempted to make a study of these jails, for example, the type of jail, the type of individuals you've met in these jails as keepers, say, or wardens? What type of human beings are these or are they different types of human beings?

KING: Well, I have gone through the process of comparing the various jails. I guess this is one of these inevitable things that you find yourself doing to kind of lift yourself from the dull monotony of sameness when you're in jail and I find that they do differ. I've been in some new jails and I've been in some mighty old ones. In the recent jail experience in Birmingham I was in the new jail. The city jail is about a year old, I think, and in Albany, Georgia, last year I was in a very old jail. In Fulton County, Georgia, I was in a very new one.

CLARK: What about the human beings who are the jailkeepers? What about their attitude toward you as a person?

KING: Well, they vary also. I have been in jails where the jailers were exceptionally courteous and they went out of their way to see that everything went all right where I was concerned. On the other hand, I have been in jails where the jailers were extremely harsh and vitriolic in their words and in their manners. I haven't had any experience of physical violence from jailers, but I have had violence of words from them. Even in Birmingham, for the first few days, some of the jailers were extremely harsh in their statements.

CLARK: Have you ever been in an integrated jail? In the South?

KING: No, that's one experience I haven't had yet.

CLARK: Well, maybe after we get through integrating public accommodations the last thing will be to integrate the jailhouses.

KING: Yes.

CLARK: I am very much interested in the philosophy of nonviolence and particularly I would like to understand more clearly for myself the relationship between the direct-action nonviolence technique which you have used so effectively and your philosophy of, for want of better words I'll use, "love of the oppressor."[1]

KING: All right.

CLARK: Dr. King, what do you see as the relationship between these two things, which could be seen as separate?

KING: Yes, I think so. One is a method of action: nonviolent direct action is a method of acting to rectify a social situation that is unjust and it involves in engaging in a practical technique that nullifies the use of violence or calls for nonviolence at every point. That is, you don't use physical violence against the opponent. Now, the love ethic is another dimension which goes into the realm of accepting nonviolence as a way of life. There are many people who will accept nonviolence as the most practical technique to be used in a social situation, but they would not go to the point of seeing the necessity of accepting nonviolence as a way of life. Now, I accept both. I think that nonviolent resistance is the most potent weapon available to oppressed people in their struggle for freedom and human dignity. It has a way of disarming the opponent. It exposes his moral defenses. It weakens his morale and at the same time it works on his conscience. He just doesn't know how to handle it and I have seen this over and over again in our struggle in the South. Now on the question of love or the love ethic, I think this is so important because hate is injurious to the hater as well as the hated. Many of the psychiatrists are telling us now that many of the strange things that happen in the subconscious and many of the inner conflicts are rooted in hate and so they are now saying "love or perish." Erich Fromm can write a book like *The Art of Loving* and make it very clear that love is the supreme unifying principle of life and I'm trying to say in this movement that it is necessary to follow the technique of nonviolence as the most potent weapon available to us, but it is necessary also

---

1. **oppressor:** One who keeps others down by the cruel or unjust use of power.

to follow the love ethic which becomes a force of personality integration.

CLARK: But is it not too much to expect that a group of human beings who have been the victims of cruelty and flagrant injustice could actually love those who have been associated with the perpetrators, if not the perpetrators themselves? How could you expect, for example, the Negroes in Birmingham who know Bull Connor to really love him in any meaningful sense?

KING: Well, I think one has to understand the meaning of "love" at this point. I'm certainly not speaking of an affectionate response. I think it is really nonsense to urge oppressed peoples to love their oppressors in an affectionate sense. And I often call on the Greek language to aid me at this point because there are three words in the Greek for "love." One is *"eros,"* which is soft of an aesthetic or a romantic love. Another is *"philia,"* which is sort of an intimate affection between personal friends; this is friendship, it is a reciprocal love and on this level, you love those people that you like. And then the Greek language comes out with the word *"agape,"* which is understanding, creative, redemptive good will for all men. It goes far beyond an affectionate response. Now when I say to you—

CLARK: That form means really understanding.

KING: Yes, that's right. And you come to the point of being able to love the person that does an evil deed in the sense of understanding and you can hate the deed that the person does. And I'm certainly not talking about *"eros";* I'm not talking about friendship. I find it pretty difficult to like people like Bull Connor. I find it difficult to like Senator Eastman, but I think you can love where you can't like the person because life is an affectionate quality.

CLARK: Yes, I have admired your ability to feel this, and I must say to you also that as I read your expounding of the philosophy of love I found myself often feeling personally quite inadequate. Malcolm X,[2] one of the most articulate exponents of the Black Muslim philosophy, has said of your movement and your philosophy that it plays into the hands of the white oppressors, that they are happy to hear you talk about love for the oppressor because this disarms the Negro and fits into the stereotype of the Negro as a meek, turning-the-other-cheek

---

2. **Malcolm X** (1925-1965): Advocate of black separatism and author of a noted autobiography.

	sort of creature. Would you care to comment on Mr. X's beliefs?
KING:	Well, I don't think of love, as in this context, as emotional bosh. I don't think of it as a weak force, but I think of love as something strong and that organizes itself into powerful direct action. Now, this is what I try to teach in this struggle in the South: that we are not engaged in a struggle that means we sit down and do nothing; that there is a great deal of difference between nonresistance to evil and nonviolent resistance. Nonresistance leaves you in a state of stagnant passivity and deadly complacency where nonviolent resistance means that you do resist in a very strong and determined manner and I think some of the criticisms of nonviolence or some of the critics fail to realize that we are talking about something very strong and they confuse nonresistance with nonviolent resistance.
CLARK:	He goes beyond that in some of the things I've heard him say—to say that this is deliberately your philosophy of love of the oppressor which he identifies completely with the nonviolent movement. He says this philosophy and this movement are actually encouraged by whites because it makes them comfortable. It makes them believe that Negroes are meek, supine creatures.
KING:	Well, I don't think that's true. If anyone has ever lived with a nonviolent movement in the South, from Montgomery on through the freedom rides and through the sit-in movement and the recent Birmingham movement and seen the reactions of many of the extremists and reactionaries in the white community, he wouldn't say that this movement makes—this philosophy makes them comfortable. I think it arouses a sense of shame within them often—in many instances. I think it does something to touch the conscience and establish a sense of guilt. Now so often people respond to guilt by engaging more in the guilt-evoking act in an attempt to drown the sense of guilt, but this approach doesn't make the white man feel comfortable. I think it does the other thing. It disturbs his conscience and it disturbs this sense of contentment that he's had.
CLARK:	James Baldwin[3] raises still another point of the whole nonviolent position, an approach. He does not reject it in the ways that Malcolm X does, but he raises the question of whether it will be possible to contain the Negro people within this framework of nonviolence if we

---

3. **James Baldwin** (1924–1987): African American author.

continue to have more of the kinds of demonstrations that we had in Birmingham, wherein police brought dogs to attack human beings. What is your reaction to Mr. Baldwin's anxiety?

KING: Well, I think these brutal methods used by the Birmingham police force and other police forces will naturally arouse the ire of Negroes and I think there is the danger that some will be so aroused that they will retaliate with violence. I think though that we can be sure that the vast majority of Negroes who engage in the demonstrations and who understand the nonviolent philosophy will be able to face dogs and all of the other brutal methods that are used without retaliating with violence because they understand that one of the first principles of nonviolence is the willingness to be the recipient of violence while never inflicting violence upon another. And none of the demonstrators in Birmingham engaged in aggressive or retaliatory violence. It was always someone on the sideline who had never been in the demonstrations and probably not in the mass meetings and had never been in a nonviolent work-shop. So I think it will depend on the extent to which we can extend the teaching of the philosophy of nonvio-lence to the larger community rather than those who are engaged in the demonstrations.

☑ **Check Your Comprehension**

1. How was King's interviewer, Kenneth B. Clark, deeply involved in the struggle for civil rights?

2. How many times does King say he has been arrested since he began to work for civil rights in Montgomery?

3. (a) What three words from Greek does King cite for the concept of love? (b) Which of these words corresponds to what King calls the "love ethic"?

4. (a) What objection does Malcolm X raise to King's philosophy? (b) What objection does James Baldwin raise?

◆ **Critical Thinking**

1. A paradox is an apparent contradiction. In his headnote to the interview, why does Kenneth B. Clark call King a paradox? **[Interpret]**

2. Why do you think Clark asks King to focus on the jails and jailers he has known? How does this topic relate to an important part of King's philosophy? **[Connect]**

EVALUATE

3. (a) How does King respond to Malcolm X's criticisms of King's philosophy? (b) Do you think King's answer is effective? **[Evaluate]**

APPLY

4. "Hate is injurious to the hater as well as the hated," says King. How might you apply this belief to a situation in everyday life today? **[Apply]**

Martin Luther King, Jr.
from Our Struggle

The segregation of Negroes, with its inevitable discrimination, has thrived on elements of inferiority present in the masses of both white and Negro people. Through forced separation from our African culture, through slavery, poverty, and deprivation,[1] many black men lost self-respect.

In their relations with Negroes, white people discovered that they had rejected the very center of their own ethical professions. They could not face the triumph of their lesser instincts and simultaneously have peace within. And so, to gain it, they rationalized[2]—insisting that the unfortunate Negro, being less than human, deserved and even enjoyed second-class status.

They argued that his inferior social, economic, and political position was good for him. He was incapable of advancing beyond a fixed position and would therefore be happier if encouraged not to attempt the impossible. He is subjugated[3] by a superior people with an advanced way of life. The "master race" will be able to civilize him to a limited degree, if only he will be true to his inferior nature and stay in his place.

White men soon came to forget that the southern social culture and all its institutions had been organized to perpetuate this rationalization. They observed a caste system and quickly were conditioned to believe that its social results, which they had created, actually reflected the Negro's innate and true nature.

In time many Negroes lost faith in themselves and came to believe that perhaps they really were what they had been told they were—something less than men. So long as they were prepared to accept this role, racial peace could be maintained. It was an uneasy peace in which the Negro was forced to accept patiently injustice, insult, injury, and exploitation.

Gradually the Negro masses in the South began to reevaluate themselves—a process that was to change the nature of the Negro community and doom the social patterns of the South. We discovered that we had never really smothered our self-respect and that we could not be at one with ourselves without asserting it. From this point on, the South's terrible peace was rapidly undermined by the Negro's new and courageous thinking and his ever-increasing readiness to organize and to act. Conflict and violence were coming to the surface as the white South desperately

---

1. **deprivation:** Loss.
2. **rationalized:** Made superficial or weak excuses.
3. **subjugated** (sub´ jə gāt əd): Put down, brought under strict control.

clung to its old patterns. The extreme tension in race relations in the South today is explained in part by the revolutionary change in the Negro's evaluation of himself and of his destiny and by his determination to struggle for justice. *We Negroes have replaced self-pity with self-respect and self-depreciation with dignity.*

When Mrs. Rosa Parks, the quiet seamstress whose arrest precipitated the nonviolent protest in Montgomery, was asked why she had refused to move to the rear of a bus, she said: "It was a matter of dignity; I could not have faced myself and my people if I had moved."

Martin Luther King, Jr.

Nobel Prize Acceptance Speech

This is the full text of Dr. King's acceptance speech on the occasion of receiving the Noble Peace Prize in Oslo, Norway, on 10 December 1964. When once asked by an interviewer what was the significance for him of receiving this much coveted award, Dr. King replied, "The Nobel award recognizes the amazing discipline of the Negro. Though we have had riots, the bloodshed we would have known without the discipline of nonviolence would have been frightening."

Your Majesty, your Royal Highness, Mr. President, excellencies, ladies and gentlemen:

I accept the Noble Prize for Peace at a moment when twenty-two million Negroes of the United States of America are engaged in a creative battle to end the long night of racial injustice. I accept this award in behalf of a civil rights movement which is moving with determination and a majestic scorn for risk and danger to establish a reign of freedom and a rule of justice.

I am mindful that only yesterday in Birmingham, Alabama, our children, crying out for brotherhood, were answered with fire hoses, snarling dogs, and even death. I am mindful that only yesterday in Philadelphia, Mississippi, young people seeking to secure the right to vote were brutalized and murdered.

I am mindful that debilitating and grinding poverty afflicts my people and chains them to the lowest rung of the economic ladder.

Therefore, I must ask why this prize is awarded to a movement which is beleaguered and committed to unrelenting struggle: to a movement which has not won the very peace and brotherhood which is the essence of the Nobel Prize.

After contemplation, I conclude that this award which I received on behalf of that movement is profound recognition that nonviolence is the answer to the crucial political and moral question of our time—the need for man to overcome oppression and violence without resorting to violence and oppression.

Civilization and violence are antithetical[1] concepts. Negroes of the United States, following the people of India, have demonstrated that nonviolence is not sterile passivity, but a powerful moral force which makes for social transformation. Sooner or later, all the people of the world will have to discover a way to live together in peace, and thereby transform this pending cosmic elegy into a creative psalm of brotherhood.

---

1. antithetical (an´ tə thet´ i kəl): Opposite.

If this is to be achieved, many must evolve for all human conflict a method which rejects revenge, aggression, and retaliation. The foundation of such a method is love.

From the depths of my heart I am aware that this prize is much more than an honor to me personally.

Every time I take a flight I am always mindful of the many people who make a successful journey possible, the known pilots and the unknown ground crew.

So you honor the dedicated pilots of our struggle who have sat at the controls as the freedom movement soared into orbit. You honor, once again, Chief (Albert) Luthuli[2] of South Africa, whose struggles with and for his people are still met with the most brutal expression of man's inhumanity to man.

You honor the ground crew without whose labor and sacrifices the jet flights to freedom could never have left the earth.

Most of these people will never make the headlines and their names will not appear in *Who's Who*. Yet the years have rolled past and when the blazing light of truth is focused on this marvelous age in which we live—men and women will know and children will be taught that we have a finer land, a better people, a more noble civilization—because these humble children of God were willing to suffer for righteousness' sake.

I think Alfred Nobel would know what I mean when I say that I accept this award in the spirit of a curator of some precious heirloom which he holds in trust for its true owners—all those to whom beauty is truth and truth beauty—and in whose eyes the beauty of genuine brotherhood and peace is more precious than diamonds or silver or gold.

The tortuous road which has lead from Montgomery, Alabama, to Oslo bears witness to this truth. This is a road over which millions of Negroes are travelling to find a new sense of dignity. This same road has opened for all Americans a new era of progress and hope. It has led to a new civil rights bill, and it will, I am convinced, be widened and lengthened into a superhighway of justice as Negro and white men in increasing number create alliances to overcome their common problems.

I accept this award today with an abiding faith in America and an audacious faith in the future of mankind. I refuse to accept the idea that the "isness" of man's present nature makes him morally incapable of reaching up for the eternal "oughtness" that forever confronts him.

I refuse to accept the idea that man is mere flotsam and jetsam[3] in the river of life which surrounds him. I refuse to accept

---

2. **Chief (Albert) Luthuli:** South African political leader who opposed racial discrimination in that country.
3. **flotsam and jetsam:** Drifting wreckage, odds and ends.

the view that mankind is so tragically bound to the starless midnight of racism and war that the bright daybreak of peace and brotherhood can never become a reality.

I refuse to accept the cynical notion that nation after nation must spiral down a militaristic stairway into hell of thermonuclear destruction. I believe that unarmed truth and unconditional love will have the final word in reality. That is why right temporarily defeated is stronger than evil triumphant.

I believe that even amid today's mortar bursts and whining bullets, there is still hope for a brighter tomorrow. I believe that wounded justice, lying prostrate on the blood-flowing streets of our nations, can be lifted from this dust of shame to reign supreme among the children of men.

I have the audacity to believe that peoples everywhere can have three meals a day for their bodies, education and culture for their minds, and dignity, equality, and freedom for their spirits. I believe that what self-centered men have torn down men other-centered can build up. I still believe that one day mankind will bow before the altars of God and be crowned triumphant over war and bloodshed, and nonviolent redemptive good will will proclaim the rule of the land. "And the lion and the lamb shall lie down together and ever man shall sit under his own vine and fig tree and none shall be afraid." I still believe that we shall overcome.

This faith can give us courage to face the uncertainties of the future. It will give our tired feet new strength as we continue our forward stride toward the city of freedom. When our days become dreary with low-hovering clouds and our nights become darker than a thousand midnights, we will know that we are living in the creative turmoil of a genuine civilization struggling to be born.

Today I come to Oslo as a trustee, inspired and with renewed dedication to humanity. I accept this prize on behalf of all men who love peace and brotherhood.

_M_artin Luther King, Jr.

from I See the Promised Land

On April 3, 1968, while organizing a labor action in Memphis, Tennessee, Martin Luther King, Jr. delivered the following speech. He was assassinated the next day.

That's the question before you tonight. Not, "If I stop to help the sanitation workers, what will happen to all of the hours that I usually spend in my office every day and every week as a pastor?" The question is not, "If I stop to help this man in need, what will happen to me?" "If I do not stop to help the sanitation workers, what will happen to them?" That's the question.

Let us rise up tonight with a greater readiness. Let us stand with a greater determination. And let us move on in these powerful days, these days of challenge to make America what it ought to be. We have an opportunity to make America a better nation. And I want to thank God, once more, for allowing me to be here with you.

You know, several years ago, I was in New York City autographing the first book that I had written. And while sitting there autographing books, a demented black woman came up. The only question I heard from her was, "Are you Martin Luther King?"

And I was looking down writing, and I said yes. And the next minute I felt something beating on my chest. Before I knew it I had been stabbed by this demented woman. I was rushed to Harlem Hospital. It was a dark Saturday afternoon. And that blade had gone through, and the X-rays revealed that the tip of the blade was on the edge of my aorta, the main artery. And once that's punctured, you drown in your own blood—that's the end of you.

It came out in the _New York Times_ the next morning, that if I had sneezed, I would have died. Well, about four days later, they allowed me, after the operation, after my chest had been opened, and the blade had been taken out, to move around in the wheel chair in the hospital. They allowed me to read some of the mail that came in, and from all over the states, and the world, kind letters came in. I read a few, but one of them I will never forget. I had received one from the President and the Vice-President. I've forgotten what those telegrams said. I'd received a visit and a letter from the Governor of New York, but I've forgotten what the letter said. But there was another letter that came from a little girl, a young girl who was a student at the White Plains High School. And I looked at that letter, and I'll never forget it. It said simply, "Dear Dr. King: I am a ninth-grade student at the White Plains High School." She said, "While it should not matter, I would like to mention that I am a white girl. I read in the paper of your misfortune, and of your suffering. And I read that if you had sneezed, you would have died. And I'm simply writing you to say that I'm so happy that you didn't sneeze."

And I want to say tonight, I want to say that I am happy that I didn't sneeze. Because if I had sneezed, I wouldn't have been around here in 1960, when students all over the South started sitting-in at lunch counters. And I knew that as they were sitting in, they were really standing up for the best in the American dream. And taking the whole nation back to those great walls of democracy which were dug deep by the Founding Fathers in the Declaration of Independence and the Constitution. If I had sneezed, I wouldn't have been around in 1962, when Negroes in Albany, Georgia, decided to straighten their backs up. And whenever men and women straighten their backs up, they are going somewhere, because a man can't ride your back unless it is bent. If I had sneezed, I wouldn't have been here in 1963, when the black people of Birmingham, Alabama, aroused the conscience of this nation, and brought into being the Civil Rights Bill. If I had sneezed, I wouldn't have had a chance later that year, in August, to try to tell American about a dream that I had had. If I had sneezed, I wouldn't have been down in Selma, Alabama, to see the great movement there. If I had sneezed, I wouldn't have been in Memphis to see a community rally around those brothers and sisters who are suffering. I'm so happy that I didn't sneeze.

And they were telling me, now it doesn't matter now. It really doesn't matter what happens now. I left Atlanta this morning, and as we got started on the plane, there were six of us, the pilot said over the public address system. "We are sorry for the delay, but we have Dr. Martin Luther King on the plane. And to be sure that all of the bags were checked, and to be sure that nothing would be wrong with the plane, we had to check out everything carefully. And we've had the plane protected and guarded all night."

And then I got into Memphis. And some began to say the threats, or talk about the threats that were out. What would happen to me from some of our sick white brothers?

Well, I don't know what will happen now. We've got some difficult days ahead. But it doesn't matter with me now. Because I've been to the mountaintop. And I don't mind. Like anybody, I would like to live a long life. Longevity has its place. But I'm not concerned about that now. I just want to do God's will. And He's allowed me to go up to the mountain. And I've looked over. And I've seen the promised land. I may not get there with you. But I want you to know tonight, that we, as a people will get to the promised land. And I'm happy, tonight. I'm not worried about anything. I'm not fearing any man. Mine eyes have seen the glory of the coming of the Lord.

☑ Check Your Comprehension

1. According to "Our Struggle," what did the uneasy racial peace in the South force the Negro to accept?

2. What reason did Mrs. Rosa Parks give for her refusal to move to the rear of the bus in Montgomery?

3. In his Nobel Prize Acceptance Speech, what idea about humanity does King refuse to accept?

4. In "I See the Promised Land," why does King say that he is happy, even though he may not live a long life?

◆ Critical Thinking

INTERPRET

1. (a) In "Our Struggle," what new discovery does King say that African Americans have made about themselves? (b) In what way did this discovery affect the South? **[Interpret]**

2. Identify two examples of cause-and-effect reasoning in "Our Struggle." **[Analyze]**

3. In the Nobel Prize Acceptance Speech, what does King mean by saying that the prize is much more than an honor to him personally? **[Interpret]**

4. In "I See the Promised Land," what do you think King means when he says that he has been to the mountaintop and seen the promised land? Explain your answer. **[Speculate]**

Martin Luther King, Jr.
Comparing and Connecting the Author's Works

◆ Literary Focus: Persuasion

Persuasion is used in writing or speech that attempts to convince readers or listeners that they should adopt a particular opinion or course of action. Newspaper editorials and letters to the editor use persuasion, as do product advertisements and political campaign speeches.

Among the methods used by persuasive writers and speakers, the following four techniques are especially important:

- logical reasoning

- imagery and figurative language

- balanced phrasing and rhythm

- repetition of key words and phrases

Martin Luther King, Jr., used all these techniques in his essays, letters, and speeches. Review the selections and identify at least one example of each of these persuasive devices.

◆ Drawing Conclusions About King's Work

When Martin Luther King, Jr., argued in favor of his philosophy of nonviolent resistance, he appealed to his listeners' reasoning powers as well as to their hearts. King was careful to distinguish his position from other people's approaches to the same problems. He also vigorously defended his position against misinterpretation or distortion.

Using "Letter From Birmingham City Jail" and "Kenneth B. Clark Interview," draw up a chart that presents the opinions and philosophies underlying four different approaches to the struggle for civil rights. On your chart, for which you can use the model that follows, fill in facts, details, and arguments related to each

individual or group's position. If necessary, use Internet or library research to supplement your answers.

Martin Luther King, Jr.	Malcolm X
Alabama Clergymen	**James Baldwin**

When you have compiled your chart, write a short essay in which you evaluate the persuasive merits of each position.

◆ Idea Bank

Writing

1. **Timeline** Using information in the biography on page 136–137 as well as library resources, create a timeline showing the major events in the life of Dr. Martin Luther King, Jr. On your timeline, also show major historical events in the nation and the world: for example, World War II, the Cuban Missile Crisis, the assassination of President John F. Kennedy, and the Vietnam War. **[Social Studies Link]**

2. **Report on Gandhi** The Indian leader Mohandas K. Gandhi profoundly influenced King's philosophy of nonviolent resistance. Research Gandhi's life and achievements. Write up your results in a brief report. **[Social Studies Link]**

3. **News Analysis** Write a news commentary on one of King's speeches: for example, "Nobel Prize Acceptance Speech," "I See the Promised Land," or "I Have a Dream" (delivered at the March on Washington in 1963). In your analysis, comment on King's major ideas and on his use of persuasive techniques. Use a news analysis in your local newspaper as a model. **[Media Link]**

Speaking and Listening

4. **Speech** Martin Luther King, Jr., was a powerful speaker. If possible, listen to a recording of King himself, and take note of the lines and ideas he emphasizes. Then, practice reading one of his speeches aloud until you can give an inspiring rendition. Present the speech to your classmates when you finish rehearsing. **[Performing Arts Link]**

5. **Dialogue** Together with a partner, role-play a dialogue between Martin Luther King, Jr., and someone with a different approach for achieving civil rights: for example, Malcolm X or James Baldwin. Look in your library or on the Internet for more information about the civil rights leader you choose. **[Social Studies Link; Group Activity]**

Researching and Representing

6. **Civil Rights Exhibit** Together with a small group, use the library and other reference sources to research the history of the civil rights m158ovement. Create a multimedia exhibit that shows a chronological progression in the battle for civil rights. **[Social Studies Link; Art Link; Group Activity]**

◆ Further Reading, Listening, and Viewing

- King, Jr., Martin Luther. *Testament of Hope: The Essential Writings of Martin Luther King, Jr.* (1986). King's work is collected in this anthology of essays, speeches, sermons, and interviews.

- Garrow, David J. *Bearing the Cross: Martin Luther King, Jr., and the Southern Christian Leadership Conference* (1986). Garrow presents a well-researched account of King's career.

- Schulke, Flip, and Penelope O. McPhee: *King Remembered* (1986). This informative biography, which includes many photographs of King's life and times, is based on interviews with King's friends and associates.

- *King: A Filmed Record . . . Montgomery to Memphis* (1970). This documentary, which covers the civil rights leader's life from 1955 to 1968, is directed by Sidney Lumet and Joseph L. Mankiewicz.

- *The Autobiography of Martin Luther King, Jr.* (1996). This audiocassette version combines excerpts from King's writings with narration by Levar Burton.

On the Web:

http://www.phschool.com/atschool/literature
Go to the student edition *Silver*. Proceed to Unit 7. Then, click Hot Links to find Web sites featuring Martin Luther King, Jr.

William Shakespeare In Depth

"Shakespeare would have made a great movie writer."
—Orson Welles, stage and screen director

WILLIAM SHAKESPEARE is widely regarded as the greatest writer in English. The power and beauty of his language continue to cast a magical spell nearly four centuries after his death.

Stratford Roots Shakespeare was born in 1564, the eldest son of a merchant in the town of Stratford-on-Avon, about one hundred miles northwest of London. He probably attended the local grammar school, where Latin formed an important part of the curriculum. In 1582 he married Anne Hathaway, who was eight years his senior. Their daughter Susanna was born in 1583. Two years later, the couple became the parents of twins: a son named Hamnet and a daughter, Judith.

A Young Writer in London
Shakespeare probably began his writing career after moving to London sometime in the late 1580's. Very little is known about him in these years. It seems likely that he held a theatrical apprenticeship, which at the time involved many different duties, including acting, writing, and learning about business management. The first printed reference to Shakespeare, in 1592, mentions a rival's attack on the young dramatist as an "upstart crow." By this time, Shakespeare had written and produced several history plays and had possibly written some of his early comedies. In 1593–94, he published two narrative poems based on ancient Greek and Roman myths and legends: *Venus and Adonis* and *The Rape of Lucrece.*

Sonnets During the 1590's, Shakespeare probably wrote most of his sonnets. A sonnet is a fourteen-line lyric poem focused on a single theme. Composing series of sonnets was popular among the leading writers of the English Renaissance, such as Sir Philip Sidney and Edmund Spenser. Shakespeare's collection, consisting of 154 poems, was published in 1609, without the poet's permission.

A Career in Full Stride During the 1590's, Shakespeare became a leading member of the Lord Chamberlain's Men. This group, which developed into London's finest acting company, began to perform in the Globe Theater after that playhouse was constructed in 1599. Although Shakespeare continued his acting career, he is most remembered as a playwright. During this phase of his career, he wrote many of his best known tragedies and comedies. In 1603, after the death of Queen Elizabeth I, the English throne passed to James I. The new monarch, like his predecessor, greatly enjoyed plays. James became the patron of Shakespeare's company, which changed its name to the King's Men.

Last Plays and Retirement In his final plays, especially *The Winter's Tale* and *The Tempest,* Shakespeare turned to another dramatic form called romance— a type of play that combined comic with tragic elements but ended happily. By 1611, when he was forty-seven, Shakespeare had achieved substantial success as a complete man of the theater. He was able to retire comfortably to his home town of Stratford. He died five years later in 1616. In 1623, two members of his company published

Shakespeare's collected dramas. It was for this work, known as the First Folio, that Shakespeare's contemporary and rival Ben Jonson praised the playwright with the following tribute: "He was not of an age but for all time."

◆ Shakespeare on Film

Orson Welles' comment that Shakespeare would have made a great movie writer reflects the fact that a Shakespearean play consists of brief scenes designed to be *viewed*, not just *read*. Possibly Welles, who was a distinguished director of both plays and films, was also referring to the phenomenal popularity of Shakespeare on screen.

Shakespeare's plays have been the basis for a remarkable number of film and television adaptations. Between 1900 and 1996, for example, there were nearly fifty film versions of *Hamlet*. One of the most highly acclaimed adaptations, directed by Kenneth Branagh, appeared in 1996.

Besides the sheer number of screen versions, an equally striking fact about Shakespeare on film is the playwright's universal appeal. For example, film adaptations of *Romeo and Juliet* have appeared in Spanish, Arabic, Hindi, French, Russian, Czech, Italian, and Portuguese. An especially popular film of the play in English, directed by Baz Luhrmann and starring Leonardo DiCaprio and Claire Danes, was released in 1995.

Recently, the playwright himself was the subject of a lighthearted film entitled *Shakespeare in Love* (1998). This film, directed by John Madden and starring Joseph Fiennes and Gwyneth Paltrow, speculates about a love affair that may have inspired the dramatist to write *Romeo and Juliet*. The screenplay for the film was co-authored by noted British playwright Tom Stoppard. *Shakespeare in Love* won the Academy Award for Best Picture of 1998.

◆ Literary Works

Poems
- *Venus and Adonis* (1593)
- *The Rape of Lucrece* (1594)
- *Sonnets* (1609)

Drama
History Plays
- *Henry VI* (Parts One, Two, and Three)
- *Richard III*
- Richard II
- *King John*
- *Henry IV* (Parts One and Two)
- *Henry V*

Comedies
- *The Taming of the Shrew*
- *The Comedy of Errors*
- *Love's Labour's Lost*
- *A Midsummer Night's Dream*
- *The Merchant of Venice*
- *As You Like It*
- *Twelfth Night*
- *All's Well That Ends Well*
- *Measure for Measure*

Tragedies
- *Romeo and Juliet*
- *Julius Caesar*
- *Hamlet*
- *Troilus and Cressida*
- *Othello*
- *King Lear*
- *Macbeth*
- *Antony and Cleopatra*
- *Coriolanus*

Romances
- *Pericles*
- *Cymbeline*
- *The Winter's Tale*
- *The Tempest*

William Shakespeare

Sonnet 17

Who will believe my verse in time to come,
If it were fill'd with your most high deserts?
Though yet, heaven knows, it is but as a tomb
Which hides your life and shows not half your parts.
5   If I could write the beauty of your eyes
And in fresh numbers number all your graces,
The age to come would say 'This poet lies;
Such heavenly touches ne'er touch'd earthly faces.'
So should my papers, yellowed with their age,
10   Be scorn'd, like old men of less truth than tongue,
And your true rights be term'd a poet's rage
And stretched metre of an antique song:
     But were some child of yours alive that time,
     You should live twice, in it and in my rhyme.

Sonnet 25

Let those who are in favour with their stars
Of public honour and proud titles boast,
Whilst I, whom fortune of such triumph bars,
Unlook'd for joy in that I honour most.
5   Great princes' favourites their fair leaves spread
But as the marigold at the sun's eye,
And in themselves their pride lies buried,
For at a frown they in their glory die.
The painful warrior famoused for fight,
10   After a thousand victories once foil'd,[1]
Is from the book of honour razed[2] quite,
And all the rest forgot for which he toil'd:
     Then happy I, that love and am beloved
     Where I may not remove nor be removed.

---

1. **foil´d:** Defeated.
2. **razed:** Erased.

Sonnet 65

Since brass, nor stone, nor earth, nor boundless sea
But sad mortality o'er-sways their power,
How with this rage shall beauty hold a plea,
Whose action is no stronger than a flower?
5   O, how shall summer's honey breath hold out
Against the wreckful siege of battering days,
When rocks impregnable[1] are not so stout,
Nor gates of steel so strong, but Time decays?
O fearful meditation! where, alack,
10   Shall Time's best jewel from Time's chest lie hid?
Or what strong hand can hold his swift foot back?
Or who his spoil of beauty can forbid?
      O, none, unless this miracle have might,
      That in black ink my love may still shine bright.

---

1. impregnable (im preg´ nə bəl): Unshakable, firm.

Sonnet 116

Let me not to the marriage of true minds
Admit impediments.[1] Love is not love
Which alters when it alternation finds,
Or bends with the remover to remove:
5   O, no! it is an ever-fixed mark,
That looks on tempests and is never shaken;
It is the star to every wandering bark,
Whose worth's unknown. Although his height be
    taken.
Love's not Time's fool, though rosy lips and cheeks
10   Within his bending sickle's compass come;
Love alters not with his brief hours and weeks,
But bears it out even to the edge of doom.
      If this be error and upon me proved,
      I never writ, nor no man ever loved.

---

1. impediments (im ped´ə mənts): Obstacles, hindrances.

William Shakespeare
Sonnet 130

My mistress' eyes are nothing like the sun;
Coral is far more red than her lips' red:
If snow be white, why then her breasts are dun;
If hairs be wires, black wires grow on her head.
5   I have seen roses damask'd, red and white,
But no such roses see I in her cheeks;
And in some perfumes is there more delight
Than in the breath that from my mistress reeks.
I love to hear her speak; yet well I know
10   That music hath a far more pleasing sound:
I grant I never saw a goddess go,
My mistress, when she walks, treads on the ground:
   And yet, by heaven, I think my love as rare
   As any she belied[1] with false compare.

---

1. **belied** (bē lïd´): Described falsely.

☑ Check Your Comprehension

1. In Sonnet 17, why does the speaker fear that future readers in the "age to come" will not believe him?
2. According to line 13 of Sonnet 25, why is the speaker happy?
3. In Sonnet 65, what are the effects of time?
4. In lines 2–4 of Sonnet 116, how does the speaker define true love?
5. In lines 1–2 of Sonnet 130, what does the speaker say about the eyes and lips of his mistress?

◆ Critical Thinking

INTERPRET

1. According to the speaker in Sonnet 17, how may it be possible for the person addressed in the sonnet to "live twice"? **[Interpret]**

2. In Sonnet 25, what is the speaker's attitude toward princes' favorites and victorious warriors? **[Infer]**
3. (a) In line 9 of Sonnet 65, why do you think the speaker exclaims, "O fearful meditation"? (b) What consoles the speaker in the final couplet? **[Interpret]**
4. What comparisons does the speaker use in lines 5–8 of Sonnet 116 to emphasize his theme about true love? **[Analyze]**
5. How would you describe the tone or attitude of the speaker in lines 11–12 of Sonnet 130? **[Infer]**

William Shakespeare

from Romeo and Juliet

from Act II, Scene viii

In the following scene, Romeo has climbed over the garden wall at the home of the Capulets, his family's most hated enemies. He is hoping to catch sight of Juliet, with whom he has fallen in love. Romeo and Juliet are in danger of discovery throughout the scene.

Enter ROMEO.

ROMEO. He jests at scars that never felt a wound.
Enter JULIET *at a window, above.*

But soft! What light through yonder window breaks?
It is the East, and Juliet is the sun!
Arise, fair sun, and kill the envious moon
5   Who is already sick and pale with grief
That thou her maid art far more fair than she.
Be not her maid since she is envious:
Her vestal livery is but sick and green
And none but fools do wear it. Cast it off.
10   It is my lady! O it is my love!
O that she knew she were!
She speaks yet she says nothing. What of that?
Her eye discourses;[1] I will answer it.
I am too bold; 'tis not to me she speaks.
15   Two of the fairest stars in all the heaven,
Having some business, do entreat her eyes
To twinkle in their spheres till they return.
What if her eyes were there, they in her head?
The brightness of her cheek would shame those stars
20   As daylight doth a lamp; her eyes in heaven
Would through the airy region stream so bright
That birds would sing and think it were not night.
See how she leans her cheek upon her hand!
O that I were a glove upon that hand
25   That I might touch that cheek!

JULIET.   Ay me!

ROMEO.   She speaks.
O speak again bright angel, for thou art
As glorious to this night, being o'er my head,
30   As is a wingèd messenger of heaven

---

1. discourses: Speaks.

Unto the white-upturnèd wond'ring eyes
Of mortals that fall back to gaze on him
When he bestrides the lazy puffing clouds
And sails upon the bosom of the air.

35   **JULIET.** O Romeo, Romeo! Wherefore art thou Romeo?
Deny thy father and refuse thy name
Or, if thou wilt not, be but sworn my love
And I'll no longer be a Capulet.

    ROMEO. *(Aside.)* Shall I hear more or shall I speak at
this?

40   **JULIET.** 'Tis but thy name that is my enemy.
Thou art thyself, though not a Montague.
What's a Montague? It is nor hand, nor foot,
Nor arm, nor face, nor any other part
Belonging to a man. O be some other name!
45   What's in a name? That which we call a rose
By any other word would smell as sweet.
So Romeo would, were he not Romeo called,
Retain that dear perfection which he owes
Without that title. Romeo doff² thy name,
50   And for thy name which is no part of thee
Take all myself.

    ROMEO.   I take thee at thy word.
Call me but love and I'll be new baptized;
Henceforth I never will be Romeo.

55   **JULIET.** What man art thou that, thus bescreened in
night,
So stumblest on my counsel?³

    ROMEO.   By a name
I know not how to tell thee who I am.
My name, dear saint, is hateful to myself
60   Because it is an enemy to thee.
Had I it written, I would tear the word.

    JULIET. My ears have yet not drunk a hundred words
Of thy tongue's uttering yet I know the sound.
Art thou not Romeo and a Montague?

65   **ROMEO.** Neither, fair maid, if either thee dislike.

2. **doff:** Put off; thrust aside.
3. **counsel:** Secret, private thoughts.

JULIET. How camest thou hither, tell me, and where
 fore?[4]
The orchard walls are high and hard to climb
And the place death, considering who thou art,
If any of my kinsmen find thee here.

70 **ROMEO.** With love's light wings did I o'erperch these
 walls
For stony limits cannot hold love out,
And what love can do that dares love attempt,
Therefore thy kinsmen are no stop to me.

JULIET. If they do see thee, they will murder thee.

75 **ROMEO.** Alack, there lies more peril in thine eye
Than twenty of their swords! Look thou but sweet
And I am proof against[5] their enmity.

JULIET. I would not for the world they saw thee here.

ROMEO. I have night's cloak to hide me from their
 eyes,
80 And but thou love me, let them find me here.
My life were better ended by their hate
Than death proroguèd,[6] wanting of thy love.
JULIET. By whose direction found'st thou out this
 place?

ROMEO. By Love that first did prompt me to inquire:
85 He lent me counsel and I lent him eyes.
I am no pilot, yet wert thou as far
As that vast shore washed with the farthest sea,
I should adventure for such merchandise.

JULIET. Thou knowest the mask of night is on my
 face
90 Else would a maiden blush bepaint my cheek
For that which thou hast heard me speak tonight.
Fain[7] would I dwell on form—fain, fain deny
What I have spoke. But farewell compliment!
Dost thou love me? I know thou wilt say "Ay"
95 And I will take thy word. Yet if thou swear'st,

---

4. wherefore: Why.
5. proof against: Invulnerable to.
6. proroguèd: Deferred.
7. Fain: Gladly.

Thou mayst prove false. At lovers' perjuries,
They say Jove laughs. O gentle Romeo,
If thou dost love, pronounce it faithfully.
Or if thou thinkest I am too quickly won,
100   I'll frown and be perverse and say thee nay
So thou wilt woo; but else, not for the world.
In truth, fair Montague, I am too fond
And therefore thou mayst think my havior[8] light,
But trust me, gentleman, I'll prove more true
105   Than those that have more cunning to be strange.
I should have been more strange, I must confess,
But that thou overheard'st, ere I was ware,
My truelove passion. Therefore pardon me
And not impute this yielding to light love
110   Which the dark night hath so discoverèd.

    ROMEO. Lady, by yonder blessèd moon I vow,
That tips with silver all these fruit-tree tops—

    JULIET. O swear not by the moon, th' inconstant moon
That monthly changes in her circled orb,
115   Lest that thy love prove likewise variable.

    ROMEO. What shall I swear by?

    JULIET.   Do not swear at all;
Or if thou wilt, swear by thy gracious self
Which is the god of my idolatry,
120   And I'll believe thee.

    ROMEO.   If my heart's dear love—

    JULIET. Well, do not swear. Although I joy in thee,
I have no joy of this contract tonight.
It is too rash, too unadvised, too sudden,
125   Too like the lightning which doth cease to be
Ere one can say it lightens. Sweet, good night!
This bud of love, by summer's ripening breath,
May prove a beauteous flow'r when next we meet.
Good night, good night! As sweet repose and rest
130   Come to thy heart as that within my breast!

    ROMEO. O wilt thou leave me so unsatisfied?

---

8. havior: Behavior.

JULIET. What satisfaction canst thou have tonight?

ROMEO. Th' exchange of thy love's faithful vow for
mine.

JULIET. I gave thee mine before thou didst request it;
135   And yet I would it were to give again.

ROMEO. Wouldst thou withdraw it? For what purpose,
love?

JULIET. But to be frank and give it thee again.
And yet I wish but for the thing I have:
My bounty is as boundless as the sea,
140   My love as deep; the more I give to thee,
The more I have, for both are infinite.
I hear some noise within. Dear love, adieu!
       (NURSE *calls from within.*)
Anon, good nurse! Sweet Montague, be true
Stay but a little, I will come again.
       Exit.

145   **ROMEO.** O blessèd, blessèd night! I am afeard,
Being in night, all this is but a dream,
Too flattering-sweet to be substantial.
       Enter JULIET *again.*

JULIET. Three words, dear Romeo, and good night
indeed.
If that thy bent⁹ of love be honorable,
150   Thy purpose marriage, send me word tomorrow,
By one that I'll procure to come to thee,
Where and what time thou wilt perform the rite
And all my fortunes at thy foot I'll lay
And follow thee my lord throughout the world.
       (NURSE *Within.* Madam!)

155   **JULIET.** I come anon.—But if thou meanest not well,
I do beseech thee—
       (NURSE *Within.* Madam!)

JULIET.   By and by I come.—
To cease thy strife and leave me to my grief.
Tomorrow will I send.

---

9. bent: Aim; force.

160   **ROMEO.** So thrive my soul—

     JULIET. A thousand times good night!
         Exit.

     ROMEO. A thousand times the worse, to want thy
         light!
     Love goes toward love as schoolboys from their books
     But love from love, toward school with heavy looks.
         Enter JULIET *again.*

165   **JULIET.** Hist! Romeo, hist! O for a falc'ner's voice
     To lure this tassel gentle[10] back again!
     Bondage is hoarse[11] and may not speak aloud,
     Else would I tear the cave where Echo lies
     And make her airy tongue more hoarse than mine
170   With repetition of "My Romeo!"

     ROMEO. It is my soul that calls upon my name.
     How silver-sweet sound lovers' tongues by night,
     Like softest music to attending ears!

     JULIET. Romeo!

175   **ROMEO.**   My sweet?

     JULIET.   What o'clock tomorrow
     Shall I send to thee?

     ROMEO.   By the hour of nine.

     JULIET. I will not fail. 'Tis twenty years till then.
180   I have forgot why I did call thee back.

     ROMEO. Let me stand here till thou remember it.

     JULIET. I shall forget, to have thee still stand there,
     Rememb'ring how I love thy company.

     ROMEO. And I'll still stay to have thee still forget,
185   Forgetting any other home but this.

     JULIET. 'Tis almost morning: I would have thee
         gone—

---

10. **tassel gentle:** Male peregrine falcon.
11. **Bondage is hoarse:** I am watched and can only whisper.

And yet no farther than a wanton's[12] bird,
That lets it hop a little from his hand
Like a poor prisoner in his twisted gyves,[13]
190 And with a silken thread plucks it back again,
So loving-jealous of his liberty.

ROMEO. I would I were thy bird.

JULIET.   Sweet, so would I,
Yet I should kill thee with much cherishing.
195 Good night, good night! Parting is such sweet sorrow
That I shall say good night till it be morrow.
      Exit.

ROMEO. Sleep dwell upon thine eyes, peace in thy
      breast!
Would I were sleep and peace, so sweet to rest!
200 Hence will I to my ghostly friar's close cell,
His help to crave and my dear hap[14] to tell.
      Exit.

---

12. wanton's: Playful child's.
13. gyves: Fetters.
14. dear hap: Good fortune.

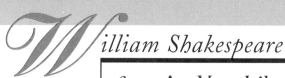

from As You Like It

Act III, Scene ii

Rosalind and Orlando had briefly met at court, fall-en in love and were then separately banished. Both independently sought refuge in the Forest of Arden. Rosalind, in order to avoid being robbed or terrorized, has taken on the disguise of a swashbuckling young man named Ganymede. She and Orlando now meet in the Forest, where Orlando has been hanging poems in praise of Rosalind on trees. Rosalind had escaped to the Forest with her cousin Celia, who observes this scene but takes no active part. Rosalind's first line is addressed to her.

ROSALIND. I will speak to him like a saucy lackey and under that habit[1] play the knave[2] with him. Do you hear, forester?

ORLANDO. Very well, What would you?

5   **ROSALIND.** I pray you, what is't o'clock?

ORLANDO. You should ask me what time o' day; there's no clock in the forest.

ROSALIND. Then there is no true lover in the forest, else sighing every minute and groaning every hour

10   would detect the lazy foot of Time as well as a clock.

ORLANDO And why not the swift foot of Time? Had not that been as proper?

ROSALIND. By no means, sir. Time travels in divers paces with divers persons. I'll tell you who Time

15   ambles withal, who Time trots withal, who Time gallops withal and who he stands still withal.

ORLANDO. I prithee, who doth he trot withal?

ROSALIND. Marry, he trots hard with a young maid between the contract of her marriage and the day it

---

1. **habit:** Guise, behavior.
2. **play the knave:** Trick him; pretend to be a young man.

20   is solemnized. If the interim be but a se'nnight,
Time's pace is so hard that it seems the length of
seven year.

     ORLANDO. Who ambles Time withal?

     ROSALIND. With a priest that lacks Latin and a rich
25   man that hath not the gout; for the one sleeps easily
because he cannot study and the other lives merrily
because he feels no pain; the one lacking the burden
of lean and wasteful learning, the other knowing no
burden of heavy tedious penury. These Time ambles
30   withal.

     ORLANDO. Who doth he gallop withal?

     ROSALIND. With a thief to the gallows, for though he
go as softly as foot can fall, he thinks himself too
soon there.

35   **ORLANDO.** Who stays it still withal?

     ROSALIND. With lawyers in the vacation, for they sleep
between term and term and then they perceive not
how time moves.

     ORLANDO. Where dwell you, pretty youth?

40   **ROSALIND.** With this shepherdess my sister, here in
the skirts of the forest, like fringe upon a petticoat.

     ORLANDO. Are you native of this place?

     ROSALIND. As the cony[3] that you see swell where she
is kindled.

45   **ORLANDO.** Your accent is something finer than you
could purchase in so removed a dwelling.

     ROSALIND. I have been told so of many. But indeed an
old religious uncle of mine taught me to speak who
was in his youth an inland[4] man, one that knew
50   courtship too well for there he fell in love. I have
heard him read many lectures against it and I thank

---

3. **cony:** Rabbit.
4. **inland:** Living close to the center of affairs.

God I am not a woman, to be touched with so many giddy offenses as he hath generally taxed their whole sex withal.

55   **ORLANDO.** Can you remember any of the principal evils that he laid to the charge of women?

ROSALIND. There were none principal. They were all like one another as halfpence are, every one fault seeming monstrous till his fellow fault came to
60   match it.

ORLANDO. I prithee recount some of them.

ROSALIND. No, I will not cast away my physic[5] but on those that are sick. There is a man haunts the forest that abuses our young plants with carving "Rosalind"
65   on their barks, hangs odes upon hawthorns and elegies on brambles, all, forsooth, deifying the name of Rosalind. If I could meet that fancy-monger, I would give him some good counsel for he seems to have the quotidian[6] of love upon him.

70   **ORLANDO.** I am he that is so love-shaked. I pray you tell me your remedy.

ROSALIND. There is none of my uncle's marks upon you. He taught me how to know a man in love, in which cage of rushes[7] I am sure you are not prisoner.

75   **ORLANDO.** What were his marks?

ROSALIND. A lean cheek which you have not, a blue eye and sunken which you have not, an unquestionable spirit which you have not, a beard neglected which you have not—but I pardon you for that, for
80   simply your having in beard is a younger brother's revenue.[8] Then your hose should be ungartered, your bonnet unbanded, your sleeve unbuttoned, your shoe untied and everything about you demonstrating a careless desolation. But you are no such man: you are

---

5. physic: Healing arts.
6. quotidian: Fever of daily recurrence accompanied by shivering.
7. cage of rushes: A prison easy to break out from.
8. younger brother's revenue: Small portion.

85   rather point-device[9] in your accouterments, as loving
      yourself than seeming the lover of any other.

      ORLANDO. Fair youth, I would I could make thee believe I
      love.

      ROSALIND. Me believe it? You may as soon make her that
90   you love believe it, which I warrant she is apter to do
      than to confess she does; that is one of the points in the
      which women still give the lie to their consciences. But
      in good sooth, are you he that hangs the verses on the
      trees wherein Rosalind is so admired?

95   **ORLANDO.** I swear to thee, youth, by the white hand of
      Rosalind, I am that he, that unfortunate he.

      ROSALIND. But are you so much in love as your rhymes
      speak?

100   **ORLANDO.** Neither rhyme nor reason can express how
      much.

      ROSALIND. Love is merely a madness and, I tell you,
      deserves as well a dark house and a whip as madmen
      do, and the reason why they are not so punished and
      cured is that the lunacy is so ordinary that the whippers
105   are in love too. Yet I profess curing it by counsel.

      ORLANDO. Did you ever cure any so?

      ROSALIND. Yes, one, and in this manner: he was to imag-
      ine me his love, his mistress, and I set him every day to
      woo me. At which time would I, being but a moonish[10]
110   youth, grieve, be effeminate, changeable, longing and lik-
      ing, proud, fantastical, apish, shallow, inconstant, full of
      tears, full of smiles; for every passion something and for
      no passion truly anything, as boys and women are for
      the most part cattle of this color; would now like him,
115   now loathe him; then entertain him, then forswear him;
      now weep for him, then spit at him; that I drave my suit-
      or from his mad humor of love to a living humor of mad-
      ness which was to forswear the full stream of the world
120   and to live in a nook merely monastic and thus I cured
      him and this way will I take upon me to wash your liver

---

9. point-device: In perfect order.
10. moonish: Changeable.

as clean as a sound sheep's heart, that there shall not
be one spot of love in't.

ORLANDO. I would not be cured, youth.

125   **ROSALIND.** I would cure you if you would but call me
Rosalind and come every day to my cote[11] and woo me.

ORLANDO. Now by the faith of my love, I will. Tell me
where it is.

130   **ROSALIND.** Go with me to it and I'll show it you, and by
the way you shall tell me where in the forest you live.
Will you go?

ORLANDO. With all my heart, good youth.

ROSALIND. Nay, you must call me Rosalind.
     Exeunt.

---

11. **cote:** Cottage.

☑   **Check Your Comprehension**

1. In the scene from *Romeo and Juliet,* why does Juliet wish that Romeo had a different name?
2. After the lovers' exchange of vows, what does Juliet ask Romeo to do the following morning?
3. Who calls Juliet from indoors?
4. In the scene from *As You Like It,* what examples does Rosalind use to support her statement that time ambles, trots, gallops, and stands still?
5. What method does Rosalind tell Orlando that she once used to cure a person suffering from the madness of love?

◆ **Critical Thinking**

INTERPRET

1. In *Romeo and Juliet,* how does Romeo react when Juliet tells him that her kinsmen will kill him if they discover him? **[Interpret]**

2. (a) In her speech at lines 85–106, what problem does Juliet consider? (b) How does she resolve this problem? **[Analyze]**
3. (a) What reason does Juliet give for re-entering the scene at line 157? (b) Is this her real reason, in your opinion? **[Analyze/Speculate]**
4. In *As You Like It,* what do you think that Rosalind's comments about time suggest about her personality? **[Infer]**
5. In dramatic irony, there is a contradiction between what a character thinks and what the reader or audience knows to be true. How does the scene from *As You Like It* illustrate dramatic irony? **[Analyze]**

COMPARE LITERARY WORKS

6. The situations in these scenes both involve romantic love. How would you compare and contrast the outlook toward love in the scenes? **[Compare and Contrast]**

illiam Shakespeare

from A Midsummer Night's Dream

from Act III, Scene ii

*In the following excerpt, Helena is upset because
she thinks Hermia has betrayed their long friendship
by getting involved in a conspiracy to embarrass her.*

HELENA. Lo, she is one of this confederacy![1]
Now I perceive they have conjoined all three
To fashion this false sport, in spite of me.
Injurious Hermia, most ungrateful maid!
5   Have you conspired, have you with these contrived[2]
To bait me with this foul derision?
Is all the counsel[3] that we two have shared—
The sisters' vows, the hours that we have spent
When we have chid the hasty-footed time
10   For parting us—O, is all forgot?
All schooldays' friendship, childhood innocence?
We, Hermia, like two artificial gods
Have with our needles created both one flower,
Both on one sampler, sitting on one cushion,
15   Both warbling of one song, both in one key,
As if our hands, our sides, voices, and minds
Had been incorporate. So we grew together,
Like to a double cherry, seeming parted,
But yet an union in partition,
20   Two lovely berries molded on one stem;
So, with two seeming bodies but one heart,
Two of the first, like coats in heraldry,[4]
Due but to one and crowned with one crest.
And will you rend our ancient love asunder,[5]
25   To join with men in scorning your poor friend?
It is not friendly, 'tis not maidenly.
Our sex, as well as I, may chide you for it,
Though I alone do feel the injury.

---

1. **confederacy** (kən fed´ ər ə sē): Alliance.
2. **contrived** (kən trīv´d´): Plotted
3. **counsel:** Confidential talk.
4. **coats in heraldry:** Coats of arms.
5. **asunder** (ə sun´ dər): Apart.

William Shakespeare

from Hamlet

from Act I, Scene iii

*In the following excerpt, Polonius, counselor to the
King of Denmark, offers advice to his son, Laertes,
before he leaves to travel abroad.*

POLONIUS. Yet here, Laertes? Aboard, aboard, for
    shame!
The wind sits in the shoulder of your sail,
And you are stayed for.[1] There—my blessing with
    thee!
And these few precepts[2] in thy memory

5   Look thou character. Give thy thoughts no tongue,
Nor any unproportioned thought his act.
Be thou familiar, but by no means vulgar.
Those friends thou hast, and their adoption tried,[3]
Grapple them unto thy soul with hoops of steel,

10   But do not dull thy palm[4] with entertainment
Of each new-hatched, unfledged courage. Beware
Of entrance to a quarrel, but being in,
Bear 't that th' opposed may beware of thee.
Give every man thy ear, but few thy voice;

15   Take each man's censure, but reserve thy judgment.
Costly thy habit[5] as thy purse can buy,
But not expressed in fancy; right, not gaudy,
For the apparel oft proclaims the man,
And they in France of the best rank and station

20   Are of a most select and generous chief in that.
Neither a borrower nor a lender be,
For loan oft loses both itself and friend.
And borrowing dulleth edge of husbandry.[6]
This above all: to thine own self be true,

25   And it must follow, as the night the day,
Thou canst not then be false to any man.
Farewell. My blessing season this in thee!

---

1. **stayed for:** Waited for.
2. **precepts:** Teachings, guidelines.
3. **their adoption tried:** Their suitability tested.
4. **dull thy palm:** Shake hands so often as to make the gesture meaningless.
5. **habit:** Clothes.
6. **husbandry:** Thriftiness.

☑ Check Your Comprehension

1. In *A Midsummer Night's Dream,* why is Helena upset with Hermia?
2. According to Helena, how did she and Hermia grow up?
3. At the beginning of his monologue in *Hamlet,* why is Polonius upset with Laertes?
4. What advice does Polonius give his son on the subject of friendship?

◆ Critical Thinking

INTERPRET

1. Identify three images used by Helena to describe her past relationship with Hermia. **[Analyze]**

2. What two reasons does Polonius give for his advice, "Neither a borrow nor a lender be"? **[Interpret]**
3. What does the monologue as a whole suggest about the character of Polonius? **[Infer]**

Evaluate

4. In *A Midsummer Night's Dream,* what upsets Helena most about Hermia's behavior? **[Evaluate]**

Apply

5. How would you apply the advice "to thine own self be true" to life today? **[Apply]**

William Shakespeare
Comparing and Connecting the Author's Works

♦ Literary Focus: Figurative Language

Figurative Language is writing or speech that is not meant to be taken literally. The following three types of figurative language are especially common:

Simile: use of a key word such as *like* or *as* to make a direct comparison between two unlike ideas. For example, in line 3 of Sonnet 17, the speaker says that his verse is "as a tomb."

Metaphor: a direct identification of two unlike things by speaking of one thing as if it were actually something else. For example, in line 11 of Sonnet 25, the name of a defeated warrior is erased from the "book of honor," which means he has lost the public's admiration.

Personification: giving human characteristics to something nonhuman. For example, Time is said to have a "swift foot" in line 11 of Sonnet 65.

Find at least one additional example of each type of figurative language in the selections you have read. On a separate sheet of paper, copy and label the passages you have chosen.

♦ Drawing Conclusions About Shakespeare's Work

Love and friendship are two of Shakespeare's most important themes in these selections. The sonnets and plays present many different insights about love and friendship. Consider, for example, the speaker's feelings toward the person he praises in Sonnet 17; the consolation offered by love in Sonnet 25; the power of love to defeat time in Sonnet 65; the definition of true love in Sonnet 116; and the praise of the speaker's mistress in Sonnet 130. In the scenes from

Shakespeare's plays, consider the different outlooks on romantic love in *Romeo and Juliet* and *As You Like It*, as well as Polonius' advice to Laertes about friendship in *Hamlet* and Helena's sorrow when she thinks her friend has betrayed her in *A Midsummer Night's Dream*.

In a brief essay, analyze Shakespeare's treatment of love or friendship in two of the selections you have read. You might find it helpful to use the diagram below in order to organize your main ideas and supporting points.

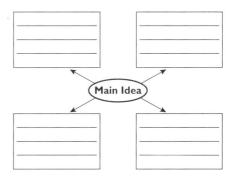

♦ Idea Bank

Writing

1. **Paraphrase** In a paraphrase, you use your own words to restate the major ideas and supporting details of a text. Choose one of Shakespeare's sonnets from the group you have read. Write a paraphrase of this sonnet. When you finish, read your paraphrase to a classmate and then use her or his suggestions to revise your writing.

2. **Plot Summary** Using information from the library or the Internet, write a plot summary of one of the following plays: *Romeo and Juliet, As You Like*

It, Hamlet, or *A Midsummer Night's Dream.* When you have finished, exchange papers with a classmate and review each other's summaries. Which play do you think you would enjoy reading most in its entirety, and why?

3. **Film Review** View a screen adaptation of a Shakespearean play. As you watch, take notes on the acting, the sets and costumes, and the sound track. If possible, compare the adaptation with the original text. Then present your findings and opinions in a film review. **[Media Link]**

Speaking and Listening

4. **Oral Interpretation** Rehearse an oral interpretation of your favorite Shakespearean sonnet. Focus on tone, pacing, volume, and emphasis. When you have polished your interpretation, present it to a small audience of friends, classmates, or family members. **[Performing Arts Link]**

5. **Role Play** Reread the monologues from *Hamlet* and *A Midsummer Night's Dream* carefully. Imagine how Laertes or Hermia might respond to each point made by Polonius and Helena. Then, with a partner, role-play a dialogue from one of the plays in which the pair of characters interact. You can find these dialogues in your school or local library. **[Performing Arts Link]**

Researching and Representing

6. **Set Design** Join with a small group of classmates to design a set for a scene in a Shakespearean play. You may choose one of the scenes from the selections in this book, or you may agree to design the set for another favorite scene. Use drawings, photographs, and, above all, your imagination. When you have finished work, exhibit your set design to the class as a whole. **[Art Link; Group Activity]**

◆ Further Reading, Listening, and Viewing

- Schoenbaum, Samuel. *William Shakespeare: A Documentary Life* (1975). This biography is a highly regarded reference work.

- Wright, Louis B. and Virginia LaMar: *Shakespeare's Sonnets* (1967). This is a complete edition of the sonnets, with notes and summaries.

- Day, Barry: *This Wooden "O": Shakespeare's Globe Reborn* (1998). This book tells the story of the modern re-creation of the Globe Theater in London.

- William Shakespeare: *The Sonnets* (1998). This audiocassette includes recordings of all 154 sonnets.

- William Shakespeare, *Romeo and Juliet* (1968). Franco Zeffirelli directed this highly acclaimed film version of the play.

On the Web:

http://www.phschool.com/atschool/literature
Go to the student edition of *Silver.* Proceed to Unit 8. Then, click Hot Links to find Web sites featuring William Shakespeare.

$\mathcal{E}.\ \mathcal{E}.\ \mathcal{C}$ummings In Depth

"in Just—
spring   when the world is mud-
luscious the little
lame balloonman

whistles   far   and wee"

—*E. E. Cummings*

E. E. CUMMINGS once said that poetry is "the only thing that matters." Cummings's ingenious, daring experiments with the look of poetry on the printed page have insured that his poems can never be mistaken for those of anyone else.

Childhood and Youth   Edward Estlin Cummings was born in Cambridge, Massachusetts, in 1894, the son of a clergyman and professor. While he was still a child, he formed the ambition of becoming a poet and began to practice toward his goal: He wrote a poem a day between the ages of eight and twenty-two.

As a student at Harvard University, Cummings started to experiment with the bold innovations that would mark his poetry throughout his career. He altered conventional syntax and punctuation; he coined new words; he experimented with complex stanza patterns; and—most striking of all—he used new visual patterns on the page to call attention to a poem's rhythm, structure, or theme.

Wartime Service   Cummings graduated from Harvard with honors. In 1917, during World War I, he traveled overseas as a member of a volunteer ambulance corps. Because of some chance comments in Cummings's letters home, French censors suspected him (wrongly) of treason, and Cummings was imprisoned in a detention camp for three months. Later in the war, Cummings was drafted into the United States Army.

Early Career   Cummings published his first book, *The Enormous Room,* in 1922. This work was a fictionalized account of his imprisonment in France during the war. In this book, Cummings stressed the importance and the dignity of the individual in mass society—a theme to which he returned repeatedly throughout his career. For Cummings, the ironic absurdity of being imprisoned by his own side during the war was balanced by the opportunity the episode gave him for contemplation and inner growth.

During the 1920's, Cummings lived in a small apartment in Greenwich Village in New York City. Active as a painter as well as a poet, he enjoyed a period of great creativity in these years, gaining numerous commissions for pictures and publishing four volumes of poetry. These collections were generally well reviewed. "No modern poet to my knowledge," wrote one critic, "has such a clear, childlike perception as E. E. Cummings—a way of coming smack against things with unaffected delight and wonder. This candor . . . results in breathtakingly clean vision." One of Cummings's early biographers commented that the poet's experiments with syntax and punctuation "are best understood as various ways of stripping the film of familiarity from language in order to strip the film of familiarity from the world. Transform the word, he seems to have felt, and you are on the way to transforming the world."

Later Years In 1933, after a journey to Russia (then called the Soviet Union), Cummings published a travel diary entitled *Eimi* (the Greek word for "I am"). In this book, he bitterly attacked the communist dictatorship for what he believed was its dehumanizing repression of the individual.

Over the next twenty years, the style of Cummings's poetry changed very little, and some critics began to question this apparent lack of development. In 1959, however, fellow poet James Dickey praised Cummings as a "daringly original poet, with more vitality and more sheer, uncompromising talent than any other living American writer." Cummings received the Bollingen Prize for poetry, a highly coveted award given by Yale University, in 1957.

The Mystery of Love In 1952, Cummings was chosen to deliver the prestigious Charles Eliot Norton lectures on poetry at Harvard. He later published these lectures in book form with a typically playful title: *i: six nonlectures*. Humor and a zest for life are seldom absent in Cummings's work, and his poetry often celebrates love. Summing up his work in the Harvard lectures, he declared, "I am someone who proudly and humbly affirms that love is the mystery-of-mysteries." Cummings died in North Conway, New Hampshire, in 1962.

◆ Typography

Typography is the art of designing and arranging material printed from type. At first glance, the most distinctive feature of a Cummings poem is its unconventional look on the page. Cummings experimented with many typographical conventions: for example, capitalization (or the lack of it), punctuation, line breaks, hyphenation, and verse breaks. Although these features frequently produce humor and give his poetry an air of playfulness, Cummings's use of graphic design also jolts the reader, often offering new insights into a poem's subject matter and new angles of vision on the poet's themes.

For example, in "spring is like a perhaps hand," the two stanzas contain many repeated words that occur in slightly different positions. The single lines at the end of each stanza—"changing everything carefully" and "without breaking anything"—stand out by contrast with the stanza blocks. Both the structure of the poem and its look on the page reinforce Cummings's main idea about spring: It is a season of gradual but wondrous change and development.

◆ Literary Works

Poetry
- *Tulips and Chimneys* (1923)
- *&* (1925)
- *XLI Poems* (1925)
- *Is 5* (1926)
- *W(ViVa)* (1931)
- *No Thanks* (1935)
- *50 Poems* (1940)
- *1 x 1* (1944)
- *XAIPE: Seventy-One Poems* (1950)

Prose
- *The Enormous Room* (1922)
- *Eimi* (1933)
- *i: six nonlectures* (1953)

Drama
- *Him* (1927)
- *Tom* (1935)
- *Santa Claus* (1946)

Cummings

Spring is like a perhaps hand

Spring is like a perhaps hand
(which comes carefully
out of Nowhere)arranging
a window,into which people look(while
5   people stare
arranging and changing placing
carefully there a strange
thing and a known thing here)and

changing everything carefully

10   spring is like a perhaps
Hand in a window
(carefully to
and fro moving New and
Old things,while
15   people stare carefully
moving a perhaps
fraction of flower here placing
an inch of air there)and

without breaking anything.

r-p-o-p-h-e-s-s-a-g-r

                        r-p-o-p-h-e-s-s-a-g-r
                    who
a)s w(e loo)k
upnowgath
    5   PPEGORHRASS
                          eringint(o-
aThe):l
        eA
          !p:
   10   S   a
                  (r
rlvlnG   .gRrEaPsPhOs)
                             to
rea(be)rran(com)gi(e)ngly
   15   ,grasshopper;

Cummings

if everything happens that can't be done

if everything happens that can't be done
(and anything's righter
than books
could plan)
  5   the stupidest teacher will almost guess
(with a run
skip
around we go yes)
there's nothing as something as one

  10   one hasn't a why or because or although
(and buds know better
than books
don't grow)
one's anything old being everything new
  15   (with a what
which
around we come who)
one's everyanything so

so world is a leaf so tree is a bough
  20   (and birds sing sweeter
than books
tell how)
so here is away and so your is a my
(with a down
  25   up
around again fly)
forever was never till now

now i love you and you love me
(and books are shutter
  30   than books
can be)
and deep in the high that does nothing but fall
(with a shout
each
around we go all)

35   there's somebody calling who's we
       we're anything brighter than even the sun
       (we're everything greater
       than books
       might mean)
40   we're everyanything more than believe
       (with a spin
       leap
       alive we're alive)
       we're wonderful one times one

E. E. Cummings

l(a

l(a

le
af
fa

5   ll

s)
one
l

iness

☑ Check Your Comprehension

1. In "Spring is like a perhaps hand," to what action or process does the speaker compare spring?
2. (a) Who or what is the subject of "r-p-o-p-h-e-s-s-a-g-r"? (b) How do you know?
3. What emotion does the poet celebrate in "if everything happens that can't be done"?
4. How does the shape of "l(a" reflect an event that takes place in the poem?

◆ Critical Thinking

INTERPRET

1. What features of spring do you think Cummings emphasizes in "Spring is like a perhaps hand"? **[Analyze]**

2. In "r-p-o-p-h-e-s-s-a-g-r," Cummings challenges you to play the game of unscrambling the letters. Why might the poet have chosen this way of catching your attention? **[Speculate]**
3. Cummings includes parenthetical material twice in each stanza of "if everything happens that can't be done." (a) In what ways are these parenthetical statements similar? (b) How do the parentheses relate to the poem's theme? **[Analyze/Interpret]**
4. What do you think is Cummings's underlying idea about life and nature in "l(a"? **[Interpret]**

if up's the word;and a world grows greener

if up's the word;and a world grows greener
minute by second and most by more—
if death is the loser and life is the winner
(and beggars are rich but misers are poor)
5   —let's touch the sky:
                with a to and a fro
(and a here there where)and away we go

in even the laziest creature among us
a wisdom no knowledge can kill is astir—
10   now dull eyes are keen and now keen eyes are keener
(for young is the year,for young is the year)
     —let's touch the sky:
                with a great(and a gay
and a steep)deep rush through amazing day

15   it's brains without hearts have set saint against sinner;
put gain over gladness and joy under care—
let's do as an earth which can never do wrong does
(minute by second and most by more)
     —let's touch the sky:
20   with a strange(and a true)
and a climbing fall into far near blue

if beggars are rich(and a robin will sing his
robin a song)but misers are poor—
let's love until noone could quite be(and young is
25   the year,dear)as living as i'm and as you're
     —let's touch the sky:
              with a you and a me
and an every(who's any who's some)one who's we

Cummings

what if a much of a which of a wind

what if a much of a which of a wind
gives the truth to summer's lie;
bloodies with dizzying leaves the sun
and yanks immortal stars awry?
5   Blow king to beggar and queen to seem
(blow friend to fiend:blow space to time)
—when skies are hanged and oceans drowned,
the single secret will still be man

what if a keen of a lean wind flays
10   screaming hills with sleet and snow:
strangles valleys by ropes of thing
and stifles forests in white ago?
Blow hope to terror;blow seeing to blind
(blow pity to envy and soul to mind)
15   —whose hearts are mountains,roots are trees,
it's they shall cry hello to the spring

what if a dawn of a doom of a dream
bites this universe in two,
peels forever out of his grave
20   and sprinkles nowhere with me and you?
Blow soon to never and never to twice
(blow life to isn't:blow death to was)
—all nothing's only our hugest home;
the most who die,the more we live

may my heart always be open to little

may my heart always be open to little
birds who are the secrets of living
whatever they sing is better than to know
and if men should not hear them men are old

5   may my mind stroll about hungry
and fearless and thirsty and supple
and even if it's sunday may i be wrong
for whenever men are right they are not young

and may myself do nothing usefully
10   and love yourself so more than truly
there's never been quite such a fool who could fail
pulling all the sky over him with one smile

the little horse is newlY

the little horse is newlY

Born)he knows nothing,and feels
everything;all around whom is

perfectly a strange
5   ness(Of sun
light and of fragrance and of

Singing)is ev
erywhere(a welcom
ing dream:is amazing)
10   a worlD.and in

this world lies:smoothbeautifuL
ly folded;a(brea
thing and a gro

Wing)silence,who;
15   is:somE

oNe.

1. What does the speaker urge us to do in each stanza of "if up's the word;and a world grows greener"?
2. According to "what if a much of a which of a wind," what will always be the "single secret"?
3. In "may my heart always be open to little," what does the speaker wish (a) for his heart, and (b) for his mind?
4. Identify four examples of untraditional capitalization and punctuation in "the little horse is newlY."

◆ **Critical Thinking**

INTERPRET

1. A paradox is an apparent contradiction that actually presents an underlying truth. What examples of paradox can you find in the first two stanzas of "if up's the word; and a world grows greener"? **[Interpret]**
2. In "what if a much of a which of a wind," what striking sound effects does Cummings use in the first line of each stanza? **[Analyze]**
3. In "may my heart always be open to little," what contrast does the speaker draw between youth and old age? **[Compare and Contrast]**
4. How would you state the poet's underlying theme in "the little horse is newlY"? **[Interpret]**

E. E. Cummings

Comparing and Connecting the Author's Works

◆ **Literary Focus: Rhythm and Meter**

Rhythm is the pattern of beats or stresses in spoken or written language. A poem's rhythmical pattern is called its **meter.** This pattern is determined by the number of stresses, or beats, in each line. Stressed (/) and unstressed (⌣) syllables make up groups called feet. The following patterns are especially common:

Iambic: ⌣/   **Trochaic:** /⌣
Anapestic: ⌣⌣/ **Dactylic:** /⌣⌣

Although E. E. Cummings was most famous for his experiments with the look of poetry on the printed page, he also filled his poems with striking, ingenious rhythms. Sometimes Cummings combines two patterns in a single poem; sometimes he deliberately alters or varies the basic pattern to create emphasis.

1. What two metrical patterns are combined in "if everything happens that can't be done"?
2. (a) In "what if a much of a which of a wind," what patterns can you identify in the first half of each stanza? (b) In the last four lines of each stanza, the metrical pattern is more regular. What is this basic pattern?

◆ **Drawing Conclusions About Cummings's Work**

One way to evaluate a poet's work is to respond to critical opinions. The modern American poet and critic Randall Jarrell offered this appraisal of E. E. Cummings's poetry: "No one else has ever made . . . experimental poems so attractive to the general . . . reader."

Do you agree or disagree? Write a brief essay in which you respond to

Jarrell's evaluation. Begin your essay with an opinion statement, and then support your position with specific quotations from the poems by Cummings in this group. Use a Herringbone Organizer like the one below to organize your thoughts. On the central line of the organizer, write your opinion statement. Then use the lines on the diagonal spines to keep track of specific quotations and details from Cummings's works that support your opinion statement.

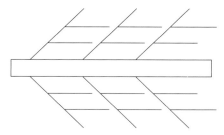

◆ **Idea Bank**

Writing

1. **Retelling a Poem** Cummings employs unusual language in many of his poems. Choose one of the poems in this group to retell in ordinary, conversational prose. In your retelling, be careful to use an appropriate tone and to capture the original essence of the poem.
2. **"What If" Poem** Three poems in this group begin with *if* or *what if*. Write your own "what if" poem, in which you playfully consider an unusual situation or a flight of fancy. If you wish, experiment with capitalization, punctuation, and line breaks in your poem to create emphasis, humor, or other striking effects.

3. **Essay** Write a brief essay in which you compare and contrast these two poems: "if everything happens that can't be done" and "if up's the word; and a world grows greener." In your essay, focus on the structure, rhythm, and theme of these poems. When you have finished, read your essay aloud to a small group of classmates.

Speaking and Listening

4. **Panel Discussion** With a small group of classmates, take turns reading aloud the longer poems in this group. Then hold a panel discussion on the topic of Cummings's use of repetition in his poems. Keep in mind that repetition can be visual and also aural, appealing to both the eye and the ear. **[Group Activity]**

5. **Music for the Seasons** In "Spring is like a perhaps hand," Cummings employs an unusual comparison to express his feelings about the season of spring. Choose a song or short instrumental piece that sums up your feelings about each season of the year. If possible, record your selections on audiocassette and then play them for a small group of classmates. Be prepared to discuss the reasons for your choices. **[Music Link]**

Researching and Representing

6. **Poster** In his poetry, E. E. Cummings often suggested new ways of looking at commonplace objects or processes in the natural world: for example, the movement of a grasshopper or the fall of a leaf. Research a natural process such as the formation of a snowflake, the breaking of an ocean wave, or the budding of a flower. Create a poster that graphically shows the different stages of this process. **[Science Link; Art Link]**

◆ **Further Reading, Listening, and Viewing**

- Cummings, E. E. *Complete Poems, 1904-1962* (1994). This volume contains all the published poetry.

- Cummings, E. E. *CIOPW* (1931). This is a collection of the poet's drawings and paintings in charcoal, ink, oil, pencil, and watercolor.

- Friedman, Norman. *E. E. Cummings: The Growth of a Writer* (1964). Friedman discusses the poems in chronological order.

- Kennedy, Richard S. *Dreams in the Mirror: A Biography of E. E. Cummings* (1979).

- Marks, Barry. *E. E. Cummings* (1963). Marks explores the relationship between Cummings's graphic art and his poetry.

On the Web:

http://www.phschool.com/atschool/literature
Go to the student edition *Silver*. Proceed to Unit 9. Then, click Hot Links to find Web sites featuring E. E. Cummings

Rudolfo Anaya In Depth

> "In a real sense, the mythologies of the Americas are the only mythologies of all of us, whether we are newly arrived or whether we have been here for centuries"
>
> —*Rudolfo Anaya*

RUDOLFO ANAYA celebrates in novels, stories, essays, plays, and poems the legacy of the Mexican American ancestral heritage. In most of his works, he explores the cultural identity of the Chicano people.

Childhood and Youth Anaya was born in the small village of Pastura, New Mexico, in 1937. When he was very young, the family moved to nearby Santa Rosa on the *llano estacado* (the high plains) in the eastern part of the state, where Anaya's father worked as a sheep and cattle rancher. Anaya's deep attachment to nature and natural beauty is rooted in his childhood, as is his fascination with the Mexican and Indian oral tradition. During Anaya's youth, his large family gathered nightly to tell stories, anecdotes, and riddles. "I was always in a milieu (social environment) of words," he recalls, "whether they were printed or in the oral tradition."

A Teaching Career Anaya graduated from Albuquerque High School in 1955 and went on to study business. Switching his major to English, he received a master's degree from the University of New Mexico in 1968. Aspiring to become a writer, he began work on his novel *Bless Me, Ultima* in the mid-1960's. Around this time, Anaya abandoned his efforts to imitate such leading American novelists as William Faulkner, Ernest Hemingway, and John Steinbeck. "I made a simple discovery," he has commented. "I found I needed to write in *my* voice about my characters, using my indigenous symbols." For several years, Anaya taught English at public schools in Albuquerque. He then began to teach creative writing and Chicano literature courses to university students.

The Chicano Movement Anaya's writing is deeply rooted in the Chicano heritage. During the 1960's, together with other writers, artists, and social activists, Anaya pioneered the Chicano Movement. The members of this movement promoted the civil rights, cultural identity, and future of the Chicano people. For many Chicanos, migration from rural communities to the cities after World War II presented a conflict between the pressure to assimilate to mainstream culture and loyalty to traditional cultural values. The Chicano Movement sought to preserve and revitalize the Chicano cultural heritage, as well as to insure workers' rights and to end existing social and economic prejudice.

Bless Me, Ultima Anaya's first novel, which took him nearly seven years to write, was published in 1972. The novel is the story of Antonio Márez, a young boy, who grows up in a small New Mexico village in the 1940's. The novel's title character, Ultima, is a *curandera* (traditional folk healer) who lives with the Márez family. Reviewers admired Anaya's skillful and imaginative handling of setting and of the main character's emotional conflicts. In addition to winning the *Premio Quinto Sol* National Chicano Literature Award, Anaya received national recognition.

Later Career During the 1970's, Anaya published two more novels. In *Heart of Aztlán* (1976), the story focuses on a family that moves from the rural countryside to live in a city. As in much of Anaya's work, the style of this novel combines realism with fantasy and mythology. In *Tortuga* (1979), Anaya dramatizes the year-long ordeal of a young boy who must undergo therapy for paralysis. The thematic similarities of these novels with *Bless Me, Ultima* are striking, and Anaya has said that the three works "are a definite trilogy in my mind."

In 1982, Anaya published *The Silence of the Llano*, a collection of short stories. He has also written an epic poem, *The Adventures of Juan Chicaspatas* (1985), as well as several plays. His most recent works include *Zia Summer* (1995), *Rio Grande Fall* (1996), and *Shaman Winter* (1998).

Commenting some years ago about his writing career, Anaya remarked: "if we as Chicanos do have a distinctive perspective on life, I believe that perspective will be defined when we challenge the very basic questions which mankind has always asked itself: What is my relationship to the universe, the cosmos? Who am I and why I am here?"

◆ Oral Tradition

Oral tradition is the passing of songs, stories, poems, legends, proverbs, riddles, lullabies, and jokes from generation to generation by word of mouth. Folk songs, folk tales, and myths all come from the oral tradition. No one knows who first created these narratives and poems, often told in different versions.

The tradition of Mexican American *cuentos* (stories) has been particularly significant for Rudolfo Anaya. The stories Anaya heard as a child in New Mexico were full of Indian mythology and folklore, overlaid with Spanish and Mexican cultural elements. He says of the storytellers he heard in his youth, "It was the magic of their words and their deep, humble humanity which must have sparked my imagination."

In two of his books, *The Legend of La Llorona* (1984) and *Lord of the Dawn: The Legend of Quetzalcoatl* (1987), Anaya explicitly addresses well-known tales from the oral tradition. He has also co-edited three anthologies of oral materials: *Ceremony of Brotherhood* (1980), *Cuentos: Tales from the Hispanic Southwest* (1980), and *Cuentos Chicanos* (1980, Chicano Stories). He upholds the oral storytelling tradition by telling *cuentos* to his grandchildren, and he has turned some of these stories into children's books.

◆ Literary Works

Novels

The New Mexico Trilogy:
- *Bless Me, Ultima* (1972)
- *Heart of Aztlán* (1976)
- *Tortuga* (1979)

Short Story Collection
- *The Silence of the Llano* (1982)

Nonfiction
- *A Chicano in China* (1986)
- *The Anaya Reader* (1995)

Plays
- *Who Killed Don José?* (1987)
- *The Farolitos of Christmas* (1987)

Rudolfo Anaya

from Bless Me, Ultima

On the first day of school I awoke with a sick feeling in my stomach. It did not hurt, it just made me feel weak. The sun did not sing as it came over the hill. Today I would take the goat path and trek into town for years and years of schooling. For the first time I would be away from the protection of my mother. I was excited and sad about it.

I heard my mother enter her kitchen, her realm in the castle the giants had built. I heard her make the fire grow and sing with the kindling she fed to it.

Then I heard my father groan. "¡Ay Dios, otro día! Another day and more miles of that cursed highway to patch! And for whom? For me that I might travel west! Ay no, that highway is not for the poor man, it is for the tourist—ay, María, we should have gone to California when we were young, when my sons were boys—"

He was sad. The breakfast dishes rattled.

"Today is Antonio's first day at school," she said.

"Huh! Another expense. In California, they say, the land flows with milk and honey—"

"Any land will flow with milk and honey if it is worked with honest hands!" my mother retorted. "Look at what my brothers have done with the bottomland of El Puerto—"

"Ay, mujer[1], always your brothers! On this hill only rocks grow!"

"Ay! And whose fault is it that we bought a worthless hill! No, you couldn't buy fertile land along the river, you had to buy this piece of, of—"

"Of the llano[2]," my father finished.

"Yes!"

"It is beautiful," he said with satisfaction.

"It is worthless! Look how hard we worked on the garden all summer, and for what? Two baskets of chile and one of corn! Bah!"

"There is freedom here."

"Try putting that in the lunch pails of your children!"

"Tony goes to school today, huh?" he said.

"Yes. And you must talk to him."

"He will be all right."

"He must know the value of his education," she insisted. "He must know what he can become."

---

1. *mujer* (mū hār´): Woman, wife.
2. *llano* (ya' nō): Grassy, treeless plain.

"A priest."

"Yes."

"For your brothers." His voice was cold.

"You leave my brothers out of this! They are honorable men. They have always treated you with respect. They were the first colonizers of the Llano Estacado. It was the Lunas who carried the charter from the Mexican government to settle the valley. That took courage—"

"Led by the priest," my father interrupted. I listened intently. I did not yet know the full story of the first Luna priest.

"What? What did you say? Do not dare to mention blasphemy where the children can hear, Gabriel Márez!" She scolded him and chased him out of the kitchen. "Go feed the animals! Give Tony a few minutes extra sleep!" I heard him laugh as he went out.

"My poor baby," she whispered, and then I heard her praying. I heard Deborah and Theresa getting up. They were excited about school because they had already been there. They dressed and ran downstairs to wash.

I heard Ultima enter the kitchen. She said good morning to my mother and turned to help prepare breakfast. Her sound in the kitchen gave me the courage I needed to leap out of bed and into the freshly pressed clothes my mother had readied for me. The new shoes felt strange to feet that had run bare for almost seven years.

"Ay! My man of learning!" my mother smiled when I entered the kitchen. She swept me in her arms and before I knew it she was crying on my shoulder. "My baby will be gone today," she sobbed.

"He will be all right," Ultima said. "The sons must leave the sides of their mothers," she said almost sternly and pulled my mother gently.

"Yes, Grande[3]," my mother nodded, "it's just that he is so small—the last one to leave me—" I thought she would cry all over again. "Go and wash, and comb," she said simply.

I scrubbed my face until it was red. I wet my black hair and combed it. I looked at my dark face in the mirror.

Jasón had said there were secrets in the letters. What did he mean?

"Antoniooooo! Come and eat."

"Tony goes to school, Tony goes to school!" Theresa cried.

"Hush! He shall be a scholar," my mother smiled and served me first. I tried to eat but the food stuck to the roof of my mouth.

"Remember you are a Luna—"

---

3. *Grande* (gran' dā): Term of respect for a wise, older person.

"And a Márez," my father interrupted her. He came in from feeding the animals.

Deborah and Theresa sat aside and divided the school supplies they had bought in town the day before. Each got a Red Chief tablet, crayons, and pencils, I got nothing. "We are ready, mamá!" they cried.

Jasón had said look at the letter carefully, draw it on the tablet, or on the sand of the playground. You will see, it has magic.

"You are to bring honor to your family," my mother cautioned. "Do nothing that will bring disrespect on our good name."

I looked at Ultima. Her magic. The magic of Jasón's Indian. They could not save me now.

"Go immediately to Miss Maestas. Tell her you are my boy. She knows my family. Hasn't she taught them all? Deborah, take him to Miss Maestas."

"Gosh, okay, let's go!"

"Ay! What good does an education do them," my father filled his coffee cup, "they only learn to speak like Indians. Gosh, okay, what kind of words are those?'

"An education will make him a scholar, like—like the old Luna priest."

"A scholar already, on his first day of school!"

"Yes!" my mother retorted. "You know the signs at his birth were good. You remember, Grande, you offered him all the objects of life when he was just a baby, and what did he choose, the pen and the paper—"

"True," Ultima agreed.

"¡Bueno!⁴ ¡Bueno!" my father gave in to them. "If that is what he is to be then it is so. A man cannot struggle against his own fate. In my own day we were given no schooling. Only the ricos⁵ could afford school. Me, my father gave me a saddle blanket and a wild pony when I was ten. There is your life, he said, and he pointed to the llano. So the llano was my school, it was my teacher, it was my first love—"

"It is time to go, mamá," Deborah interrupted.

"Ay, but those were beautiful years," my father continued.

"The llano was still virgin, there was grass as high as the stirrups of a grown horse, there was rain—and then the tejano⁶ came and built his fences, the railroad came, the roads—it was like a bad wave of the ocean covering all that was good—"

"Yes, it is time, Gabriel," my mother said, and I noticed she touched him gently.

---

4. **Bueno!** (bwā´ nō): Good!
5. **ricos** (rē´ kōs): Rich people.
6. **Tejano** (tay ha´ nō): Texan of Mexican descent.

"Yes," my father answered, "so it is. Be respectful to your teachers," he said to us. "And you, Antonio," he smiled, "suerte[7]." It made me feel good. Like a man.

"Wait!" My mother held Deborah and Theresa back, "we must have a blessing. Grande, please bless my children." She made us kneel with her in front of Ultima. "And especially bless my Antonio, that all may go well for him and that he may be a man of great learning—"

Even my father knelt for the blessing. Huddled in the kitchen we bowed our heads. There was no sound.

"En el nombre del Padre, del Hijo, y el Espíritu Santo—[8]"

I felt Ultima's hand on my head and at the same time I felt a great force, like a whirlwind, swirl about me. I looked up in fright, thinking the wind would knock me off my knees. Ultima's bright eyes held me still.

In the summer the dust devils of the llano are numerous. They come from nowhere, made by the heat of hell they carry with them the evil spirit of a devil, they lift sand and papers in their path. It is bad luck to let one of these small whirlwinds strike you. But it is easy to ward off the dust devil, it is easy to make it change its path and skirt around you. The power of God is so great. All you have to do is to lift up your right hand and cross your right thumb over your first finger in the form of the cross. No evil can challenge that cross, and the swirling dust with the devil inside must turn away from you.

Once I did not make the sign of the cross on purpose. I challenged the wind to strike me. The twister struck with such force that it knocked me off my feet and left me trembling on the ground. I had never felt such fear before, because as the whirlwind blew its debris around me the gushing wind seemed to call my name:

Antonioooooooooooooooo. . .

Then it was gone, and its evil was left imprinted on my soul.

"¡Antonio!"

"What?"

"Do you feel well? Are you all right?" It was my mother speaking.

But how could the blessing of Ultima be like the whirlwind? Was the power of good and evil the same?

"You may stand up now." My mother helped me to my feet. Deborah and Theresa were already out the door. The blessing was done. I stumbled to my feet, picked up my sack lunch, and started towards the door.

"Tell me, Grande, please," my mother begged.

"María!" my father said sternly.

---

7. **suerte** (sū ar̃′ tā): Luck.
8. **En el nombre . . . Santo**: In the name of the Father, Son, and Holy Spirit.

"Oh, please tell me what my son will be," my mother glanced anxiously from me to Ultima.

"He will be a man of learning," Ultima said sadly.

"¡Madre de Dios!"[9] my mother cried and crossed herself. She turned to me and shouted, "Go! Go!"

I looked at the three of them standing there, and I felt that I was seeing them for the last time: Ultima in her wisdom, my mother in her dream, and my father in his rebellion.

"¡Adios!" I cried and ran out. I followed the two shegoats hopping up the path ahead of me. They sang and I brayed into the morning air, and the pebbles of the path rang as we raced with time towards the bridge. Behind me I heard my mother cry my name.

At the big juniper tree where the hill sloped to the bridge I heard Ultima's owl sing. I knew it was her owl because it was singing in daylight. High at the top by a clump of the ripe blue berries of the juniper I saw it. Its bright eyes looked down on me and it cried, whoooo, whoooo. I took confidence from its song, and wiping the tears from my eyes I raced towards the bridge, the link to town.

I was almost halfway across the bridge when someone called "Race!" I turned and saw a small, thin figure start racing towards me from the far end of the bridge. I recognized the Vitamin Kid.

Race? He was crazy! I was almost half way across. "Race!" I called, and ran. I found out that morning that no one had ever beaten the Vitamin Kid across the bridge, his bridge. I was a good runner and I ran as hard as I could, but just before I reached the other side the clatter of hoofbeats passed me by, the Kid smiled a "Hi Tony," and snorting and leaving a trail of saliva threads in the air, he was gone.

No one knew the Vitamin Kid's real name, no one knew where he lived. He seemed older than the rest of the kids he went to school with. He never stopped long enough to talk, he was always on the run, a blur of speed.

I walked slowly after I crossed the bridge, partly because I was tired and partly because of the dread of school. I walked past Rosie's house, turned, and passed in front of the Longhorn Saloon. When I got to Main Street I was astounded. It seemed as if a million kids were shoutingruntingpushingcrying their way to school. For a long time I was held hypnotized by the thundering herd, then with a cry of resolution exploding from my throat I rushed into the melee.

Somehow I got to the schoolgrounds, but I was lost. The school was larger than I had expected. Its huge, yawning doors were menacing. I looked for Deborah and Theresa, but every face

---

9. ***Madre de Dios!:*** (ma drä de dē ōs): Spanish exclamation meaning "Mother of God!"

I saw was strange. I looked again at the doors of the sacred halls but I was too afraid to enter. My mother had said to go to Miss Maestas, but I did not know where to begin to find her. I had come to the town, and I had come to school, and I was very lost and afraid in the nervous, excited swarm of kids.

It was then that I felt a hand on my shoulder. I turned and looked into the eyes of a strange red-haired boy. He spoke English, a foreign tongue.

"First grade," was all I could answer. He smiled and took my hand, and with him I entered school. The building was cavernous and dark. It had strange, unfamiliar smells and sounds that seemed to gurgle from its belly. There was a big hall and many rooms, and many mothers with children passed in and out of the rooms.

I wished for my mother, but I put away the thought because I knew I was expected to become a man. A radiator snapped with steam and I jumped. The red-haired boy laughed and led me into one of the rooms. This room was brighter than the hall. So it was like this that I entered school.

Miss Maestas was a kind woman. She thanked the boy whose name was Red for bringing me in then asked my name. I told her I did not speak English.

"¿Cómo te llamas?"[10] she asked.

"Antonio Márez," I replied. I told her my mother said I should see her, and that my mother sent her regards.

She smiled. "Anthony Márez," she wrote in a book. I drew closer to look at the letters formed by her pen. "Do you want to learn to write?" she asked.

"Yes," I answered.

"Good," she smiled.

I wanted to ask her immediately about the magic in the letters, but that would be rude and so I was quiet. I was fascinated by the black letters that formed on the paper and made my name. Miss Maestas gave me a crayon and some paper and I sat in the corner and worked at copying my name over and over. She was very busy the rest of the day with the other children that came to the room. Many cried when their mothers left, and one wet his pants. I sat in my corner alone and wrote. By noon I could write my name, and when Miss Maestas discovered that she was very pleased.

She took me to the front of the room and spoke to the other boys and girls. She pointed at me but I did not understand her. Then the other boys and girls laughed and pointed to me. I did not feel so good. Thereafter I kept away from the groups as much

10. *Como te llamas?*: (cō′ mō tā ya′ mas) What's your name?

as I could and worked alone. I worked hard. I listened to the strange sounds. I learned new names, new words.

At noon we opened our lunches to eat. Miss Maestas left the room and a high school girl came and sat at the desk while we ate. My mother had packed a small jar of hot beans and some good, green chile wrapped in tortillas. When the other children saw my lunch they laughed and pointed again. Even the high school girl laughed. They showed me their sandwiches which were made of bread. Again I did not feel well.

I gathered my lunch and slipped out of the room. The strangeness of the school and the other children made me very sad. I did not understand them. I sneaked around the back of the school building, and standing against the wall I tried to eat. But I couldn't. A huge lump seemed to form in my throat and tears came to my eyes. I yearned for my mother, and at the same time I understood that she had sent me to this place where I was an outcast. I had tried hard to learn and they had laughed at me, I had opened my lunch to eat and again they had laughed and pointed at me.

The pain and sadness seemed to spread to my soul, and I felt for the first time what the grown-ups call, la tristeza de la vida.[11] I wanted to run away, to hide, to run and never come back, never see anyone again. But I knew that if I did I would shame my family name, that my mother's dream would crumble. I knew I had to grow up and be a man, but oh it was so very hard.

But no, I was not alone. Down the wall near the corner I saw two other boys who had sneaked out of the room. They were George and Willy. They were big boys, I knew they were from the farms of Delia. We banded together and in our union found strength. We found a few others who were like us, different in language and custom, and a part of our loneliness was gone. When the winter set in we moved into the auditorium and there, although many a meal was eaten in complete silence, we felt we belonged. We struggled against the feeling of loneliness that gnawed at our souls and we overcame it; that feeling I never shared again with anyone, not even with Horse and Bones, or the Kid and Samuel, or Cico or Jasón.

---

11. *la tristeza de la vida* (la triss tā´ sa de la vē´ da): The sadness or sorrow of life.

☑ Check Your Comprehension

1. Why is the day on which the story is set important for Antonio?
2. What career does Antonio's mother hope that her son will follow?
3. (a) What does Antonio feel as Ultima blesses him? (b) What does he hear on the way to school?
4. (a) What does Antonio find that he can do by noon? (b) Why does he feel lonely at lunch time? (c) Who gives him strength?

◆ Critical Thinking

1. What are two details that hint at conflict between Antonio's mother and father? **[Support]**
2. How do the family regard Ultima? **[Interpret]**
3. (a) What are two reasons that Antonio feels lonely and apprehensive at school? (b) How does he overcome these feelings? **[Analyze]**
4. Rudolfo Anaya often includes elements of folklore in his writing. What passage in the story shows the influence of folklore? How do you know? **[Interpret]**

Rudolfo Anaya

from Take Tortillas Out of Poetry

In a recent lecture, "Is Nothing Sacred?," Salman Rushdie[1], one of the most censored authors of our time, talked about the importance of books. He grew up in a household in India where books were as sacred as bread. If anyone in the household dropped a piece of bread or a book, the person not only picked up the piece of bread or the book but also kissed the object by way of apologizing for clumsy disrespect.

He goes on to say that he had kissed many books before he had kissed a girl. Bread and books were for his household, and for many like his, food for the body and the soul. This image of the kissing of the book one has accidentally dropped made an impression on me. It speaks to the love and respect many people have for books.

I grew up in a small town in New Mexico, and we had very few books in our household. The first book I remember reading was my catechism book.[2] Before I went to school to learn English, my mother taught me catechism in Spanish. I remember the questions and the answers I had to learn, and I remember the well-thumbed, frayed book that was sacred to me.

Growing up with few books in the house created in me a desire and need for books. When I started school, I remember visiting the one-room library of our town and standing in front of the dusty shelves lined with books. In reality, there were only a few shelves and not over a thousand books, but I wanted to read them all. There was food for my soul in the books, that much I realized.

As a child I listened to the stories of the people, the cuentos the old ones told. Those stories were my first contact with the magic of storytelling. Those stories fed my imagination, and later, when I wrote books, I found the same sense of magic and mystery in writing.

In *Bless Me, Ultima*, my first novel, Antonio, my main character, who has just started to school, sees in books the power of the written word. He calls books the "magic of words."

For me, reading has always been a path toward liberation and fulfillment. To learn to read is to start down the road of liberation. It is a road that should be accessible to everyone. No one has the right to keep you from reading, and yet that is what is

---

1. **Salman Rushdie:** Contemporary British author, born in Bombay, India.
2. **catechism book:** Handbook of questions and answers for teaching the principles of a religion.

happening in many areas in this country today. There are those who think they know best what we should read. These censors are at work in all areas of our daily lives.

Censorship has affected me directly, and I have formed some ideas on this insidious activity, but first, I want to give an example of censorship which recently affected a friend of mine. My friend is a Chicano poet and scholar, one of the finest I know. For some time I have been encouraging Chicano writers to apply for the National Endowment for the Arts literary fellowships.[3] A number of poets who use Spanish and English in their poetry applied but did not receive fellowships; they were so discouraged they did not reapply. This happened to my friend. He is an excellent poet, mature, intelligent, and he has an impressive academic background. He knew that when you apply for a fellowship you take your chances, so he did not give up after being turned down twice. He also knew, we all knew, that many of the panels that judged the manuscripts did not have readers who could read Spanish or bilingual manuscripts. In other words, the judges could not read the poetic language that expresses our reality. My friend rightfully deduced that his poetry was not receiving a fair reading.

"You know," he told me, "if they can't read my bilingual poetry, next time I apply I'm sending them only poems I write in English. My best poetry is bilingual, it reflects our reality, it's the way we speak, the way we are. But if I stand a better chance at getting a fellowship in English, I'll send that. But the poems I write only in English are really not my best work. It's just not me."

I was dismayed by my friend's conclusion. How he coped with the problem has tremendous cultural implications. It has implications that we may call self-imposed censorship. My friend was censoring his creativity in order to fit the imposed criteria. He sent in his poorer work because that was the work the panelists could read, and therefore consider for reward.

My friend had concluded that if he took his language and culture out of his poetry, he stood a better chance at receiving a fellowship. He took out his native language, the poetic patois of our reality, the rich mixture of Spanish, English, pachuco[4] and street talk which we know so well. In other words, he took the tortillas out of his poetry, which is to say he took the soul out of his poetry. He still has not received a fellowship, and many of those other poets and writers I have encouraged to apply for the fellowships have quit trying. The national norm simply does not want to bother reading us.

I do not believe we should have to leave out the crucial elements of our language and culture to contribute to American lit-

---

3. **literary fellowships:** Grants to support writers.
4. ***pachuco*** (pa chū´ cō): Mexican American kid.

erature, but, unfortunately, this is a conclusion I am forced to reach. I have been writing for a quarter century, and have been a published author for eighteen years. As a writer, I was part of the Chicano Movement which created a new literature in this country. We struggled to change the way the world looks at Mexican-Americans by reflecting our reality in literature, and many eagerly sought our works, but the iron curtain of censorship was still there.

Where does censorship begin? What are the methods of commission or omission that censorship employs? I analyze my own experiences for answers. Many of my generation still recall and recount the incidents of censorship on the playgrounds of the schools when we were told to speak only English. Cultural censorship has been with us for a long time, and my friend's story suggests it is with us today.

If we leave out our tortillas—and by that I mean the language, history, cultural values and themes out of our literature—the very culture we're portraying will die. Publishing has often forced us to do just that.

☑ Check Your Comprehension

1. What image from Salman Rushdie's essay made a special impression on Anaya?
2. According to the essay, what kind of path is traveled by someone who learns to read?
3. What example of "self-imposed censor-ship" does Anaya give in the essay?
4. What method did Anaya and other writers in the Chicano Movement use to change the way the world looks at Mexican Americans?

◆ Critical Thinking

1. What do Anaya's memories about his childhood suggest about the way he regards books and storytelling? **[Infer]**
2. What evidence did Anaya's poet friend use to conclude that his poetry was not receiving a fair reading? **[Interpret]**
3. Why does Anaya conclude that his poet friend's decision "has tremendous cultural implications"? **[Analyze]**
4. (a) What does Anaya mean by "taking the tortillas out of poetry"? (b) What is his reaction to this concept? **[Synthesize]**

Rudolfo Anaya

Comparing and Connecting the Author's Works

◆ Literary Focus: Imagery

Imagery is the use of words and phrases to create pictures in the reader's mind. These images help the reader to relate vividly to the experience being described.

Successful descriptive images appeal to one or more of the five senses: sight, sound, taste, smell, and touch. For example, in the excerpt from *Bless Me, Ultima*, young Antonio describes says that his new shoes "felt strange to feet that had run bare." The school building is full of "strange, unfamiliar smells and sounds that seemed to gurgle from its belly."

1. In the selection from *Bless Me, Ultima*, identify two images for each of the following. On your paper, write the sense(s) to which each image appeals.
   (a) Gabriel's description of the *llano*
   (b) Ultima's blessing of Antonio
   (c) Antonio's walk to school
   (d) lunchtime at school
2. In "Take Tortillas Out of Poetry," explain why the writer Salman Rushdie uses the idea of books being like bread. What does he communicate with this image?

◆ Drawing Conclusions About Anaya's Work

In "Take Tortillas Out of Poetry," Anaya argues that Chicano writers must remain true to their culture and their heritage. Anaya writes, "If we leave out our tortillas—and by that I mean the language, history, cultural values, and themes out of our literature—the very culture we're portraying will die." In addition, Anaya has often referred to the importance for his writing of the storytelling tradition of *cuentos,* or oral tales.

One way to evaluate an author is to compare his or her works to statements expressing the author's ideas about writing. Create a chart like the one below for the selection from *Bless Me, Ultima.* On the chart, list specific words, phrases, and passages from the selection that match Anaya's ideas.

	Anaya's Ideas About Writing	Examples from *Bless Me, Ultima*
Chicano language	_____	_____
Cultural values	_____	_____
History	_____	_____
Oral tradition and folklore	_____	_____

◆ Idea Bank

Writing

1. **E-Mail** Write an e-mail message to Rudolfo Anaya giving your reactions to the essay "Take Tortillas Out of Poetry." In your message, also tell the author what you enjoyed most in the selection from *Bless Me, Ultima.*
2. **Analysis** Conflict has been called the mainspring of a good story. In a paragraph or two, identify and discuss the external and internal conflicts in the excerpt from *Bless Me, Ultima.* How do you think these conflicts were resolved in the novel?
3. **Sequel** Write a sequel to the passage from *Bless Me, Ultima,* set on Antonio's graduation day from high school. In your sequel, include Antonio's parents, Ultima, and one or more teachers. Also feel free to invent some new characters if you like.

Speaking and Listening

4. **Oral Storytelling** Working with a small group, take turns telling stories about an important event in your childhood. Find different ways to hold your listeners' attention. After everyone has told a story, discuss the various methods of storytelling demonstrated and decide which ones were most effective. **[Performing Arts Link] [Group Activity]**

5. **Panel Discussion** In Part Four of his autobiographical work *Barrio Boy* (1971), Ernesto Galarza tells about his first day of school as a child in Tucson, Arizona. Ask a teacher or librarian to locate this passage for you. (An excerpt is available in Prentice Hall Literature *Timeless Voices, Timeless Themes*, Bronze.) Together with a small group of classmates, take turns reading the passage aloud. Then hold a panel discussion in which you compare and contrast Galarza's recollections with the story of Antonio in *Bless Me, Ultima*. **[Social Studies Link] [Group Activity]**

Researching and Representing

6. **Visual Report** Research the Pueblo Indians of New Mexico, looking for photographs or pictures that show their way of life. Create your own artistic rendering of the culture of the Pueblo Indians. You can make a model, drawing, painting, collage, or any kind of visual representation. Present your work to the class, explaining how your report represents the Pueblo Indians' way of life. **[Art Link; History Link]**

◆ Further Reading, Listening, and Viewing

* Anaya, Rudolfo, and José Griego y Maestas, translators. *Cuentos: Tales from the Hispanic Southwest* (1980).

* Anaya, Rudolfo, and Antonio Márquez, editors. *Cuentos Chicanos: A Short Story Anthology* (1980).

* Dick, Bruce, and Silvio Sirias, editors. *Conversations with Rudolfo Anaya* (1998).

* Bix, Cynthia Overbeck. *New Mexico: The Spirit of America* (1998).

On the Web:

http://www.phschool.com/atschool/literature
Go to the student edition *Silver*. Proceed to Unit 10. Then, click Hot Links to find Web sites featuring Rudolfo Anaya.

Photo Credits